10,000,000,000,000.00 in DEBT, Nothing Fixed and Broke!!!!

Are we finally tired of all the Politically correct HYPOCRACY, GIMMICKS, SELLOUTS, RIPOFFS, CRIME, AND HELPLESSNESS? Don't let the big spending People in Power and their Parasites make their 10 Trillion Problems your Problem!!! Protect your family during their coming crisis and don't count on Government Welfare. Just . . . .

Let me share with you one simple solution to solve 70% of our country's problems with your **Wages And Assets Quadrupled In Value, Social Security Fully Funded, Healthcare ¼ the Cost**, crime is reduced 75%, our 10 Trillion is paid off in 4 years, over 160,000,000 new high pay jobs created, National Security is vastly improved as your Freedom and American Dream becomes reality, **NOW!!!!** Not in 30 more years!! And Politicians the people will love you!

"Scrape up the Hope you can,
Come join the Freedom Man,
Asking you to Demand,
the AMERIPLAN, today!!"

This plan will defeat Parasitic **SOCIALISM** in any country and keep a political party in office for 60 years. After 60 years, you are on your own!

Learn How To

I. Let me help you stop Parasitalism as you make or save an *extra $70,000* a year by working smarter, not harder and longer (Now you will have the time for your family and friends and achieve your goals)!

II. With the 10 Commandments of Job Growth, create *160,000,000 New High Pay American Jobs* (Now we can have Foreign Trade in the low pay jobs)!

III. *Reduce our Crime Rates 75%*, end the drug trade, eliminate most Welfare and Poverty as our people respect one another and trust their Public Servants again!

IV. *Pay off the $10 Trillion Debt* in 4 years with 10% GDP growth rates for 20 years straight, huge productivity gains, 2% 30 year interest rates, absolutely no inflation, Medicare and Social Security made solvent immediately without breaking any promises as the Stock Market Booms. Now your spouse can stay home and raise your family, instead of working for nothing, paying Tax homage for the Parasites!

V. Vastly improve our *National Security* and how to end most illegal immigration in 30 days! But can we all agree on keeping our door open for the best and the brightest who will contribute and not be Parasites?

VI. 6 Secret (and easy) Habits to greatly *Improve your Intelligence, Health, and Wealth*. Also some Simple Actions to make an incredible improvement to your life in over 30 ways! TODAY!

VII. *Eliminate Income and Consumption Taxes* and slash all the rest with a high level of Government Spending: All with a Balanced Budget **as Your Paycheck Quadruples!**

VIII. *Reduce our Pollution 90%* as we feed millions of the world's poor for free!

IX. Your *6 Silver Bullets* to guarantee you and your family much better lives!

X. Get Government to compete for our interests with the simple *70% Solution* (the KEY) to all our current problems, as Capitalism is once again legitimized and dysfunctional Neo-Liberalism, Communism, Parasitalism and Fascism (which are forms of Socialism) are dealt a major set-back!

Fixing and doing the above solutions will guarantee you an excellent environment to obtain your American Dream. Believe it and if anyone says you can't have all the above, they are shortchanging themselves and don't you believe them. With a new environment and common sense, simple solutions are possible today with the AMERIPLAN. This is the United States of America we can do it now! Are you with me? It's not rocket science, as you will soon see! And if this seems too complicated, don't worry, just doing the simple 70% Solution will start a chain reaction and everything will be fixed as your pay multiplies 4 TIMES!

AMERIPLAN vs. Death of the American Dream

Uncle Jim

Library of Congress Control Number: 2010901782
ISBN: Hardcover 978-1-4500-4010-5
Softcover 978-1-4500-4009-9

This book was printed in the United States of America.

****Bookstores, this book should be stocked on the shelves in All the following general categories—Political Science, Economics, Business and in the Self-Help book sections.****

To order additional copies of this book, contact:
Xlibris Corporation
1-888-795-4274
www.Xlibris.com
Orders@Xlibris.com
68445

The Ameriplan

Table of Contents

Dedication

My friends, you are the heroes that make the Freedom and True Capitalism work. You do most of the working, taxpaying, raising our children and dying in our country. You are the only ones playing by the rules, working harder every year for less and less as the abuse, lack of respect and arrogance grows, some Parasites get richer and the Welfare crowd grows, contributing less and less each year as you support them more and more with the fruits of your labors. Patriot, from the greed and jealousy, you are being taxed into extinction as they sell you out.

My Patriots, in dedication to those of you who make the country work, finally, easy solutions to save your family, freedoms and wallets from the People in Power with their Communists, Fascists, Criminals, Warped Environmentalists, Socialists, *(dis)Liberals*, Foreign Lobbyists, Arrogant Bureaucrats, Multi-National Businesses, Predators, and many other nasty Parasites. And maybe, just maybe, one day when the Parasitalism stops, with respect we can all work together, again, in one Nation, Under God, with Liberty and Justice for *ALL*! Be brave and strong . . . . it's every man for himself.

You are about to partake on a journey of education in which you will never see Government the same, FOREVER . . . .
Scrape up the hope you can,
Come get your freedom, Man!

Introduction

Many of you work harder, longer, and with more competition at your job than your parents when they were your age, even with all our advanced technology to improve the quality of our lives. You are better educated. Both you and your spouse work full-time, you have less children than your parents, you don't have time for friends and most of you have fewer assets, higher taxes, have less time to guide your children, are in debt up to your ears, Social Security is broke, you have higher crime, drugs, and other perils your children need protection from and you are worse off in other most important qualities of life compared to your parents, even after the Liberals (*(dis)Liberals*) 10 Trillion spending spree. It boggles the mind! The risks of their economic collapse are real! Unfortunately, the money in your accounts, Pensions, Social Security, Stocks and Real Estate is shrinking, and one more lefty boo-boo and you can be totally wiped out. Although the National Debt is now much higher than when I originally planned on publishing this manuscript, the theories, principles and solutions apply more now than ever. Look at the National Debt not so much as the amount but the direction it is moving in. The debt is rising which means our economy is getting sicker. If we were investing this debt it would be one thing but we are squandering our future and putting our children into debt servitude.

You are assaulted from the injustices of Free Trade idiotology shipping your businesses, jobs and wealth overseas, illegal immigration *Crowding Out*, massive inflations, taxes, wage deflations and confiscatory interest rates to scalp off your labors, exploding lawsuits and regulations and money policies to destroy all but the unproductive multinational businesses, regulators, drug lords, and criminals. This costs you job security as you run even faster on the treadmill, causing you to fold in exhaustion as they rip your family apart, hemorrhaging our society. They don't get it, except your tax money! And not even a thank you of appreciation. You are nothing but livestock and their expendable resource until you become self-sufficient (sovereign). Don't become a victim, just stop sniveling, get off the pity pot, pull yourself up by the bootstraps, read on and get educated.

You ask how we can fix this mess? Simply, with specific knowledge in this book. Unfortunately, we have increasingly become a more specialized and politically ignorant society with little understanding of Socialist

Government in which the needs of the few supposedly outweigh the needs of the many. The growing numbers of freeloaders will take whatever you let them get away with. It's every man for himself in this era. The last to react and to protect their family from the People in Power domination and Parasitic environment will get clobbered and end up broken. Their tax strategies are only a tax on you. The rich have lots of money. If they lose most of it, they are still rich. If the rich are taxed more, they cut jobs, lower production, raise prices and totally pass the cost of the tax on to you. In other words, there is and always will be one tax and it is a tax on you and the fruits of your labors and the increased work pressure to produce for the Parasites. All taxes work their way through the system and are still a tax on you! Worse than you paying all the taxes and working longer under more stress, is when your job is cut. You still need a job to support your family, so you take what you can get. Most people today are ***"half-frightened to death in fear of losing their job"*** (there aren't many extras laying around). Our Socialists and their Parasites got the system set up this way, keeping your pay low, with limited opportunities. Don't let them get away with a system based on fear, punishment and Parasitalism. This has been great for those who keep dominating, vulturizing and exploiting you with their mitts in your wallet. They want zero population growth and have encouraged 200 million American Abortions in their family planning. What a shame! But they love illegal immigration to keep your salary low. They're sick! Get away from this disease! Survive by becoming self-sufficient, so they can't parasite off you. Don't be like the rest of the gullible and suckers; you smarten up. Have your own family. Stop the rip-offs of your fruits of labor, with their ever-rising borrowing, then inflation and taxes as your heritage is destroyed. I have dedicated an entire chapter, giving you my best strategies to prevent our Socialists 10,000,000,000,000.00 problems from becoming your problem! I'll show you how to thrive during their day of realism! Hint: if nothing dramatic is done, the stuff hits the fan the day when enough baby boomers retire! Maybe sooner. So PLAN NOW!

The unproductive and dependent classes have exploded and are hooked like dope on the freebies: now the baby boomers will be retiring, demanding paid in advance services and with a mushrooming elderly class and a much smaller work force except for the uneducated, welfare crowds, drug peddlers and illegal aliens sneaking over our unprotected borders, it all spells trouble. The numbers don't add up! And what do the greedy Politicians do? They take campaign money and raise taxes on our producers as families are rotting at the core and the National Debt skyrockets. Like Nero fiddling on the violin while Rome burned: it isn't working people! Liberal Socialism ran amuck! The 10 Trillion Austerity will start soon. You see it coming. You didn't get their windfall; so don't let the Parasites stick you with their bill. Don't let their party be your hangover.

Dear Patriot, you should be thrilled about our future, however, we don't have much time and must act now with the AMERIPLAN's 70% Solution. Every day our problems are compounding at a nefarious pace from Socialism. If you don't know it, you will, and soon. The book style is negative in the beginning because we are teaching about a nasty subject . . . Socialism and its Parasitalism. The nature of the book turns dramatically positive when we learn the solutions to our problems. This common sense book provides our current solutions with Personal Responsibility, the Wisdom of History, the *Laws of Nature*, and our Heritage. You won't learn reality from the Politicians In Power. They think they can ignore history and logic. They say things are more complicated and different now, but you've heard that a thousand times. This book simplifies the problems with the "*KISS Formula*" (keep it simple, stupid), so we know what's happening and maybe this book isn't so simple after all.

Do you maybe think we are in a New World Order? Sorry, it's the same Old World Order with elites, foreign countries and selfish interests, fighting over our wealth, dominance, prestige, jobs, culture, religion, etc. So you think you are smarter than your forefathers long gone? There is very little new in our time that hasn't happened throughout history. Sure, we have more technology and volumes of loopholes in the laws for special interest factions (Parasites), but that is it. Genetically, we might have slightly higher IQs than our bloodlines 10 generations ago, but still, with all the junk food and brain washing from the Parasites, I doubt many of us are as smart or honorable as our Founding Fathers. It's all the same old stuff with small privileged groups exploiting the masses as it has been since the beginning. There is still a right and wrong. Actions still speak louder than words. There will always be rich and poor, smart and not so smart, good and evil, and finally in the end, hopefully fairness.

So, you want to know what went wrong in America? Look in your wallet, Patriot. I think you bought this book to learn how to obtain a better life and become strong. Maybe you are desperately seeking knowledge on how to keep the fruits of your labors, regain your freedoms, improve

Government, protect your family from the Parasites, uncomplicate and understand your life so you have time to properly raise your family and work on worthy goals to reach your American Dream. This book is for you, especially the 10 Commandments of Job Growth and Crime Reduction, as we pay off the 10 Trillion Debt with Debt Transfers to spare our children debt servitude and **Multiply Your Pay 4 Times.** Finally, the AMERIPLAN hands you 6 Silver Bullets to defeat the Socialist Parasites and a 7th if all else fails.

Poor and rich people won't find a better life by rioting, shady business tactics, looting, or regulating and taxing away another's wealth and then consuming it like the Parasites and the elite pulling the strings in Washington and local Governments. Nope, you need a better environment. I don't waste time naming specific Politicians, Parasites and Predators in this book or their gimmicks and tricks. You are smart enough to figure them out. There is plenty of blame to pass around, including you and I. For starters, learn to smarten up and improve your health, with the 6 Simple Habits. Then learn to create and protect your own capital. Hang on to it and invest it wisely for your self-sufficiency. Only with discipline and a clear mind can you keep from being tricked out of it. One action may improve your life 30 ways as you escape the Socialist tentacles. When the Socialists extract your wealth without your blessing, they are stealing the clothing, shelter, and food out of your children's mouths. They lay waste up to 70% of what they extract.

Dear Patriots, join me; shake the Parasites off your back! Granted, there are a lot of them. You can cry excuses, but you will remain their servant and exploited until you are ready to take responsibility for yourself. Start with this book, learn what the Parasites are doing to you and wake up! You are more of the problem than you think (an Enabler). With the power of knowledge and eternal discipline, you will become and stay a freeman and save our country for our children. Cheer up! You can easily defeat the Parasites with the AMERIPLAN which are the long-term solutions which get us moving in the right direction immediately. We have already defeated the massive evils of Fascism and Communism, but now, it is our patriotic duty and destiny to defeat the 3rd leg of Socialism called Parasitalism!

Do not grow to hate the Socialists. They have an immature philosophy where they think they can violate ancient and obvious patterns in Nature. They are filled with arrogance, jealousy, fear and distrust. Instead of encouraging our fellow men, they would rather join a political clique, dominate and tear us down. But, never fear, the simple 70% solution in the last chapter will cure their Socialist-Parasitic disease and this is something great to celebrate! Only here will you find the answer! The solution is simple, but understanding the problem will take four hours of reading. Don't spoil the journey by jumping to the last chapter, keep reading. You will learn unpleasantries about life that you desperately need to know to protect yourself.

Here is a dishonest excuse the Liberals and Socialists use over and over as they tax and confiscate your assets, putting them under Government domain: "We need more Government spending (of your money) to fix our problems (really their problems), our economy is mature, people can't find work and the 10% growth rates are gone forever. Well, how true for them, not us! Do the AMERIPLAN and all is possible right now; not in 30 years! Watch growth rates over 10% for 20 years straight as our salaries skyrocket. Now you can afford to happily give to your favorite charities!

The AMERIPLAN will school you on the "***Economic and Social Problems Total Interrelation Theory***". With this most powerful Economic Theory, you will have the foundation to understand the *Laws of Human Nature* and how they relate with Government, jobs and crime, which will enable you to run a 1st class Government without excess Socialism, inflation, tax oppression, job killing legislation, payoffs, mortgaging our children's future or misappropriation of the Social Security Trust Funds with commingling scams and diversion of funds.

Learn how to dramatically grow the "*American Pie*" with *Debt Transfers* as **Crime drops 75%** and **160,000,000 new high pay jobs** are created. Now we have the money to clean up our pollution, greatly improve our National Defense, pay debts and much more all at once. To take things to this high elevation, I outline the AMERIPLAN, giving basic actions to excel our country well beyond our current status.

Maybe your Faith is low and you are wondering if you can ever help fix our problems? Maybe your hope for the American Dream has been dashed? Maybe you have lost your love for our citizens and country? Can the AMERIPLAN really stop the Parasitic abuse? Are we doomed? Scrape up the Hope you can! Come join the Freedom Man!

The 4 major Goals I challenge you with are attainable and you deserve the best, Magnificent Patriots. It's your life and your children's future! The 10 Trillion Debt holds in the Balance and not for long. The baby boomers will soon retire to a Bankrupted Social Security Ponzi Scam. We need a

10 Trillion stockpiled surplus in the next 15 years. Let us have surpluses in the budget today, with tax cuts! Not in a few more years, don't settle for less! We gave the Socialists plenty to spend already and they wasted it on their Parasites, but no more.

Be strong, live the good life with an abundance of *Hope, Faith,* and *Love.* These three little words and the feelings behind them are what matters most in life. They are more than enough and more rewarding than a mountain of Gold! And who knows? This unique book in your hands may be worth a mountain of gold (at least 10 Trillion). (I better raise the price of the book!). Anyway, I hope this book is as enlightening and fun for you as it is for me. Dear friends, join me, you are about to partake on a journey of possibilities few have ever dared to imagine, let alone blaze a trail to our hopes and dreams!

With our efforts we and *our* Government can do much better for our families. Ask it, Expect it and Demand it!

Patriots, with the knowledge in this book, Empower yourself!

If you only believe, all things are possible, especially your American Dream!

(Dreamer / Patriot,
And part-time Author)

1

TEASERS

We can truly have a better life for our families.

Tell the People in Power (PIPS) who are over taxing you to stop the rip-offs! When you send tax money to the PIPS with only 30% getting to the deserving recipient or project, where is the other 70%? Where is the Social Security Surplus? And isn't a $10,000,000,000,000.00 debt on top of it enough? And isn't another 40 Trillion of your money promised to the Parasites enough to make you sick? With the AMERIPLAN, everyone will have a good job. Even the PIPS will see their **Pay Increase 4 Times** in value! This Parasite Socialism doesn't cut the mustard. The Cold War is Over! Patriot, I know we can have a better way of life. Dear friend, I am glad you are here. You can do it! Learn well the AMERIPLAN and get your deserved Peace Dividend! One other thing, you shouldn't have to work a job over 8 hours a day, 5 days a week to provide for your family or something is deeply wrong.

But now Patriots, it's every man for himself. Socialism has run amuck in Parasitalism. Learn how to break their chokehold, keep the fruits of your labors and get your American Dream. Learn what you've been missing. With a little knowledge you can escape the bondage cage and start calling your own shots or you will be running till you die of exhaustion on their treadmill as you try and fail to pay all their bills (50 Trillion)! Make a solemn oath to take back your life, today, right now, this second. Last I checked, you are living and it is your life, isn't it?

Why U.S. Socialism Will and Must Die

Hold your flag high, we are going to cut through the Socialism and get a life you never dreamed possible. For starters, be on guard against Parasitalism (a side effect of Socialism). Parasitalism is not Capitalism, fairness and growth, but a regressive jealous sickness, where greedy Parasites eat the labors and steal the hope out of the productive class and their families. The greedy Parasites produce nothing you can see, hold or use which is real. Instead, they try to cut a share out of your labors. I'll show you how to stop it today and forever. Socialists, *(dis) Liberals*, Elitists, Lobbyists, many Trial Attorneys, Environmental Extremists, all Monopolies, many Bureaucrats, Big Union Bosses, many Multinational Businesses, all Foreign Campaign Contributors and their Lobbyists, many Journalists, Predators, Communists, Fascists, and many other phonies to beware of in Washington, D.C. You won't find the solutions to our problems from the Socialists and their multiplying moochers. They like the feast. But now, they bit off more than they can chew (10 Trillion)! Remember that our productive bake a cake and the unproductive eat it. That cake rotted years ago and the Vultures are still scavenging for its rancid crumbs. Too bad, but the Socialists and their Parasites have to go back to work and help bake a new cake. You can't get something for nothing forever!

You better pay attention Patriots, before you get bulldozed. If the PIPS were really "Of, By, and For the People," they would stop taking foreign money, abolished the income tax, have passed Term Limits and the Balanced Budget Amendments years ago. However, they say these are unconstitutional. "Since when did the PIPS follow the Constitution?" They don't want you to limit their power, they want to continue limiting your freedom and milking your salary, keeping you dependent on their kindness (NOT). Fortunately, PIPS have a major problem, MONEY! With the Baby Boomers retiring, the Gulf War about over and their phony protection racket unmasked, the jig is up. How could they continue to buy off their growing Cliques and clubs of Parasites, PACs, and Special Interest Groupies? Patriot, they are desperately using every trick, lie, deceit, and scam in the book to suck your freedoms, salary, time, life, and children into a black hole of hungry Parasites (and if you don't have a pot to piss in, they will make sure you never get one). Could it be our Socialists are the other "Evil Empire"? I hope not. To be sure, vote the rest of the career PIP Socialists out and watch the Lobbyists scramble for a new food source. Join me; scrape the Parasites off your back! And never forget . . . .

“CAPITALISM DIDN’T FAIL OUR PEOPLE, OUR PIPS IN WASHINGTON FAILED CAPITALISM”

DUNCE
SOCIALIST
LIBERAL
PIPPY
PSSST! Carl Marx and our intellectuals lied or don’t understand human nature. They never told us about the dark side of Socialism . . . .PARASITES!!!
Shhhhh! Let them figure it out on their own!

The Parasitic 30-70 Rule

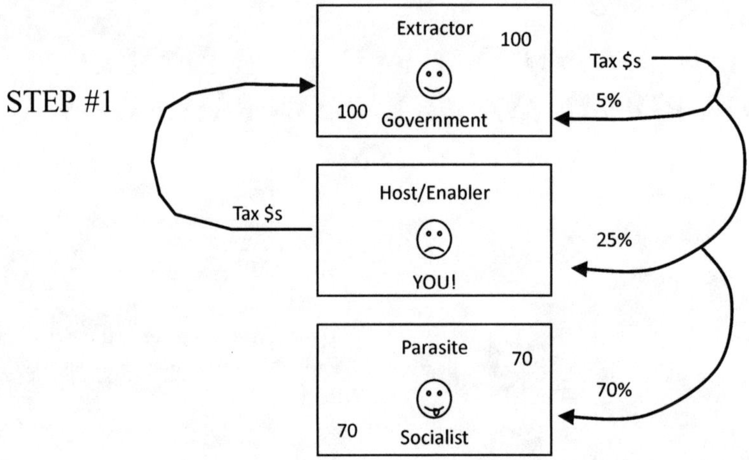

You = Host
Socialist = Parasite
Government = Extractor/Siphon Tool of the Socialist

STEP #2 **Do it again and again forever until you smarten up.**
If you ever do . . . . smarten up.

By the way . . . each cycle you grow weaker.

How Long Can The Game of Parasitalism Last?

Oh what will I tell my dependent subjects?
PIPPY

Our PIPS have No clothes!
They spend money like drunken Sailors but . . .

They are

BROKE!

and in Debt by

$10,000,000,000,000.00

For Pippys sake, hopefully, the foreigners and our rich will continue to ignore this debt, support the Government and buy bonds. As long as someone keeps buying, inflation rates stay low, while PIPs can keep running the printing presses, taxing labor and capital, spending fiat, feeding their growing Parasites, buying off voters. Right, Pippys? Don't do what's right for your country. Just stick to your Liberal politics over principles and get re-elected, then you forget about your people as the Social Security Ponzi scam and Debt Bubbles eventually blow up in our faces. But you'll be long gone, "so who cares?" Everyone will soon enough, (Put your clothes on Pippy!)

"Regain Your Hope, Faith, Love and Peace of Mind"

I. THE PROBLEM—PARASITALISM

A. A shortage of High Pay Jobs to support our families who are overworked, under-employed and in debt, barely hanging on and in our weakened state, with the Parasites clinging to our backs as our people collapse from exhaustion!
B. Excessive Crime rates 4 times too high!
C. The $10,000,000,000,000 Debt Bubble and Bankrupt Social Security System, all with enormous wasted tax extraction at the same time!
D. The spreading unchecked illegal drug trade, with drug addictions, dysfunctional families, broke judiciary and abusive arrogance from many bureaucrats!
E. Cancerous Illegitimacy and Illegal Immigration!
F. Exploding Welfare for the rich, poor, foreign trading countries and Parasitic Special Interests!
G. Dangerous National Security problems and trade dependency as our self-sufficiency and sovereignty are squandered for a paltry short-term gain!
H. The Unstable, Unsound, Undisciplined and Dishonest Money Policies causing bankruptcies, unemployment, pensions wiped out, home and business foreclosures all from the dislocations.
I. Bloated, Non-competing self-serving Government at all levels as it jealousy regulates, taxes and rots our productive! It's them against you. They only win when you lose. This is the Nature of all Parasites. Wake up! These nicely dressed and kindly talking snickering Parasites aren't your friends. They are cutting a pound of flesh off your body as soon as you turn your back. Do you see the similarities between these Socialists and a crackhead?

II. TOOLS TO SOLVE THE PROBLEM

A. "*Government Competition Theory*" with incentive.
B. "*The Nature of Parasitalism*"

C. "*American Pie Theory*"
D. "*Economic and Social Problems Total Interrelation Theory*"
E. "*4X Job Theory*"
F. "*Crowding Out Theory*," "*Government Corruption Theory*," "*Competition Theory*," "*Containment Theory*," and "*Complication Theory*."
G. "*Loose Money equals Loose Morality Principle*" which equals *(dis)Liberalism* run amuck.

III. THE SOLUTIONS

A. The Government's **70% Solution** to all our current problems.
B. Your ***6 Silver Bullets*** to guarantee you a better life, regardless of Socialist interference.
C. The **AMERIPLAN**.

Yes, aren't the PIPS something? They tried every gimmick except to fix their mess. Don't look to Indonesia, Europe, China, Japan, Middle East, or Mexico for answers! They are laughing at the folly as it destroys our people and country. But we can fix the above problems with the AMERIPLAN! Then we can prance all over the planet, telling everyone else how to live and do the Free Trade. But not until! Fair enough?

Where do we start? By pulling Socialism out by the roots with the 70% Solution in the last chapter. Don't jump to it. The solution is simple, but understanding the problems will take a little work (about 4 hours of reading.) Most important, you will soon know how creeping Socialism has spawned Parasitalism. With this knowledge, you can reclaim your American Dream as it becomes reality!

EXTRA, EXTRA, READ ALL ABOUT IT!

Patriots, wake up the Economic Genius within you!

Want Ad: FREEDOM SECTION

Feel burned out and stunted from all the Greedy People feasting off the fruits of your Labors? Feel like they are holding you back in stagnant stifle from your true potential? Can't afford to help your family or friends or find a good job? Getting a divorce or thinking about an abortion? Are you giving up the quest for the American Dream, sliding into a life of drugs, crime, immorality, Welfare and despair as you badmouth your country? No time for your children? Is your health shot from all the junk food and your mind mixed up from the misinformation and propaganda? Are you ready to jump off a cliff?

Hold onto your Dreams! Never give up! Never! Dear friend, join me as we scrape the Socialists off our backs and live a whole New World with more happiness than you ever believed achievable. With a New Environment, we can overcome the most impossible obstacles by finding surplus opportunity and incentive to enable you to reach your goals in life! Study well, The AMERIPLAN. Also check out the Website after you have read every page for some great books and magazines Uncle Jim enjoys. *www.unclejimameriplan.com*

Shoot for the Stars—Settle for the Moon!

Let's create **160,000,000 New American Jobs! Payoff the 10 Trillion Debt in 4 Years! Eliminate 75% of all crime**! No income or sales tax! Have 2%-30 year interest rates, no inflation! **Raise Living Standards 4 Times!**

So what if we mess up (but haven't) and only make a 50% grade, which even in public school is an E, but still that's 80,000,000 jobs, 8 years to pay off the 10 Trillion Debt, a 50% tax reduction, 40% crime reduction, 100% increase in your salary, 3% interest rates with 1% inflation. Are you ready?

And the Leftys and Rightys in power think they are so great (trying and failing) sucking up all our assets in a Socialist Government with NAFTA to create 200,000 jobs, as they pay 50 Billion of your money, not theirs to prop up the PESO to give free money to a few already rich Hot Dogs and further run a 600 Billion Trade Deficit, as they shell out trillions of your money in bailouts to pay for their self-inflicted (on purpose) policy boo boos.

This money could have been given to create 100,000,000 New American Millionaire Families; did you want to be one?

I really wish you were! It comes down to this . . . do you want your wealth back or more Socialism?

Stick with me. Uncle Jim will show you how we do this and oh so much more.

100,000,000 New American Millionaires!

$1,000,000 | $100,000,000,000,000.00 in Government Assets

Better Odds than the Lottery!

WHERE ARE THE SURPLUS JOBS AND OPPORTUNITY?

The PIPS (People in Power) and their Statests boast for every $1 Billion dollars in American exports, they created 20,000 new jobs! But they conveniently forget to tell you that every Billion in imports takes away 20,000 American jobs that they let slip through their fingertips.

So, if we have a 600 Billion Trade Deficit, which means that they lost us (600 x 20,000) = 12,000,000 jobs and they created nothing, just lost 12,000,000 high pay jobs! The next time they boast how many jobs they saved and created, question them and ask them how many millions of our children's jobs they had to throw away to foreigners in crummy trade deals with 600 Billion deficits to create their puny 20,000 jobs? And how many more *Billions of Debt* did they pile up for our kids to pay in the process?

Even worse than losing 12 Million jobs, you have to account for all the support and secondary jobs that are deflated or eliminated according to the "*4X Theory*" of Job Creation. So each primary job multiplies, losing needed secondary jobs! For a gross total of 48,000,000 High Pay American Jobs! (Very gross!)

For a change, let's try a 600 Billion Trade surplus and create over 96,000,000 real, *real* high pay American jobs! Hey, did you want one of these high pay jobs? I sure want you to have one! Or how about a big fat raise at your job? Or a big signing bonus like the entertainers and athletes? You don't want Socialist phony minimum wage laws, paltry unemployment compensation, Medicare Taxes, Socialized Healthcare, Illfare or Social Insecurity. Nope, you want all the fruits of your labors that they took and keep taking, so you can afford to pay your own bills. How do you like the book so far, Patriot? You will when we learn how to eliminate the Socialist disease called Parasitalism which is destroying our families by ripping off ¾ of your salary!

Patriots, work smarter, not harder, for less. Make twice as much doing half as much or **Make 4 Times More** and watch the value of your assets skyrocket! Help the True Conservatives (Jeffersonian Liberals) with the AMERIPLAN so you can afford to spend time properly raising your family in a better life![1] "You deserve a break today, so get up and get away from the Taxers!"

When we throw away good jobs in twisted trade deals and goofy regulations, is it any wonder our young are stuck working in dead end worker bee jobs, wasting their lives with no future? But not anymore as you defeat Parasitalism with the AMERIPLAN! Or do you want more *(dis)Liberal* Socialism and their 5,000 page Free Trade Laws? If they really wanted Free Trade, just start trading! 10 trillion in debt and nothing solved. The emperors have no clothes.

If it's free, why do we owe 10 TRILLION!
Put your clothes on Liberal

[1] The language "Jeffersonian Liberal", I first heard of it from the famous radio talk show guru and proponent of States Rights in a Limited Republic by Mark Scott.

WHOSE MONEY AND WHERE IS IT?

How come in Washington a spending cut is an increase in spending, but just not as high as they wished they could spend?

Oh, where is all the money going?
Put your clothes on PIP!

Sorry Socialists, Freedom Won! And you Lost! We are 10 Trillion in Debt, plus you owe another 40 Trillion off budget in guarantees. There is no money left to buy voters anymore. Money isn't the root of all evil, but the waste of it!

Lefty
Ah, where did all the money go?
U.S.D.A. Pork
Oink! Oink! Put your clothes on.

It's time to get real with the philosophy of realism. Let us stop telling white lies, grow up and fix our problems. We can start with the "*K.I.S.S. Formula*" (keep it simple, stupid.) Our citizens have become cynical from the simple laws the *(dis)Liberals* draft into 5,000 pages. Nobody understands Government anymore, hence distrust, more scandals and obviously there will be! Just another rip-off from the Socials.

Here's a good one: Leftys say they give you an entitlement like a home mortgage deduction! This proves their arrogance. They think they own your entire salary and they think out of the goodness in their hearts they are giving you more money . . . how kind. Instead of the paltry tax credits, capital gain tax reductions, tax deferred I.R.A. contributions as they wipe out your pensions and other gimmicks, let's just **Increase Our Pay 4 Times** and eliminate income and consumption taxes. Yes, totally!

Liberal is a derivative that comes from the word Liberty, which means Freedom and Self-determination. Then why do Liberals pass all these laws taxing and taking away our freedoms, opportunities and private property? We don't get it. Maybe they really aren't Liberal, but Socialist Statests, who prey on your gullibility. If they won't even tell you the truth about who they are, what makes you think they are telling the truth at election time?

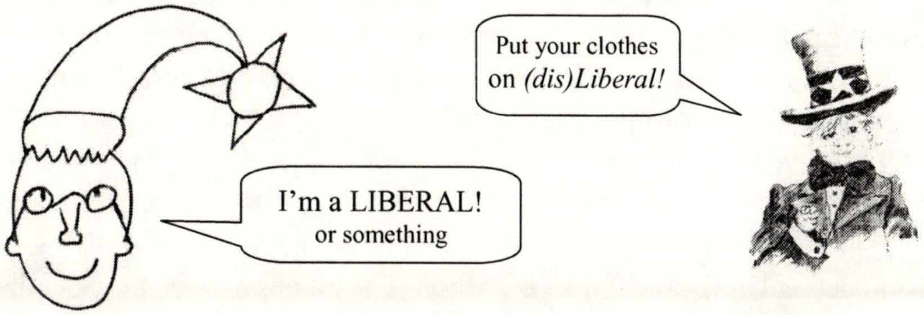

I'm a LIBERAL!
or something
Put your clothes on (dis)Liberal!

THE CYCLE OF DEMOCRACY

The people get involved in Government;

Which causes	The environment to improve,
Which causes	Surplus jobs and opportunities,
Which causes	Crime to diminish,
Which causes	The budget to become balanced,
Which causes	Surpluses in the Treasury,
Which causes	Complacency in the people,
Which causes	A deteriorating environment of Parasitalism,
Which causes	A job shortage and lack of opportunities,
Which causes	Crime to increase, with even more Parasites,
Which causes	The budget to become unbalanced (even with higher taxes),
Which causes	Raids on the Treasury, resulting in Massive Debts and Bankruptcy!
Which forces	The people to get involved, demanding better Government,
Which causes	The entire cycle to begin anew!

Do we really have to have a full-blown depression like now or riots before we fix anything? I hope not.

You own the country. Do you want more of the PIPS' shenanigans? We can balance the budget today with tax decreases and spending increases. It's up to you. Believe in the Parasites or start believing in yourself and the AMERIPLAN, as told by your Uncle Jim.

So be weary when you hear the bleeding heart Politicians tell you our problems are inherent and been with us for generations and we need more time to fix them (and your money!). This is bull. They love the domination over your life and salary. They don't need even 1 more cent. Tell them to put their clothes on and fix their messes today, not in 30 more years. Come join the Freedom Man!

Riddle: What does it mean when the Federal Reserve says the Economy is overheating? It's a nice way of saying the Socialists screwed it up again. Way to go. Bring in the next bunch of warped economists to fool the public. Time to get real and pay off the 10 Trillion. The joke is now on the Socialists: their Parasites are splitting and Parasiting on each other. It's every man for himself. Patriot, this manual is a guide on how to protect yourself and profit during their crisis. Don't let the PIPS drag the country down, turn you into a brain-dead zombie, and make you pay for their foolish campaign pay-offs, vote buying, social experimentations, sellouts, and tinkering with the system. They broke it; we have to fix it for ourselves.

PATRIOTISM LIVES!

Patriots, we are a slave to the 10 Trillion Debt!

"Give Me Economic Liberty
or Give Me Death!"

If the PIPS won't help, then tell them to stay out of the way!
It will be tough but, we are paying off their debts fair and square with no Fiat! And no tricks!

Inflate, Tax, Borrow and Spend! I'm giddy!
Pippy

Humpty Dumpty Pippy,
Sat on the Wall.
Humpty Dumpty Pippy,
Had a Great Fall.
Pippy got 10 Trillion in Debt,
Another 40 Trillion and He will be set.
But Pippy tried more borrowing yet,
One thing certain he's sure to regret,
I'm sure you will bet,
One more Dollar Pippy couldn't get!
All the Socialist Lobby Horses and
All Pippy's Tax and Spend Parasite men,
Wouldn't and Couldn't Put Humpty Dumpty
Pippy Government Back Together Again.

10 Trillion in Debt. Oh, my!
Pippy

Pippy fell down,
And broke his crown.
Then he left town,
And made not another sound!

Good Morning. I'll pick up the pieces and clean up their mess.
We can fix this country without deceit as the *(dis) Liberals* spent our Social Security funds and put us 10 Trillion in debt, squandered our savings, gave away our jobs and made us dependents of the Socialists.

Aristotle said.."Know thyself"
Plato said.."Be thyself"
Ralph Waldo Emerson said.."Trust thyself"

Uncle Jim said .... "Work thyself"

SO YOU WANT NATIONALIZED HEALTH CARE?????????? GET READY TO SACRIFICE AND WORK ANOTHER 4 HOURS A WEEK TO PAY FOR THE EXTRA WASTE AS THE COSTS GO UP EVEN MORE!!!!!!!!!!!!!!!!!!!!!! OR, GOOD LUCK TRYING TO PAY FOR LITTLE JOHNNYS SCHOOL LUNCH, PAYING THE RENT OR MORTGAGE, NO BIRTHDAY OR CHRISTMAS PRESENTS, AND FORGET THAT VACATION. All from your bungling, borrowing, conniving, big spending, reckless money sneaking, double speaking, figure tweaking, inflation leaking, poll peaking, tax seeking, control freaking, wreaking PIPPYS! IT'S YOUR CHOICE OF COURSE.

50,000,000,000,000.00 REWARD! Yup! That's Trillions!

FBI Most Wanted:
Danger! Hide your wallet. Suspect is accused of turning over 300,000,000 U.S. citizens into dependent slaves, skimming off over 50% of your paycheck, running Ponzi Scams, counterfeiting with Fiat, regulating zealotry, payoffs, bribes, shipping our jobs overseas, cornering the Bond Market, exposing and drowning your family in drugs, crime, disease, illegal immigration, unemployment, propaganda brain washing, despair and destroying your American Dream.

Hey, gang. We need more Socialism so I can CASH IN and suck!

Aliases—Lefty, Socialist, Righty, Plutocrat, Collectivist, Statest, Commie, Cannibal, Fascist, Progressives, *(dis) Liberal*, Wacky Eco Environmentalist, Vulture, Free Trader, Elites, Lobbyist, Parasite, Vampire, Predator, Leech, Complacent Bureaucrat, Bloodsucker, Uncompeting Union Boss, Monopolies, Speculator, Welfarian, and all the others getting a free ride.

Pssssst! I forgot the New World Order groupies, with their fingers in your pockets . . . Big group, sorry.

BUG SPRAYING

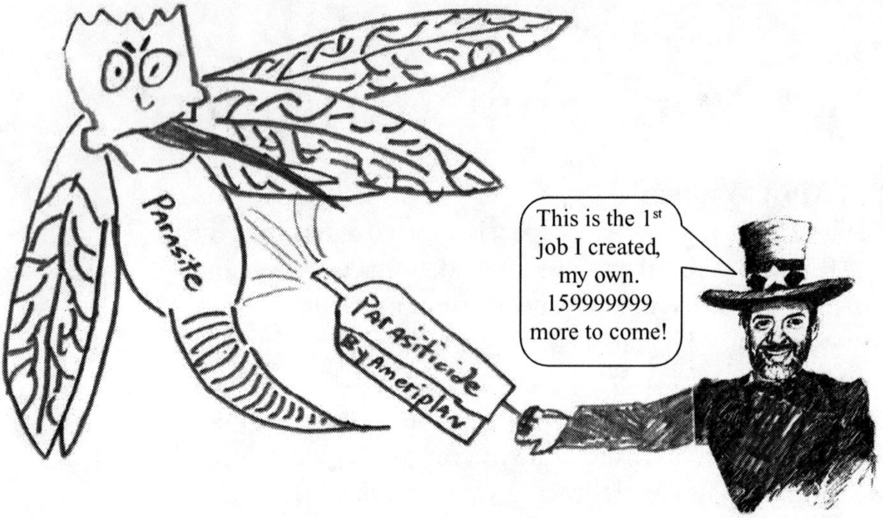
Parasite
Parasiticide By Ameriplan
This is the 1st job I created, my own. 159999999 more to come!

PARASITICIDE—THE CURE

Dosage:	4 hours of reading the AMERIPLAN
Warning:	Keep away from PIPS.
Danger:	Will put Socialism in a Coma!
Disclaimer:	Do not place much meaning on any number in this book. I could be wrong on any number. For example, I say we may create 160,000,000 new high pay American jobs, well if we do everything in the AMERIPLAN, we may end up creating 2.5 Billion jobs! This book can multiply your wealth as it creates millions and millions of new opportunities, but is dangerous to the 10 Trillion debt, Poverty, Unemployment, Welfare Programs, criminals, and the greedy, all stinking thinking of Socialists and Parasites dishing it out but keeping 70% for themselves, not to mention Pessimism, Racism, Jealousy and Fear. Another disclaimer is the 70% wasted in the bureaucracy and 40 Trillion in future promises. These may be less and again they could be higher! A whole lot higher!

The ideas in this book can stop most of our crime. This book is dangerous to drug pushers and criminals (including illegal immigrants flooding across our borders) with dope, disease, crime and transient behavior patterns which are trashing our country as they spread their problems around instead of fixing their own mess back home in their own communities and countries. These people want one thing, by whatever means—MONEY! Have you, your family and friends had enough abuse yet? You will one day. In the meantime, let them suck out your entire paycheck with taxes to fix everything. NOT!

This material contained in this manual is deadly to the 10 Trillion Debt and once paid will cause the people to again respect their Government as it becomes Capitalistic, not more Parasitalistic. And I don't mean exploitation, but True, Honest, Fair Capitalism! Win-Win!

The material in this book is dangerous to Despotism, Collectivism, Fascism, Elitism, Socialism, Parasitalism, Lobbyism, Neo-Liberalism, and Communism. If you belong to one of these categories, maybe this isn't the place for you. Pack your bags and immediately leave for sanctuary in Cuba, Afghanistan, Iran, Somalia, Madagascar or North Korea. Don't let the door hit you on the way out. Don't worry; the Foreigners have plenty of positions for you. How about working alongside the prison labor, Comrade? And bring your family. Even your 10-year-old son and daughter will work 12 hours a day. Forget about keeping the fruits of your Labors. See what it's like getting Parasited on yourself for a change, next to the Commies.

YOUR CIVIC DUTY—TAKE SOME RESPONSIBILITY TO SAVE OUR WAY OF LIFE

Here is one of the dirty little secrets of the Socialists and their Parasites. They are an extreme segment of our population. They are a very small, overly vocal and pushy clique growing larger daily. They have an infatigable determination and greed for their cause. However, they have a twisted focus with a direction which is incompatible with the Laws of Nature and a shallow, petty, selfish and immature philosophy. They know most people strongly reject their policies, so with their propaganda they have moved very cautious over the last 80 years, as they methodically tightened their chokehold (read the *Frog Boil* and the *Nibble techniques*.)

When these zealots get their candidates elected, their policy perversities damage the entire country, setting in motion cancerous ripples with irreparable damage. Read the definition of a Parasite. The PIPS don't care about you; they will do any unprincipled act, scare tactics or whatever, like buying votes with Welfare to get elected. Getting elected is more important than helping and doing what is good for our people. To them, it's position over principle. We believe these Lefty Politicians are speaking for the entire country. They are not. Only their political backers. When you hear their magnificent speeches, do you still really believe they will fix their messes after all these years? Will you even vote? When good people do not get involved and keep the Politicians and their Parasites in check, staying forever vigilant, the Parasites will rip you off blind. Like now! (Restudy the *Cycle of Democracy*.) Do you like the 10 Trillion Debt and would you like more Socialism? I hope not! Stop depending on false PIP promises and depend on yourself. How did you like their stock market crash in 2008? Remember the wise saw the Socialist takeover well before the elections of November 2008.

My friend, we probably can't wake up the country until a total disaster. However, I hope this book will help, especially you. But, don't you throw in the towel; things in our country will get worse. Our Socialists are increasingly eating our young, saddling them with debts and Parasiting with a vengeance. Besides, getting good citizens elected for short-terms in office to help reduce the Parasitalist Environment, I want you to protect yourself from their tentacles.

This book is your medicine. Eventually, when the rest of the foolish in this country get abused enough, they will wake up, but why wait another 30 years? Live a good life now!

Don't forget, you deserve tax cuts now, don't let the *(dis)Liberals* fool you into thinking the sky is falling. It's not. Only their sky is falling as Socialism is destroyed and they lose all their gains over the last 80 years! And their loss is **Your Quadruple In Pay** and your quality of life. Your American Dream! Demand the AMERIPLAN! Immediately!

THE NOBLE PLEAS OF THE SOCIALISTS, BUT WHO SHOULD DO THE SPENDING OF YOUR MONEY? AND IF THEY WON'T COMPETE, THEY ARE PARASITES!

We must change the corrupt Socialist environment. This disease is spreading like a cancer on our children. Without competition and rewards for people to produce, this stinkin'-thinkin' philosophy always fails sooner or later. Look at the U.S.S.R. We are at the later stages with the 10 Trillion Debt, plus the Politicians promised another 40 Trillion of your money, not theirs. They don't produce wealth, only spending. This rip-off is the equivalent of 1,000,000,000 Bonnie and Clyde's. Incredible! This scam will go down in history as the greatest rip-off the world has ever seen! What an embarrassment even when our Great, Great, Great, Great, Great, Great Grandchildren read this 300 years from now! It is unbelievable! Now you know where the crooks are in this country! Spawned from excess Socialism.

Now come the Socials creating more addictions and dependencies, wanting more of your tax money to give Welfare for the growing underclass (they created), so the "affected" don't riot. Can't you hear the disingenuous pleas for the homeless, the abused and battered, the disadvantaged children, taking care of the sick and dying, the old, money for rehabilitations, stopping AIDS, saving the Spotted Owls and salamanders, funds for the U.N. and World Bank, locking up criminals in soon to be built air-conditioned prisons, ever increasing taxes for the Social Security Ponzi Scam, Corporate Illfare, Affirmative Action, Free Government Services for illegal immigrants, healthcare, education loans and grants, wanting money to protect Somalia and Bosnia from themselves, policing the world, feeding Africa, building the foreign economies (even as it destroys ours), raising taxes to finance roads, bridges, Government projects, more Policeman and Bureaucrats, and school funding, all as their Parasites siphon off 70% for themselves first! Are they kidding? Tell them to put their clothes on! Let us increase all of our paychecks 4 times and we can buy and support all this stuff at 30% of the cost the PIPS charge us (1/12th the cost), plus it will get done a lot better. We pass. No thank you very much! Stop the Parasitalism.

Don't believe it? Look at their 10 Trillion Debt you get to pay. Believe *me*, *you*, *us*; *they* will do their best concentrating all their time and energy figuring how *they* will fleece and make *you* pay for their party (50,000,000,000,000). Socials spend more time hiring Spin Doctors, Handlers, Speech Writers, Attorneys, and Pollsters than they do solving the country's problems. Join me before their train wreck brings down the whole country in destruction. I'm not here to feel your pain, but eliminate your pain, with the AMERIPLAN.

Here's a reason why our country is going broke. One thing that ought to really disturb you is the taking of foreign jobs, money and loans by the PIPS and their kin and buddies. It's all legal, they say. They passed the law. But is it right? Surely Politicians must be of the highest moral standards and never, ever even give the impression, appearance, or be involved in a situation where their public behaviors are questionable. Some Politicians have stooped to the lowest level by taking this money and selling out the American people. It is treason. Taking foreign money and foreign loans by politicians and political parties, for any reason is wrong, even after Government service (or was it dis-service?) This is not a "*Government Of, By, and For the People*" these politicians pretend to serve. This is bribery at its worst, equal to a Benedict Arnold Turn Coat. In the old days, these Politicians and Parasites would be hung by the neck from the nearest tree. Let's hope these culprits shape up. And you can fix them with the first Silver Bullet!

PATRIOTS VS. PARASITES

Time to separate the Men and Women (Patriots) from the boys and girls (Parasites).

	The Patriots want	***The Parasites want***
1.	Lower taxes and create 160,000,000 high pay jobs.	Increased taxes and create Welfare programs
2.	Balanced budget amendment and fiscal responsibility.	More unbalanced budgets and fiscal irresponsibility, without any Cost/Benefit Analysis
3.	Personal responsibility and freedom of choice.	Less personal responsibility and more Government mandates.
4.	More private ownership of assets and wealth.	More Government and monopoly ownership over tools and production. (Power Mongers)
5.	Decentralized Government bureaucracy.	Centralized Government bureaucracy control (which ultimately is done with oppression.)

6.	The enforcement of laws already on the books.	Another crime bill and another Campaign finance law they write but don't follow and obey.
7.	Low inflation and low interest rates—cheap capital, available to all.	High inflation and high interest rates—expensive capital, available only to the very wealthy and the anointed.
8.	Doing the right thing, more than getting elected.	A winner, more than doing the right thing.
9.	Principle over position. (Not swayed by special interest Parasites.)	Position over principle. (Preoccupied with pleasing special interest Parasites.)
10.	No more borrowing and wasteful spending.	Higher borrowing to increase spending on themselves.
11.	Less illegal immigration and see the horrors.	More illegal immigration and see the temporary short-term gain.
12.	See no advantages of mind-altering drugs.	Free experimenting with drugs for recreation.
13.	No worship of the State; personal religion is important.	Total worship to the state; religion is unimportant.
14.	The Bill of Rights and Constitutional Principles (limited Government).	No reliance on the Bill of Rights and the Constitution (unlimited Government).
15.	School Competition	Socialist public schools for the masses, their children get the choice of private schools.
16.	More defense spending for National Security	Less defense spending, believe the U.N. will save and protect the U.S. in time off need.
17.	Less dependence on Government	More dependence on Government.

18.	More Capitalism and fair markets	More favoritism and vote buying with Government discrimination, quotas, bureaucracy control, Welfare, Bailouts, Pay-offs, lobbyist tax breaks, loopholes, grants, centralized Government planning with taxes on production and regulation for the unanointed so they don't have the ability to compete in freedom and succeed but are controlled.
19.	Fairness and equal opportunity with no discrimination.	Want to jealously take the productives' wealth with no desire to acquire their own through work (Socialism and Parasitalism).
20.	Believe in the American people.	Believe in the Socialist Government Bureaucracy.

WE HAVE NOTHING TO FEAR EXCEPT GOV'T SOCIALISM ITSELF!

You Decide

No Crime No Drugs No Illegal immigration Massive Jobs Pay Rates 4 Times Higher No Taxes Freedom Growth and Opportunity	OR	Crime Drugs Illegal Immigration Massive Welfare Low Pay Rates Huge Taxes Parasitic Control Decay

It's Your Life and Your Country

To Oppress . . . . or Not to Oppress?

This is the question.

The 70% solution is the answer. Look it, Patriots, we can't afford more of the 10 Trillion borrowing, 40 Trillion in Government promises and the 60 plus years of social insecurity deceit. We need 160 million new jobs, the 10 Trillion Debt paid off and Asset Sale Incentives for the next 60 years as you regain your self-sufficiency.

Tax and Spend on Themselves
Borrow and Spend on Themselves
Inflate and Spend on Themselves
Hurrrray!
Then Start Over
When It Stops Fooling the People,
Deflate the Economy into Depression
and Spend on Themselves

What do you think of those sneaks? Even a crackhead will smile and tell you all the great things they will do and how they will help you if you give them a little money. But as soon as you leave, the thieving Judas mentality takes over and they immediately are buying drugs again. Just like your Socialist Government when it taxes you but it never stops and they never solve anything. Get away from the Socialists and Marxists in our country. I'm warning you they will suck out everything good in this country and our people. You will be left with their waste. Can you smell it yet?

How do you stop these Government crackheads? You take away all the money! Don't earn a surplus to invest, except in yourself and family. They will steal it. Become self-sufficient! Protect your Pensions, Income, Wages, Stocks, Businesses, Real Estate, and Home, everything decent and honestly earned. They will dishonestly steal from you; leaving you crushed in penniless want and despair in your old age! "It is your duty as a citizen to protect your capital at all costs from a Socialist Government."[2]

Besides Uncle Jim's 2 favorite solutions to fix our messes, here are 2 really simple solutions that really work. Try this—raise a 10% tariff across the board. This will create 200 Billion in extra revenue paid totally by the foreigners. This will also create 48 Million American Jobs! This will reduce worldwide pollution and finally the trade rip offs by the foreigners will stop as they pay a pollution tax and pay to use our ports, railroads, roads, use our police protection, pay for going through our customs to catch their dope smuggling and access to our markets. This will not create inflation as we need less Government for drug abuse, crime diminishes, energy costs decline, pollution goes down, and our interest rates go down as capital becomes more abundant for us. If the foreigners want to sell in our markets, they need to compete and pay for their fair share of taxes! Maybe 10% is too low and they need to pay 50% like our American people!

Ok, I know this is too easy but there is a 4th solution to solve their mess. Give every adult $40,000.00 right now in their bank account! Forget trying to prop up the Parasites and Predators trying to pick out losers and winners rewarding bad behavior! This is only 8 Trillion. Our Government is sitting on over 100 Trillion in assets. The Socialists can afford it. Now! Not in 30 years. But then again, they don't really care about helping you, your children or reducing poverty.

Awwww . . . what the heck, here's a 5th . . . give tax amnesty for all tax cheats and tax evaders. This will destroy the income tax system by any President of the People in an hour!

---

2 The great industrialist Henry Ford of Ford Motors made a profound statement to this effect and affect.

You really have to ask yourself about all the abusive suffering when our Government could have fixed all its messes in 5 minutes. Yeah, you go ahead and believe the bull about how this is impossible, irresponsible and all the excuses why it won't work. The PIPS and Socialists are the irresponsible. Look at their 10 Trillion debts! Go ahead, make their day and be their pawn. Let's just do it! Put $40,000.00 in your pocket. Now watch the Bank crisis end instantaneously, with your 40,000 in the bank. Then we can worry about how this solution can't work! Are you beginning to smell a Socialist Rat yet?

We've got to get away from these Socialists and their Parasitic Elites.
I don't know about you, but I am exhausted from the regressive *(dis) Liberalism* over the last 60 plus years. Sometimes I think these Parasites are making me croak! I don't have 30 more years, maybe 10. Can we fix this mess now?
Keep reading. Don't skip ahead but read faster. And when you get to the Freedom chapter, get the Silver Bullets and shoot the chains and shackles **free** as ***you jump off their treadmill!***

The Economic Stimulus[3]

At sometime taxpayers will receive an Economic Stimulus Payment. This is a thrilling program that I will explain using the Q and A format:

Q: What is an Economic Stimulus Payment?
A: It is money that the federal government will send to taxpayers.

Q: Where will the government get this money?
A: From taxpayers.

Q: So the government is giving me back my own money?
A: No, they are borrowing it from China. Your children are expected to repay the Chinese.

Q: But isn't that stimulating the economy of China?
A: Shut up!

Below is some helpful advice on how to best help the US economy by spending your stimulus check wisely:

> If you spend that money at Wal-Mart, all the money will go to China.
> If you spend it on gasoline, it will go to Hugo Chavez, the Arabs, and Al Qaida.
> If you purchase a computer, it will go to Taiwan.
> If you purchase fruit and vegetables, it will go to Mexico, Honduras, and Guatemala (unless you buy organic).
> If you buy a car, it will go to Japan and Korea.
> If you purchase prescription drugs, it will go to India.
> If you purchase heroin, it will go to the Taliban in Afghanistan.
> If you give it to a charitable cause, it will go to Nigeria.

---

[3] This wonderful information came from an anonymous source off the internet.

And none of it will help the American economy. We need to keep that money here in America. You can keep the money in America by spending it at yard sales, going to music concerts, Broadway shows, a baseball game, or spend it on prostitutes, beer (domestic only), or tattoos, since those are the only businesses still in the United States.

Patriots, email me with your Parasitic experiences, jokes and stories. I may put it in a book. By sending it, you allow me to publish your info. I can't pay you, but I'll try to include your name and city for acknowledgement.

unclejimameriplan@yahoo.com

2

THE 10,000,000,000,000.00 PROBLEMS

Wow! We sure have a lot of problems. The Politicians spent a lot of money, but unfortunately for our wallets, nothing else was reduced. They are morally, intellectually, spiritually and fiscally bankrupt. And they have their crime, Parasites and 10 Trillion Debt to prove it. It is time to end their Welfare Parasitalism and Socialism. These philosophies have become an extreme disappointment and a dismal failure. We need a new philosophy which is called "Realism." We need a philosophy which works and is based on the Laws of Nature. Here are the major Parasitic Problems:

1. Pathetic Job Shortage
2. 10 Trillion National Debt
3. Dangerous Levels of Crime
4. Unprotected Borders
5. Degradation of American Citizens
6. The Parasitic Culture Where We Eat Our Children by Destroying the American Dream
7. Paltry Pay Rates
8. Mushrooming Drug Culture and Abuse
9. Exploding Welfare Society
10. Illegal Immigration
11. Free Trade Rip-offs
12. Bizarre Over-Regulation
13. Government Official Pay-Offs and Bribes
14. Confiscatory Taxes, Inflation and Extremely High Borrowing Costs
15. Oil Dependency
16. Government Bloat, Dishonesty, Scandals and Deceit
17. Low G.D.P. Rates
18. Parasitic Health Care Costs
19. Poverty
20. Foreign Strangle Hold on our Politicians

21. Trade Imbalances
22. High Energy Costs
23. Expensive Student Education & Test Scores Too Low
24. Socialist Mentality and Cliques
25. Excessive Pollution and Global Warming

I have the solution!!! Keep reading . . .

3

THE NATURE OF PARASITALISM

"Before one may know Himself, Others, Governments, or Economics,
He must know nature." *quote by Uncle Jim*
"Nature never lies or is mystic, and its principles and teachings are timeless Truths of Life."[4]

Most likely the political environment trend and the growing problems we have in this country will continue to worsen until a catastrophe. We have had over 60 years of growing Socialism, with its Parasitalism. This "stinkin' thinkin'" is so ingrained in a large group of our citizens that they can't even see the forest from the trees and how this is screwing up our country. This won't change until the disaster strikes, forcing them in line. You can change yourself though. But before we go further with how to protect your family in freedom from Social oppression, let's define a Parasite, so you know what to watch out for, thus you can quickly recognize the peril and avoid the danger with your *6 Silver Bullets*.

"Parasite"— A.) An organism living in dependence on another for existence without making a useful return. To infest and consume on. An entity, which survives by using force with destructive procurement of benefits and resources from a Host that it critically injures and harms.[5]

B.) A Parasite is a creature that cannot see damage done to its Host. A Parasite can only survive by scavenging and feasting off a Host. A Host refuses or is unable to understand the nature of a Parasite and is helpless in preventing a Parasital attack. A

---

4 Marty Stauffer of "Wild America" said a profound statement something like this; a true Genius of Ecology.

5 Merriam-Webster Dictionary.

Host can only survive by destroying the Parasite or warding off a Parasital attack. There is no respect, just arrogance from the Parasite and ignorance from the Host. *Definition by Uncle Jim*

Parasites are a byproduct of Socialism but they don't get it. But you get it. You—Host; Socialist—Parasite and You—Prey, Them—Predator.

Socialists, their elite Robber Barons, Multi Nationals and others on the dole, will say anything to continue the feast and to get their man elected. They are flourishing in our current government environment. They are laughing behind your back. Oh sure, fall for those great speeches and be their suckers. You think they believe in Capitalism? Give me a break! **Parasitalism is the name, tax extraction is the game.** Remember that Capitalism is fairness, growth and honesty. Parasitalism is favoritism, regression, domination and dishonesty. Do you think the 10 Trillion Debt was money spent honestly? Then why is crime higher? Why do we have so many people working in dead-end jobs with little opportunity? Why don't we have surplus jobs? Why isn't your take home pay and net worth 4, yes **4 Times Higher**? And finally, why did they make 40 Trillion in promises of your money, not theirs? Just think, you've got to earn this money first, but they already spent it! Now you know what a Parasite is! Believe me, this chapter was no picnic or pleasure to write and fun to learn, but it's time for all of us to grow up and deal with these unpleasantries.

We have accomplished nothing great by expanding Socialism over the last 60 years and any good we have, happened despite it. The accomplishments and legacy of Socialism are government domination (of your life and money) a 10 Trillion Debt and another 40 Trillion in promises by their politicians to buy off voters. Don't forget their lousy system siphoned off your pension and Social Security benefits and caused Healthcare costs to be 4 times higher than necessary. Oh? These people aren't Socialists or Parasites? Then why do *(dis)Liberals* want to put our healthcare totally under their dominion and control? You want more of their regulation and monopolistic prices as the Parasites skim off even more? They don't even have a clue how socialized medicine is screwing up the country. They don't get it. Re-read the definition of a Parasite right now. If you don't like the word Parasite, how about Predator, which means "one that preys, destroys or devours; a mode of life which food is ruthlessly obtained by killing and consuming, a plunderer, ravager, to take by force, and wrongfully in the process steal, sack and lay waste" (not any better is it?).[6] How about Cannibals, where they eat our young and their waste is a 10 Trillion Debt? And how about another 40 Trillion in promises; your money, not theirs! And worse, your children get the bill and they didn't even vote! (Taxation without Representation). Predators, Cannibals, Vultures, Crackheads, Vampires, etc. are all the same to me and for convenience will be labeled Parasites in this book.

It's a cruel world out there, so be on guard. Parasite people talk nice, but don't expect fairness. Get smart. You will never get an education on this in your public schools! But hang tough; with the AMERIPLAN you beat the Parasites with the Silver Bullets, which help you change your environment! When you finish this journey today, you will be enlightened and with confidence move forward with each step. And don't get hung up on the little stuff. All you need to remember are the 70% Solution and the *6 Silver Bullets* in the AMERIPLAN and they are clearly outlined and simple to do! With these, cure your Parasitosis, prepare for success, thrive in FREEDOM, and of course with an **Increase in Your Pay 4 Times!**

All your entire life you were told to be positive and see only the good in people, but in the real world, you must also see the dangers and negative side to make it in life. Growing Socialism seems to be compassionate, but in reality they are creating dependency. Once the people become dependents, they can be Parasitized. If you want to blindly trust them, then skip this chapter. It made me sick to write it, but I felt compelled to bring the nefarious dark side of Socialism out of the closet to be exposed in the spotlight. Granted, most Socials don't think they are Parasites, causing any of our problems, but this is the Nature of the Beast. A Parasite is the very last to discover the extreme and critical harm it causes. This is the "arrogance." The American people are the Hosts to the Parasites but don't know how to stop it. This is our "ignorance." Socials have great ideas, but disastrous side effects, like trying to help a few poor by forcibly sucking out a small portion of the fruits of your labors, (where 70% is unfortunately siphoned off going to Parasites). But alas, the few destitute lost souls taking the easy bait, multiply into an army of millions of starving dysfunctional, dependent creatures. Now they consume most of your labors, as you work four times longer at your job, barely noticing your own malnourished and unsupervised children. Sure, things could be worse, but think of the positive and how much better things should be.

---

6 Merriam-Webster Dictionary.

"Within our sanitized and civilized world, mankind doesn't have to worry about the Parasites in the animal kingdom, but other human Parasites fill these voids very well indeed." See below some of the Parasitic behavior of creatures which are paralleled in humanity and why Socialism is not the way to go.

THE PARASITAL WASP

With a Capitalistic environment, we should have 160,000,000 high pay surplus jobs, 75% crime reduction, 50% less pollution, the 10 Trillion debt paid off in four years and vastly improved National Security. We don't have any of these and it is because of the Socialist Parasitic environment in our country, produced by a few arrogant and millions of ignorant hosts. Your pay and asset values should be **4 Times Higher** or you should only have to work ¼ as long so you can solve problems properly, raise your children and give them all the love and experiences of a first class childhood they can look back on with gratitude. But you don't have the time as your children fall into dope, diseases, sex, crime, and your TV is the babysitter! All of these ills are from Parasitalism and it is getting worse. Pay attention as this may be the most vivid and everlasting warning you will learn about the Parasites, who include many so called big spending and taxing Liberals, arrogant Bureaucrats, Multinational big businesses, hedge funds, many misguided Environmentalists, many Entertainers, OPEC and other twisted traders abusing the American people, all Welfare classes, some Union bosses, Monopolies, early Parolees, many Attorneys, Lobbyists, big Drug companies, some Foreign governments, Socialist zealots, Drug pushers, Illegal immigrants and other classifications of vultures, bloodsucking on the fruits of your labors. Most of these people and creatures don't even know they are Socialists, let alone Parasites, so "be wary". The abuse they bear on you is as serious as survival itself. Do you really believe when the Socials give their great speeches that they *can* really fix their mess? C'mon! They set things up this way and like it. Parasites don't care about you or your children. They only want to live off their wits and suck your fruits.

The Freeloaders have discovered the power of Government tax increases, borrowing, controlled spending to increase their power, loopholes, fiat funny money, regulation and loose immigration for wage deflation, all extraction techniques, all sucking off the family parents to control and leech off their labors. Just like a caterpillar, which is stung by a wasp implanting eggs in the caterpillar's very own body. Soon the eggs hatch and the larvae grow by eating the inside tissues of the still living caterpillar! The larvae inject a chemical, turning the caterpillar into a giant eating machine, producing large tasty flesh to be consumed by the Parasites. The caterpillar fights in pain ever harder for its very survival. It fights on seriously wounded in agony for each breath as the situation becomes more and more perilous and hopeless. After much misery, the caterpillar dies and the wasp larvae parasites finish off the flesh. The caterpillar doesn't reach maturity and produce offspring, so there is no future investment or further generation. This species becomes extinct. Now all the food nourishing the Parasites is gone, forever. The Parasite larvae must eat each other in anarchy. It's every Parasite for itself. Most kill one another as they cannibalize each other Pac-Man style. Possibly, a few will live if they migrate to a new food source and can find a new host.

We are trapped on a punishing environment treadmill, producing for the Socials and we neglect or forego families as their Parasites suck on our labors. One of the chemicals their PIPS inject in us is fiat money, which fuels their feast as you work harder for less. Fiat causes inflation and according to the *Loose Money Equals Loose Morality Principle* leads to destruction and eventual collapse into depression and anarchy. This is just what they are doing to you and our baby boomers! Illegal immigration will not fill the void, only sicken the situation as our respect diminishes and life is devalued with more and more Parasites joining the feast.

Patriots, it's every man for himself. We have a 10 Trillion debt the Parasites voraciously ran up. They ate up all our capital and this is why interest rates are not 2%. The Socials polluted the business environment with their byproduct called Parasitalism and this is why we have so many foreclosures, bankruptcies, lawsuits and unemployment with their twisted regulation. This is why you can hardly succeed in your own small business. They don't want you to be self-sufficient or a free man, like a sturdy oak. They want you dependant, without capital. Social Security was an excuse to raise your taxes, take away your capital and spend the money on themselves. Social Security is broke and they ate it! When you are old and tired, good luck fighting to get it out of them! Your family is small and sacrificed as you work longer and longer hours for nothing. But the Parasites have multiplied out by sucking off your labors and jeopardizing your children's future with a 10 Trillion debt burden and their other 40 Trillion promises. Forget about the Socialism and working together for a common cause, they shot themselves in the head as they destroyed their own philosophy and all possibility of a compassionate society. The Socials are cracking up the country! I see when you are 70, you want a strong heritage and legacy, with your successful offspring at your side. You certainly don't want to see a bunch of Vultures, Tax collectors, Bureaucrats, Monopolies, greedy Hospitals, Social workers, Attorneys, Pickpockets, Big Insurance companies, greedy Charities, Dope Addicts, Alcoholics, Wall Street Fat Cats, illegal immigrants and Illfare Parasites clinging to your veins eating the fruits of your labors as you sacrificed your life in vain to save! And watch their garlic eaters as they kick and spit in your face when you grow tired and decrepit in your last few lonely, painful years, like a dying caterpillar being eaten inside-out from Parasitic larvae, unable to continue their flesh feast from the fruits of your labors. Die your sorry, miserable death in agony and deepest regrets. Toodles.

Compassionate Socialists, congratulations with your Welfare on destroying part of this country. The exploding dysfunctional unproductive and elite Parasites you spawned that do not produce a surplus, like maggots, must now bite the hand that feeds it and eat the Liberal flesh right off your bones. Poetic justice?

THE STURDY OAK

In nature, the strong get stronger and the weak get weaker. In Nature, the weak are susceptible to the siphoning Parasites. The strong have defenses and can ward off Parasites and force the Parasites to hunt for another victim. Now that you know what a parasite is, you need to know what it takes to defeat them. Here is a parallel in Nature.

A small insignificant singled out sapling is unprotected and exposed to Parasites. Bores suck the sap and energy out of the young tree, bagworms devour its foliage, night beetles consume its tender leaves, the deer chew the forming buds, and the sun bakes its roots. The sapling has no immune system to fight off bacteria and diseases. Without the strength to produce sap and chemicals to repel the Parasites, soon the sapling bends and withers to death from all the attacks. This is kind of what the PIPS are doing to our productive children and the fruits of your labors (you must learn how to stop it).

On the other hand, a tall strong sturdy oak has plenty of branches, shade and roots which are planted deep in the soil and can absorb nourishment and water even in droughts. The bark is thick and protects the tree from fires, which would scorch and critically singe a sapling. This tree is self-sufficient, with thousands of leaves to prevent the sun from baking and drying out the roots. The bores try sucking the life's blood out of the tree, but are repelled by the tree's chemical releases, bagworms devour some foliage, but the sturdy oak has staying power and if not this year, in a couple years the birds will come to the rescue and feed on the caterpillars. Night beetles and aphids try their feast but there are so many leaves and shelter, the damage is minimal as resident tree frogs and other beneficial insects like Lady Bugs keep them in check. The deer and other herbivores try to stretch for the tender buds, but the sturdy oak is 5 feet in diameter and over 120 feet tall. The multitude of leaves and branches by their overwhelming numbers virtually guarantee survival. This mighty oak is blessed with reserves and self-sufficiency (for you, like a loving, supportive family and friends). Plus, the roots are so extensive; the grubs eating on root sap are insignificant. The stout size of the roots anchors the tree against any tornado, flood or hurricanes. This tree won't be broken and it can withstand the harshest environments.

The uncompassionate, cruel Parasites never hear the desperate cries of our families as they single out and break our people one by one like a sapling, tearing them down and when each one of us is beaten, just watch the violent Parasite feasting binge to the bone marrow like piranhas. Help your Uncle Jim stop these horrific atrocities. Religiously follow the *6 Silver Bullets*, and tell your friends.

The rich and elite Parasites can survive harsh circumstances. In this book, I show you how to also survive and outlast them, until the environment is changed, as they parasite on themselves in a cannibalized implosion. This is the way of nature as the strong become stronger and weak become food for the parasites. When there aren't any weak left, the parasites parasite on themselves in self-annihilation. We can stop this Parasitalism anytime we want. Join me, you soon to be sturdy oak of the ages! We don't have to wait for a major disaster like a depression, drought, war or plague to straighten them up, like usually happens. Sure you are a little sapling child lost in the wild. Learn your *Silver Bullets* and be a mighty oak tree, indeed! This is your book! This can be your path to your future, your hopes, your faith, your love, your American Dream. It's all here if you can only understand the simple solutions which the Elites, Government, Schools and Plutocrats could never share with you to allow your continued growth, even though this ultimately benefits them, just as much! Hint—learn your *Silver Bullets* well, my patriot. Your life is truly in your hands. All you needed was a tiny bit of knowledge.

There is more of course. A weak sapling in a field is easily crowded out by weeds and can easily be choked off and never grow to bear fruit. Weeds are weeds, which mean they don't produce a surplus, like the sturdy oak, which makes thousands of acorns to feed the entire woodland creatures. If the weeds are left unchecked, the small sapling will die or become stunted and never mature to a great surplus producing valuable tree. Remember, weeds don't grow into sturdy oaks. This is why Illegal immigration is so costly to our society as proven by the "*Crowding Out Theory*". Legal immigration, by the best and most responsible adults? YES. Illegitimate immigration? NO.

So, be a mighty oak, soaking up the daylight sun (knowledge and freedom), beyond the Parasites assault and stop being the unenlightened weak sapling fighting for daylight under a dense canopy of Parasites and don't let them sap your strength with taxes, confuse you with misinformation, getting you hooked on their dope, Welfare, junk food, gambling and other vices. Raise your own family, not support the unproductive or lazy through their tax extraction. Socials must raise their own young in honesty and from their own labors, not cutting a share from your fruits, especially without your blessing. Tell them to get a real job!

THE BEAST OF BURDEN

It is usual for a government to extract surpluses from people who have perverse behaviors according to the laws of nature, such as Drunks, Gangs, Pedophiliacs, Pornographers, Drug addicts, Monopolies, Influence peddlers, Lobbyists, Gamblers, Greed mongers, the Dishonest, lazy, Oppressive and Sneaky Foreign Trading Countries with closed home markets, Prostitutes, other unethical people, Criminals, and Welfarians (rich and poor), but when the Parasitalism instead is infestuated onto the productive and their children, the government has become corrupt! It is your responsibility and duty to save our country and protect your family from falling into a black hole of eternally hungry Parasites, as they take the cream and you are stuck with the leftovers of spoiled milk.

This reminds me of a calf that is born and fed in preparation of the eventual slaughter. The newborn cow is given shots (vaccinated), branded (finger printed and given a social security card), trained (a Socialist public education), prodded into its stall (job), milked (exploited) and finally shipped to the glue factory for salvage (nursing home and finally, death with inheritance taxes). If there are any calves (children), they will be veal (dead meat, look at the 10 Trillion debt the Parasites hung around their necks). Patriot, you and your children are nothing more than livestock to be consumed, unless you wake up. Remember, Socials arrogantly think they nurtured you for their harvest. You are their HUMAN RESOURCE TO BE CONSUMED!

Do you still wonder why interest rates aren't 2% and why we don't have 160,000,000 new high pay surplus American jobs? Why is healthcare so expensive? Why is the environment so crummy you can't start a new business without over 90% failing in a few years? Why do we have so much regulations, litigations, taxations and inflations? Do you think they like the system this way? The Socials said they needed all these crazy taxes to fix our messes and needed to borrow another 10 Trillion to solve everything. Then why isn't anything solved? All these problems they said they would fix are even worse, needing more money and bureaucracy, now and every year after, forever. Hey? Do you think they did this for an excuse, so they could get money out of you for the purse snatchers? They have no clothes.

The Socialists had their party, now they can help pay their own indecent 10 Trillion bills! They wanted to stay in power because they were better and so much smarter and compassionate than the stupid working women and men and greedy small business owners. Where in the heck is the compassion now, as we are broke and forced to pay as slaves the Parasites 10 Trillion bill! The Socialists and Liberals bought the parasite vote with your money as they sold their souls for a few more blood sucking years. Their grand "Pie in the Sky" ideals of government and collective ownership have blown up in their faces as their philosophy is mortally wounded and has become an unhappy, nauseating 10 Trillion joke, a bankruptcy at best. Maybe these Socials aren't so smart after all. They spent an extra 10 Trillion but solved nothing, only stuck their filthy mitts in your wallet and helped themselves and their buddies. Remember, anybody can talk a good game, with all their practice. Too bad they didn't spend all that time finding out the solutions, but fortunately, the AMERIPLAN solved their problems, well, at least yours.

THE GARDEN

When you change the government environment, you change people's behaviors, but it all blows up sooner or later if the environment is not in alignment with the "*Laws of Nature*" or as some call it "*Universal Law*".

Taking this statement a step further, with our directions, the Federal Government can change the environment in our country. This in turn will change behaviors. Our crime rates are high, our illegal immigration is high, our drug and alcohol abuse is high, our Parasites are too many, etc. These high rates tell you the environment is unacceptable. These and millions of other problems are solvable if you only know how to change to a better environment. You may not solve individual isolated incidents, but you will prevent a majority of the individual occurrences from ever happening. For example, to lower drug use, we can try with education and with rehabilitation, one by one. However, the crime has already been committed and the taxes to pay the costs are Parasitic. But if you weed the garden, eliminating the supply of drugs and the costs of drug use are too high, the citizens won't want to know the dangers they are missing and won't get hooked through repeated use. Thwarting the supply being smuggled over our borders, whistle blower fees, bounties and strict self-sufficient profit making prison sentences to uproot the spread is cost-effective. After a generation, the costs of preventing drug abuse will plummet, as the acceptability of drug use is intolerable. Education is nice, but making drugs scarce and the costs high is a sure bet to reducing most of the problem. We can do so much more to stop drug abuse (with less wasted tax money) and the secondary crimes from this Parasitalism. The question is, should the drug trade be stopped, as this will worsen the "*Crowding Out Theory*" if other structural changes are not made to the environment? The Socials don't want to solve these massive but simple to solve problems, like rampant drug abuse and illegal immigration or they already would have. Now, the Garden and its environment.

Look at our country as a *Garden*, where we collectively form a government to be our *Farmer*. The Farmer (government) has the responsibility to protect the garden environment for the *vegetable plants* so they may continually bear produce, just like our government has the responsibility to protect our productive families from Monopolies and other Robbers like Foreign trade nations buying influence parasiting on our families, dumping and siphoning off our jobs and wealth, etc.

When our New World Order Socials give our industries and jobs away in their trade deals, this is like *rotor tilling* our vegetable plants under and destroying them. At this point, the farmer has an obligation to sow a new crop for a better future yield (higher paying surplus jobs and industries). Our Socials never get enough new seed planted. By this I mean providing an environment causing surplus jobs and opportunities where infant businesses can grow and bear fruit. We have a bad environment and a waste of garden space as it fills with weeds (Illegal Immigration).

Remember, weeds don't produce a surplus. This is why they are weeds. They only suck up the nutrients and crowd out a good life for our productive citizens. Weeds consist of Drug pushers, Illegal immigrants, Criminals, unethical Attorneys, a growing segment of our Media, Pornographers, Gamblers, Prostitutes, Socialists, and others with useless vices that sap our time, energy, money and cause us harm.

Parasites such as worms and beetles eating the plants are like our Lobbyists, arrogant Bureaucrats, rich and poor Welfare classes and Illegal immigrants, getting your government services, all trying to cut a share off the fruits of someone else's labors. These growing cancers rot the partially eaten fruits, as the disenchanted productive are unable; quit or won't produce surpluses. Our farmer is unnaturally encouraging more Parasites with free feed of our services and wealth. It is the enabler spawning ever greater numbers of Parasites!

Other destructive creatures attacking the garden while the farmer is asleep are *varmints*. These consists of raccoons, rabbits, deer, ground hogs and are the predator class like monopolies, Robber Barons, Wall Street crooks, bloated unions, foreign governments with one way trade deals, special interest groups, some bureaucrats, and illegal immigrants unlawfully up here, all to take booty back home by whatever means. This bunch goes directly for the fruits of the productive, unapologetically cropping off the best nutritional parts, leaving you and your children undernourished, financially dependent and susceptible to diseases, unable to obtain the good life your forefathers provided and promised.

Diseases are the inevitable result of a negligent farmer, who allowed the garden to be overrun with *Weeds*, who allowed the life's blood of the plants to be siphoned off by *Parasites* and who allowed the *predators* to steal away with the fruits in the middle of the night. Don't forget the derelict *rototilling* by the farmer as he tilled under the producing crops called free trade, and his blatant laziness by not planting new seed. The *diseases* which destroy the garden plants are what is happening to our society today as our people have the virus of jealousy, the loss of hope, the lack of respect, lost work ethics, the disorder of greed, we have malignant Socialism, excessive Crime, and a Parasitic Plague.

Another danger is the over pruning of the plants. The hedging and pruning are like our overzealous regulations, stagnating our potential and stifling our freedoms. This is called regulation creep, an ever-tightening tourniquet, along with the crippling taxation extraction which is eaten by the Parasites.

The farmer must be sensitive to the plant requirements of fertilizer and water. To our people this means providing the needed incentive and job opportunities for all our citizens, young and old. The catch is it must not be done by our welfare, government programs, and our taxing and borrowing and fiat money creep, or Parasitalism takes over and you cause more damage than you solve. In the garden, you don't chop off the valuable garden plants that are doing well, feeding them to the sick, slower growing plants do you? For a moral government to be sensitive to its citizens, surplus jobs are the fertilizer for our people to grow. An honorable farmer deserving trust and respect in running our garden would pull the *weeds* out by the roots, use insecticide (parasiticide) to eliminate insects (*Parasites*), fence off the garden from the *Predators*, saw off the *branches* stealing sunlight from the plants, and finally provide the proper amount of *fertilizer* and *water* (resources) to keep the plants healthy and free of diseases. Hello? Anybody home? You think we need a better environment (Govt.'s system or rules)?

Your **pay should be 4 times greater** and your **assets worth 4 times more**. If you doubt me then just look at the outrageous cost of healthcare, bankrupt social security, 10 Trillion debt, our crime and deflated retirement accounts! Do you still think it all happened because of a recession? Get real patriot! How would you like to not have a recession for 60+ years! It's up to you, you know!

THE PHEASANT

I knew an Ann Arbor area Michigan farmer who liked pheasants. He kept buying them with hard earned money, releasing them and he even set up several feeding stations. Unfortunately, the birds kept dying and disappearing.

The pheasants had little ground cover for shelter from the long cold winter weather. Without more brush and tall weed fields, the pheasants didn't have seed to browse on when they became hungry or shelter from the wind. They soon froze to death. Also, without tall grasses in the fields, there weren't any grasshoppers in summer to supplement their diets. Without cover, the pheasants were an easy target for the hawks, owls, foxes and stray dogs that systematically attacked the flock, picking them off one by one. It really devastated the birds when the farmer went on vacation each year for a month in the middle of winter. The feeding stations ran out of food quickly and needed to be replenished every week. Obviously, most of the birds became dependent on the easy pickings at the feeders and lost their self-sufficiency. When the food supply ran out and the free lunch was over, it was over for them too. (Hint—make sure you are self-sufficient and not dependent on Socialist handouts. The gift of welfare is a Trojan horse).

After a few years, the farmer listened to me about the importance of the environment. He discovered the environment he was providing for the birds was weakening their survival skills. The birds lost the ability to feed themselves and secondly, by luring them unnaturally into the open fields, they were easy prey for the predators. (This is our country's environment, produced from Socialism. The Socials cure is more Illegal immigration to increase our labor pool even as they crowd our own children out.

Finally, the farmer realized how to improve the pheasant environment. Instead of constantly buying and stocking new birds in his fields (Illegal immigration) and then unnaturally supporting them with bird feeders (Welfare, free healthcare and other wasteful government services), the farmer stopped cutting his fields in various spots, allowing different plants to grow tall and produce dense cover and seeds for the pheasants to sustain themselves. Soon the birds thrived and were much better equipped with strong survival and self-sufficiency skills, instead of dependant on Illfare. Let us return private ownership, job expansion and the ability of our productive to keep the tools of production and keep the fruits of their labors and not Parasited on by Socialists, foreign lobbyists, trial attorneys, and big businesses, with their tax extractions, regulations, lawsuits, trade deals and subsistent Welfare subsidies. The environment doesn't work and is in debt by 10 Trillion! Their feast has bankrupted the country. Forget Illegal immigration to increase the productive population and raise your own children as you flourish. Let us respect the "*Breeding Rights Theory*" and once again become a government OF, BY, and FOR the people, *our* people.

The moral of the story . . . let us change and improve our Socialist environment in government (well at least our own) and stop being birdbrains.

FISH ANYONE?

To measure compassion; don't take a workingman's fish by force (taxes), and don't give a non-working man that fish (liberal welfare). Let each man keep his own fish (freedom from tax Parasitalism), and show all men how to fish (self-sufficiency)! Don't fence and close off the lake to fishing (Socialism)!

By making men dependent on welfare for their next fish is growing a class of pathetic slaves. This doesn't seem very compassionate to me. Remember *this* when the *(dis)Liberals* cry for more taxes to show compassion. Do you see how they use your kindness and compassion as a weapon to Parasite on you? If you really want to help the poor, start spending your own money and start helping poor people. I'll bet you'll get 4 times more done at 10 cents on the dollar! Or, let the Socialists keep raising taxes and then we all can be poor and miserable together.

LEFTY NIBBLING—SOCIALISM CREEP

This reminds me of a Host who took a friend to dinner. The guest was asked by the waiter what he wanted for dinner. He said "Oh no, I'm not hungry, I don't want anything". The Host tried to get the guest to order without success and finally ordered dinner. When the appetizer came, the Host politely offered the guest a bite. The guest said, "just a small nibble". The guest kept taking small nibbles and before you knew it, he ate the whole appetizer. When the Host's salad came, he asked if the guest wanted a taste. "Well, just a nibble" as the guest inhaled the whole salad. When the Host's diner came, the guest became pushier even as the Host politely offered the guest to have a small nibble. The guest scarfed down the Host's entire dinner. The waiter seeing this inquired if the guest would like dessert. Full of irritation, the guest protested, "No, I told you I wasn't hungry!"

This is like our Socials who say they don't want to parasitize the fruits of our labors to our faces, and then behind your back aggressively siphon off our money with huge tax increases, borrowing and inflations. When they get caught, they play up to our kindness and gullibility, telling us the regulations and tax increases are for some noble cause. They call you a bigot; mean spirited or whatever, if you disagree. They keep tightening the grip, taking away our wealth, putting it under their control, trying to run businesses and failing, spending 70% on themselves, without giving the people back a useful return. "You earn it, they spend it. This is Socialism and the creeping demands are getting awfully strong. This is the problem with our country that our people haven't been able to identify, but they sense something is awfully wrong with the direction this country is heading in. Keep in mind, the government is our biggest growth industry and it is at the expense of our productive. For every Government job created we have eliminated 4 real jobs because the government doesn't produce, only consumes and redistributes, often unfairly. When the Socialists have to pay the customary 70% in Parasital homage, there aren't many spoils left to dish back out for your benefit or the needy. This is why Socialism can only work for a few decades. Eventually the populace wises up and sees the hypocrisy, and refuses to continue laboring for freeloaders, being the fools."

THE FROG TECHNIQUE

We don't see the effects of long-term Socialism creep and its hangerons side effects, as it methodically grows, siphoning away our freedoms, extracting the fruits of our labors, confiscating our assets and property rights, and further suffocating our families. This reminds me of the frog that was dumped in a pot of boiling hot water. Immediately, the frog leaped out feeling the danger of being exposed to the killing environment. Our Socials soon learned they must move very slow and in shadows without bringing attention to themselves. This time they gently set the frog in a pot of cool water and ever so slightly and calculating, they raise the temperature to a boiling death trap. The frog doesn't notice the incremental water changes as it continues swimming in the pot at a slower and slower weakening state. Eventually, the frog is boiled to death.

The frog never knew what was happening and never thought to jump out of the pot when it still had the strength to act. At the very last moments before death, the frog realizes it was nefariously tricked in an evil plot, but alas, it is too late for this frog. It is boiled meat. Stick a fork in, he's done, lunch time for the Parasite feast! Turn out the lights. So it is with Social Security . . . suckers!

In a past Congress, Socials in Power got over anxious and they tried to force their monopolistic healthcare on us too quickly. They got caught and a lot of these PIPS lost their next election. Many just made up a phony excuse and retired. If they would have tried to run they would have got trounced and the crud beat out of them. They didn't run because they don't want you to realize you have the power to fix their mess, starting by firing them. "And here they go again" but remember, "Freedom is never more than one generation away from extinction."[7] So wake up to their deceitful power grab.

Above is a parallel of what their environment is doing to our own children. Our children don't know any other or better way or see the creeping changes. They don't have the imagination or a healthy sense of skepticism. They are easily swayed by others and don't have any experiences beyond their own young years. TV and Socialist public school brain washing hasn't equipped them to judge reality, only making it easier to be exploited and harvested by the Parasites and their zombie followers who are blinded from all the disinformation and propaganda. Our people think the current high disrespect, crime rates, drug and alcohol abuse, violence, etc., is normal. It is not! We can change it, a lot quicker than they took to mess things up. Scrape up the Hope you can, come join Uncle Jim, the freedom man.

Again, with a proper environment, I believe your **Salary Should be 4 Times Higher,** No Govt. Debts, with **75% less crime**, as you raise your own children in love, safety and security, with more freedom and happiness than you could possibly and currently imagine. This is Capitalism. Don't wait for the disaster when they finally discover their ideas and Socialist philosophy is corrupt, according to the "*Laws of Nature*". Fix your own problem, so they can't make their 10 Trillion problems your problem. And oh yeah, their other 40 Trillion in promises. Just wait for the coming austerity! Smarten up now.

---

7 President Ronald Reagan.

THE MOTHER DUCK

Many years ago, when I had a summer job in Grosse Pointe, Michigan to pay for my tuition, I would walk along a nearby shoreline at Lake St. Clair during breaks.

I remember clearly a mother duck with eight ducklings. One duckling was always last in line following the mother and tended to stray a few yards behind the flock all hovering close around the mother. One day, suddenly the mother circled aggressively toward the last duckling. The last duckling sensing the danger tried to flee as the mother snatched it in her beak and viciously shook the duckling. I interjected with a stick, poking the mother until she relented. Then all the ducks followed her in line, even the attacked duckling. For the next ¼ hour, all was fine, until the last duckling wandered astray a few short yards. The mother again shot toward the duckling, crushing the fledgling's neck, violently shaking it. I ran to find a stone, and then threw it at the mother. She released the duckling, but it was floating limp and lifeless. I eventually retrieved it and convinced it was dead, buried it.

Why would a mother kill her own offspring? This is totally against the "*Laws of Nature*" and inbred instincts. This took much pondering, as I required myself to completely understand this lesson of nature and how to relate it, if possible, to human nature.

I contemplated my observations of the mother duck. Perhaps the harsh environment without much food caused her to destroy one of the offspring; and because the wandering duckling was such a distraction and threat to the survival of the other young and herself. However, there was plenty of vegetation for sustaining the ducklings and no hungry predators such as turtles, hawks, large fish, etc. The reason for the wrongful death of the duckling must be that this duckling was from another brood and no relation to the mother. I soon found this to be unlikely.

I continued my study of the resident family of ducks. On the second morning since the first death, I witnessed, to my horror, the discovery of yet another dead duckling floating near the shore. The mother who originally had eight ducklings was shockingly now down to four. There were no other adult ducks in this area, so I felt convinced this mother duck killed at least four of her own offspring.

I didn't see them again to continue my observations, but I can't help wondering in sadness about the outcome of the remaining four ducklings.

Did their fate end up like the other four siblings? And if any of these siblings live to bear offspring, will they in turn kill off their young?

Many strange events occur in nature. If the behaviors and actions of a creature are wrong according to the *Laws of Life*, they are eventually corrected by nature, as this animal will become extinct from inferior instincts. This behavior, either learned (environment) or inbred (genetics) will not continue. Our Social government, with condonement of drug abuse, welfare for the non-working causing unnatural population expansion, illegitimate immigration policy, and the over tax extraction of our shrinking productive class, excessive borrowing and spending are suicidal violations of nature and will soon blow up in their Socialist faces. Show compassion, don't hate them. You don't have to produce a surplus they can suck out of you by forcing our Government to do their dirty work. Become self-sufficient and this legal theft will all end in a couple of years as you thrive in FREEDOM! Even now, the Pendulum has changed direction, where we have too many consumers and not enough producers. Shortages will soon result as the baby boomers retire and all will be exposed to *Darwin's Survival of the Fittest.*

Don't punish the promoters and practitioners of these lifestyles, with the jealous Parasiting on the productive families. These groups are headed for extinction, along with their Socialist Liberal Party. The question is "Since we live in a Limited Republic, should they be able to crowd out your family with their philosophy, propped up with fiat money theft, your taxes, over leveraged borrowing, buying votes with welfare as they destroy jobs, illegal immigration, and teachings to entice and indoctrinate your children into their way of life? Again, run for your life! Natures' strongest instinct is survival. There is no room for hate; they have the right to be here just as much as anyone else. Just accept it and flee the abuse. You can't change them. They can choose what they want as long as they don't Parasitically interfere with your freedom. All you can do is compassionately watch as they destroy themselves. Again, stay out of their way with the *6 Silver Bullets* so you can't be hurt from the behavioral epidemic of *(dis)Liberalism*.

SUNFISH

In Farmington Hills, Michigan where I grew up, there was a nearby pond. When I was about 12, I decided to go fishing in it. Unfortunately, this pond was dug about two years earlier and didn't contain any fish.

However, I now had a goal to keep me busy the next few years—stocking the pond! All the free time I had, especially in the summer, I went fishing at a small creek to catch sunfish to release in my neighbor's pond. The rest of my free time was spent observing the new pond inhabitants.

After three years, I began catching some of the biggest and healthiest sunfish, in the stocked pond, that I have ever seen. I returned them to the water so they could repopulate the pond. The fishing was good a couple more years. After the 5th year, I noticed there were sunfish everywhere I looked in the pond, but they all appeared very small. Each year after, I caught fewer and fewer big sunfish and more stunted bait nibblers. At seven years from the beginning of my experiment, most all of the fish I caught were stunted, unhealthy, and ¼ the size of the fish caught a few years back. This made me ponder . . . fish are animals and subject to nature like man. I looked for comparisons and a question arose, "What happens to people if there are not enough resources and too many people are packed into an environment without room for growth?"

Obviously, people will be stunted physically and mentally if they avoid or can't obtain proper nutrition. But what if there are too many demands placed on government services like education, Welfare payments for the rich and poor, etc., causing an increase in taxes, leading to limited resources, more crime and aggressive competition (like rats) for food, shelter, clothing, jobs and a better quality of life? Does the crowding out manifest in parental deprivation where our children suffer the consequences and become stunted themselves?

An intelligent species or an intelligent segment will lower its population procreations when a harsh external environment has shortages. However, a competitively stressed dysfunctional species or a segment thereof from the challenges of survival will over breed, trying to make up in numbers what it lacks in quality. Our elite want Welfare fuel for the underclass to stimulate breeding and illegal immigration, which means more markets, cheap labor and deflated American wages. With cheap labor, a country will never stay number one especially with 4 billion people who will kill to get in here and work for $8.00 a day. To make it worse, our parents, during their child-rearing years, are Parasited on with heavy taxes to sustain the job transfers to the poor foreigners and wealth transfers, which then end up in the rich elite's pockets. The productive are unable to build capital, which allows for their self-sufficiency, reserves for recessions and emergencies. They are not experiencing the satisfaction of Capitalism and growth, but compete harder and harder on the treadmill of life for less and less, as they feed more and more Parasites, rich and poor. This is Parasitalism, not Capitalism. Our productive middleclass is being ripped apart with a few joining the rich Parasite club and a multitude joining the ranks of the downtrodden or just dying out in numbers over the years, foregoing a family possibly having abortions. This is a long-term type of *Productive class genocide*, which dooms any society moving in this direction of decay. This philosophy seems quite uncompassionate and stupid to me. What do you think?

The expanding taxes, drugs, decaying education system, growing government ownership, 10 Trillion debt, Pick Pocket Socialism, loss of surplus opportunity and growing dangers to our national security is a bizarre environment trend which puts our country at risk of social and economic upheaval. When our stabilizing large baby boom class of wealth producers retires and without great changes, this country will rot in self-destruction. Sadly, the elites should be **Four Times Richer** themselves, without having to look over their shoulders paranoid and worrying about the next regulation, new tax, lawsuit, drive-by shooting or their kids becoming drug abusers. What a regressive wretched society with lifeless expressionless humans wandering as strangers passing one another. There is no community, friendship or nationalism. Nobody greets you with a smile; just another worker bee walking by in miserable silence.

By encouraging a growing dependant class that cannot produce a surplus and consumes more than it contributes will cause a stunting as all suffer and are poorer from the "*Crowding Out*" with increasing taxes for Welfare and crime control. The point is, if you help the unproductive, you must go the distance and help prevent the unplanned procreating and Illegal immigration or the result will be slow or negative growth, from the stunting. The cure to the unproductive's overcrowding in the past has been wars, birth control, starvation, riots or diseases. (AIDS and Ebola are proof the "*Crowding Out Theory*" has been violated). It's too bad people must now be exposed to *Darwin's Law*; however, our country is broke and unable to continue the Welfare feast for rich and poor. Socialism must now end. Without using the techniques in the AMERIPLAN, this country will experience a very harsh existence, along with the surplus trading nations we gave a temporary advantage. It won't last forever. The irresponsible Socialist tinkering is cruel punishment and they pretend to be compassionate? Do you still believe Welfare is kindness or is it a cruel evil joke on the productive Hosts for the benefit of the Parasites, as the self-sufficiency and future survivability of the poor is destroyed? Do we live in a country of Capitalism or Parasitalism? Which environment do you prefer? Who are the real racists, the Socialist Liberals or those wanting to reduce Welfare with no taxes and surplus real jobs?

Back to the sunfish. During the 7th and 8th years I took all the small fish I caught and returned them to the river. I culled the breed to reduce the Over-Crowding pressures. By the middle of the 9th year, I was pleased, as I was again catching a stock of large, healthy sunfish. I was satisfied my childhood experiment was a success! From this adventure in my early life, I developed a clear understanding of the importance of the environment and its effects on all living creatures.

The solutions to end the "*Crowding Out*" which is ruining a good life for our people and the solutions to returning to the American Dream are some of the same problems and simple to solve once you clearly have identified the problems.

Below are some responsible, simple and compassionate solutions to stop this disaster and keep a country moving forward.

1. No dangerous prisoner early parolees or reduced sentences for good behavior. When caught, "you do the time for the crime" and stop Parasitalism with self-supporting prisons.
2. End most Welfare, causing illegitimate procreation dysgenics (*breeding rights* violation), but be compassionate by creating 160,000,000 new jobs. Our charities and churches will help the destitute, unless they are crackheads, thieves, liars, or dangerous.
3. End all illegal immigration and reduce legal immigration to the best and brightest. No more mass irresponsible granting of citizenship. Let us stop exporting our jobs and importing people and illegal drugs. Let's raise our own children in a decent life.
4. Reduce all social services and government jobs which are unessential as they spawn a growing Socialist lazy culture, which will destroy the productive with ever higher taxes, extracting the fruits of our labors as the 10 Trillion debt blows up in bankruptcy or hyperinflation (your choice). Probably both.
5. Better teaching in school about responsible parenting and the disasters of unplanned pregnancies is crucial. The schools and churches have to work together. Try same sex schools and weekly clergy visits to the schools for starters.

6. Anyone taking welfare accepting government aid must have mandatory birth control (tubal ligation and vasectomies). When they pay the Socials a big fee and payback the welfare, the dependents can then have a reverse operation. To control this breeding rights violation, you can always go to China where there is no welfare but you get an abortion anyway.
7. Banishment. If anyone in this country can't play by the rules—offer a one-way ticket to another country. It's a privilege to live in the United States, not a right to Parasite and get a free ride at the suffering of another.

Surely you can see the Social Politicians haven't begun to solve any of the critical problems and their actions have worsened all of these. We can't stop every isolated problem or crime in this country; however, with a proper environment most of these problems will never occur. We can then have Government concentrate on the remaining problems, instead of just wasting all our lives and money to prop up the hangerons.

Years later, as an adult, I went back to the pond to see what had become of the sunfish that had consumed a large part of my childhood. I hadn't culled the sunfish for several years and had great curiosity as to what became of them. To my horror, the pond was practically empty with only a few tiny little sunfish and several small dead fish on the shore. During other summers at this time I saw thousands. My mind was racing to understand what happened. Was this pond affected by winter kill from an over-populated environment of sunfish, which depleted the oxygen in combination with dying vegetation and heavy snow over the winter ice? Were there new Predators or Parasites? Or possibly a disease had stricken the pond sunfish? Was this an eventual check and balance by nature, according to the "*Crowding Out Theory*"? Could it be soon nature will correct the excesses of our Socialist philosophy? We can easily change our environment but sunfish can't.

I strongly believe there are lessons from this ecology that parallel mankind. Today, we have nature giving us subtle hints of a forthcoming major disaster. Look at AIDS, Ebola, T.B. and Legionnaires disease, etc. and how quickly they can spread. It is quite possible the irresponsible sex and procreating of the third world and the underclasses with the artificial help of Welfare could wipe out most of mankind by accelerating the spread of some incurable disease. The "*Laws of Nature*" surely work on mankind just as on sunfish.

Natural Law has eminent domain over government. A successful government must stay within the envelope of nature or nature will slap down a Humpty Dumpty government hard, with a disaster that no men can collectively solve. At this point it will truly be every man for himself.

BETTER YOUR PROBLEMS THAN MINE

By some intellectuals, it is determined beneficial to have at least one country to accept the spillovers of surplus humans or a small war in the world happening at all times. The thrill and danger seekers bent on high-risk adventure will gravitate to these areas taking their violent ways with them. This will be one less problem the dysfunctional nations will have to deal with in their own lands. However, the accepting nation is put in a very dangerous and precarious position.

The thrill seekers can be encouraged to migrate to the action and some people think if they themselves fall victim to the carnage, so much the better. This is a most effective way to cull the human breed without using force, if they should happen to later get out of line. The undesirables could stir up the pot, agitating and unraveling the co-habitative peacefulness in the community. Much better to let them migrate to someone else's country. Remember all the looting and rioting in L.A.? Won't happen again? Right. Is this why Mexico and other countries are content letting all the illegal aliens from Central America migrate up here?

Why are illegal aliens bad news and what is the danger in not protecting our borders? They do exacerbate the "*Crowding Out Theory*", don't they? Do they ever sell drugs? Do they ever deflate wages? Do they absorb government services which drastically raise your taxes, keeping you working longer to pay for them as you have less time and neglect your own children, if you can afford any (or have abortions)? They don't spread diseases, do they? Do they ever steal, rob, become violent, prostitute, shoplift, form gangs, or threaten you and your children? Are they always peaceful law abiding humans? Right? They don't work for cash, trying to avoid our tax system, do they? They don't migrate up here bringing their problems with them instead of fixing their own messes back home, do they? None of them are wanted by the law? In case you don't know it, this is the *Silent*

War.[8] The greatest human instinct is self-preservation and survival, all you can do is flee. Get out of their way before these Predators destroy you and your family. Or, will you wait for help from the politicians' big lethargic ineffectual government solutions instead of them calling you a racist, xenophobe or bigot? Their sticks and stones *will* break your bones, but their names will never hurt you.

THE CICADA

The Periodical Cicada emerges from the ground every 17 years from its larval stage into a large bodied adult to seek a mate and reproduce. The cicada is a most tasty bug, which is a favorite for Parasites like Killer Cicada Wasps and predatory birds to feed themselves and their young. The Cicada by coming out of the ground once for only a brief spell has improved its survival odds. This periodical emergence has foiled many a Predator. There is no Parasite which can withstand and match its way of life. Parasites looking for a feast on the 18th year are in for a rude awakening. Not until another 17 years will Cicadas appear in mass for a great feast. Lucky will be the few Predators around for the 17th year feast!

As adults, our baby boom generation has been feasted on by the Parasites of Foreign Lobbyists, OPEC, Big business, insiders and other Special interest groups. Raising a family in the current conditions with all the drugs, crime, high taxes, diseases, Socialist red tape, trade deficits, job dislocations, Illegal immigration *Crowding Out*, alternative lifestyles, etc., is making survival unnaturally difficult in our country. Our productive, by feeling the effects of this Parasitic environment, are cutting back on their families. This will reduce the amount of surplus wealth and investment available to be extracted in the future. This is when the Parasites will cannibalize themselves. They can't live for free forever.

We had a good environment after WWII and during the early adolescent baby boom years, which was the result of our citizens keeping the Parasites in check. Our men and women who made great sacrifices during the depression and World Wars, understood it was more important to protect

---

8 I read this in a book over 10 years ago and don't know who coined this phrase.

our own children than to appease and give homage to the foreigners that cost us so many of our people during their wars. We couldn't be bribed, bullied or beaten. But now the good times are gone and life is a harsh existence, as our young do not understand how they are the pawns used to prop up a world economy without regard to fairness and respect. There is no fairness and respect in running a 600 billion yearly trade deficit. This only punishes our people as it falsely rewards sloth. Keep reading, I think you are beginning to smell a Social rat and our problems aren't so tough to solve when you get the big picture.

The punch-drunk People in Power don't have a clue how they are causing critical damage. It is thought by our Socials the man-made government stress put on our productive will force us to be more competitive and create further wealth in new industries and technologies, but not for over 20 years straight! Unfortunately, they tried to cross the razors edge, got cut and the result is a massive transfer of wealth and jobs with slower growth and a debt driven economy full of disheartened Welfare recipients and other Parasites feasting off a smaller and smaller "*American Pie*". Why even our Parasites could see their pay dramatically increase 4 times, if they could only wake up, but the Social *(dis)Liberals* can't.

So, now our population is shrinking except for the growing Parasites. There won't be many human Cicadas to be consumed in the future. Our productive families are waiting to raise children when the environment improves, which you can improve starting today. Don't wait for them or you may never have a family, wealth or freedom. Remember, our Socials put government in debt by 10 Trillion, taxed your surplus for social insecurity, which they spent, and promised 40 Trillion or so more. In the next major depression, with the 10 Trillion debt, our government will be a liability, not an asset. The clock ticks into the 18th year and soon our baby boomers will retire in mass into the stock market crash and plummeting real estate values as they all try to liquidate at once like lemmings, with a bankrupt Ponzi social security scam. Don't let their problems be your problems. Study your *Silver Bullets* in this book and prepare while you still have time.

One day if we aren't wiped out, when they stop exporting jobs, wealth and industries in exchange for drugs, illegal aliens, borrowing and welfare, then like the Cicadas, our people will prosper and produce another baby boom generation of magnificent children and future world leaders. Unfortunately in the next generation, without using the 70% solution, I see the U.S. decaying as its prestige evaporates and other countries taking the lead of world leadership; all because of the policies we have today.

It is the Author's opinion, our remaining baby boomers and Echo Boomers of child rearing age should dramatically increase their number of children. It is also believed by Uncle Jim the bureaucrats in Washington are making a catastrophic mistake in trying to smooth out our population birth cycles. They believe the economic dislocations and changes in demographics are bad for a society. I think this is ignorant thinking, which violates the "*Laws of Nature*". It can just as easily be said by trying to tinker with our lives is a disaster exacerbating the cycles worse than if they just let this natural phenomena work to its own design. Human reproduction by responsible adults is the strongest instinct after self-preservation and survival. The Socials don't have the intellect to make informed policy over the "*Laws of Nature*" when they can't even fix their own debts and dysgenic Parasitalism. Then they make you weak with health costs 4 times too high, massive unemployment and poverty. And you want more Socialism? Remember . . . **"We have nothing to fear except Socialism itself." "Do not ask what your country can do for you, but ask what you can do for yourself!"**

I am convinced the baby boom cycle and the next mini-baby boom cycle is a positive event in nature we must nourish. As the boomers advance into different stages of their lives, there is great change and energy causing innovation, ingenuity and creativity with endless opportunities! Sure these changes put stress on People in Power as they try to corral and tame the restless spirits of the young adults. But then the Parasites have a field day as the middle aged productive adults try to raise their young through the growing trend of Parasitalism. And finally, after the child rearing has been curtailed and the adults become older, exhausted, but much wiser, the Parasites are shaken off with the power of knowledge. Now a new cycle will begin. The 18th year! Watch, we will destroy their Parasitic Socialism and its abomination of nature! Join me! Learn well my Patriot . . . THE AMERIPLAN.

THE CUCKOO BIRD

The Cuckoo bird is one of the most bizarre and most diabolical Parasites of them all. The female Cuckoo bird mates with its opposite sex, then seeks out a Hosts' nest to drop in its egg when the male and female bird of another species are out foraging for food. The Cuckoos, won't take the responsibility of raising their own offspring, they force or trick another to do the labor, like the Parasitic Socialists. The Cuckoo bird removes, kills, and eats one of the Host eggs so there is still the same number of eggs in the nest. The new parents sit on the eggs not knowing one is not of their own. When the eggs hatch, the Cuckoo fledgling is much bigger and more aggressive, eating all the food as the other legitimate babies starve and cry for nourishment. The baby Cuckoo bird is a killer, and when the Host parents are away searching for food to feed the voracious appetite of the growing Cuckoo, the baby Cuckoo Parasite pushes the much smaller chicks out of the nest to their certain death. Now the Cuckoo gets all the spoils. The Host parents do not understand the wicked trick played on them. They were fooled by the egg planted in their nest that looked like their own, so they continue to feed this killer Parasite even as it grows twice the size of the adult Hosts. Eventually, the exhausted childless Hosts' discover this hideous Parasite is not their offspring and abandon the nest and curtail feeding the Parasite. After a day or two waiting in hunger, the Cuckoo flies away and begins feeding itself. Now you know why it is imperative we abolish the income tax with an amendment.

This is what happens from Welfare and illegal immigration. The Illegals come up here for free Government services, healthcare for their families, Welfare and take jobs. Our parents work harder and harder to pay the higher taxes with deflated wages to support the feast. Our own children are neglected from the longer hours we work and they fall into the wrong crowds, dope, crime, diseases and are *Crowded Out* from the good life they deserve. Many of our children who are now adults forego a family, have abortions or have very small families as they try to cope with the tax Parasitalism which feeds and nourishes the Illegal immigrant Cuckoos. To stop this, our Parasitic taxes, Welfare, Illegal immigration and government services must be cut to the bone, so each family is allowed to keep the fruits of their own labors. Now, the evil Cuckoo Parasitalism crowding out your children can be stopped. And what are the *(dis)Liberals* doing now? Enticing the illegals with free health care! No wonder this country is a broke joke!

If you can't see the immorality and insanity of Welfare look to nature. A male and female dove must expend all their time and energy nurturing and protecting their nest of fledglings. There is never enough time and resources to run around to all the dysfunctional birdies nests and feed other stranger offspring or their own offspring are put at risk of predators, are not taught survival skills and risk perils of starvation. With our Socialist Welfare our children are undernourished, unsupervised and suffer the pitfalls of drugs, crime and a pathetic education in front of the boob tube as we work longer hours to pay taxes before we can sustain ourselves and our children. When the Socialists pay the unproductive their cut and the remaining spoils are redistributed, you will find their 30% back for Welfare, Daycare, Head Start, Social Security, education, etc., is no match compared to your loving nurturing. You do it from love; they do it to get in your wallet. If you still believe in the merits of Socialism, you have sold yourself short, lost your freedom, hope, love and true compassion for our children and Humanity!

The moral of the story, stop being a Parasite's Birdbrain (again) and work smarter, not harder, as your **Pay Increases 4 Times** with the AMERIPLAN and your own children thrive in an economy growing at 10% a year!

TURKEY FLOCKS

Turkeys function mostly on instinct. They have very small brains and are not one of the more intelligent members of the animal kingdom. They have a survival instinct of flocking together with other turkeys, as there is safety in numbers. They have less odds of being singled out and a few extra sets of eyes might come in handy. Turkeys don't go it alone in a nasty environment full of Predators or they are quickly eaten up.

Minors in the ghetto form gangs for the very purposes, as do turkeys. Once gangs become prevalent, a youngster must choose a gang or face the danger of going it alone. Survival and self-preservation are in the forefront of these kids' minds. With the current environment in the slums with all the violence, jealousy, drugs and carefree attitude about crime, a gang is a crutch and a form of protection, which increases ones safety, or at least kids think so.

If gangs were only about protecting each other, it would be a good thing. Unfortunately, this is not the case. Paradoxically, the very things the kids wanted protection from, which made them join a gang, are the very things the gangs are doing to others, such as intimidation, theft, physical attacks, vandalism, pushing dope, sexual assaults and other crimes. Gangs can be stopped with some simple environmental changes such as curfews, same sex schools for less teen pregnancy, school and class rotation among children so they don't develop strong bonds with their gang members, year round schooling to eliminate idle time and reducing minimum wage rates and regulations to increase summer job opportunities. If they drop out of school, then catch them and put them in a home. Stiff juvenile penalties with trials as adults ending two-tier justice, with a long time away from home for possession of drugs and guns will help. Of course, eliminating Illfare and providing the parents job opportunities so they will have to become responsible will make them become a good role model and example for the children. Ending Welfare subsidizing the illegitimate procreation and sufficient birth control will help solve the "*Crowding Out Theory*", thus reducing a lot of the crime from these people fighting over limited resources. If human offspring are planned, the parents take pride in them and properly supervise them. Giving unearned "*Welfare Breeding Rights*" is disastrous and will doom a civilized people. It's your choice . . . Subsistent Welfare or **160 Million new high pay American jobs**. Which do you think is more compassionate?

LIFE OF A SALMON

After over 35 years of Salmon, Steelhead and Brown Trout fishing on, to me, the greatest fresh water river in the world (The Big Manistee), I have a few parallels more. Salmon deposit their eggs on a gravel bed and immediately fertilize them, at which point life begins. After a month or two, Frye can swim and begin the migration downstream into the Great Lakes. After four years a grown adult returns to the exact spot of its birth to breed the next generation of salmon. If in the four years before its return, the spawning beds are destroyed, or a dam has been built restricting its passage, the next generation is doomed. Our Socials have erected a tax dam which has created a lousy environment with scarce resources, high crime, lack of good high pay jobs and limited capital available for only a small band of privileged adults between the child rearing ages of 25 to 45. This is when the family men and women need to keep all the fruits of their labors to properly raise their offspring. Many intelligent adults will forego a family because of the harsh environment. This fits in with the PIP Zero Population Growth agenda. But, unfortunately, a large segment such as illegal aliens and those getting Welfare will over breed to make-up in quantity when they lack quality resources in a stressed environment according to the *Laws of Nature*. It is surprising the PIPS don't use the "*Birth-Slotting Technique*", but this is another matter.

I have previously mentioned, in my opinion, the baby boomers and echo boomers need to raise more offspring as stated in the Cicada subchapter. Nature always weeds out any excesses without tinkering. The

Socials prefer the *Dumbing Down of America* method by penalizing the productive at the same time they have encouraged Illegitimate birthing with lousy policies and Welfare subsidies. These practices are resulting in dysgenics and civilized genocide. But there are more mistakes, by opening the flood gates with the lure of free government services to the Illegal aliens who quickly fill the population void, grabbing the prize and laying claim to the rights of our heritage (this is the evil *Cuckoo bird Parasite phenomena*). Now that we have stifled the breeding of the productive baby boomers, a significant portion of our future generation has been destroyed. The next generation will have to work even harder just to keep their place as there will be less producers, more consumers and of course, more debts and more Parasites. The question is why are we importing drugs and Illegal aliens as we export our wealth and jobs? Why don't we want to raise our own families in a good life? Is it to get cheap labor? Because Illegal aliens work cheap, do they deserve to be citizens? Are they really working cheap when you figure they work for cash, avoid taxes, smuggle dope, they increase taxes, crime, diseases, insurance and security costs for our individuals, companies and government, not to mention the abuse on our own children. What about the costs of free health care, free schooling, government services and Welfare they soak up, which they never pay for, but we subsidize their freebies with our higher costs? Wouldn't our people do these lower pay jobs if we didn't have all this wage taxation? Couldn't we pay our own people more if we didn't have all these hidden costs and problems? Wouldn't our taxes go down? Wouldn't the cost of everything we bought drop in price over 50%? Couldn't we then have 110% employment, ending Welfare and Socialism? Couldn't we automate with robotics, most of these tedious jobs, which could make us even richer with more leisure time for everybody to create new technologies? Wouldn't Capitalism flourish? Why do we have to take the spillover of Central Americas' over procreation problem? So they don't riot down there like they did in L.A.? Is it wrong to stand up and say you don't want any more Socialist productive genocide and anti-American familyism? What about getting off the treadmill and raising our own children with compassion and love, instead of all the Parasites? What about living your own destiny without the Parasitic Oppression?

To prove Illegal immigration is good for you, hurray for the *(dis) Liberals*! They found one Illegal immigrant, out of millions who made a small contribution. Again, hurray! They boast their NAFTA has solved our problems. How could anyone possibly believe them with the 10 Trillion debt, 50 Billion bailout to prop up the peso and their 600 Billion a year trade deficit? Back to the salmon.

When a Salmon is tired, weak and resting, it is at risk of a Parasital attack from a Lamprey Eel. The Eel is an opportunist, waiting for a chance to cling with its sharp teeth to a tasty salmon and suck some blood and flesh. If the Salmon is tired, it won't have the strength to shake off the Parasite. Once the Eel has had a chance to really sink in its teeth, the Salmon is doomed to a stunted existence and early death. This fish will not breed to carry on the next generation, but is food for the Parasites. Just like you Patriot.

So, it is with our baby boomers and next generation. They have massive debts to payoff from the New World Socialists and many problems to fix. Our people will become exhausted at times. The peril is the growing class of Parasites who will try and cut a large share out of our labors, if we drop our guard. Believe me; our children will have it worse than you do without massive idiotology changes! Our best defense is the *6 Silver Bullets* in this book. When the times get tough, make sure you and your family are prepared. Don't let them stunt your children and crowd out your children's chances for a good life. Right now I see it as even money there will be a depression worse than the 1930's, when the baby boomers begin to retire. This time government will not be an asset, but the cause from all the foolish policies over the years.

Get off their treadmill. You don't need all that junk they push on you. And don't believe that stupid TV, full of disinformation. Grow up and face it. All you ever had, have or will have is Hope, Faith, and Love. And if you haven't guessed it by now, have your four children. Just like the Cicada, we will soon be starting the 18th year! Sure, we are going to soon have a lot of pain and possibly one heck of a depression! But, this isn't your problem, it's the Socialist implosion. Their sky is cracking and beginning to fall. Let them pick up the pieces. They didn't help you, but created a tax dam which stunted you and caused over 20 years of declining wages, enticed Illegal immigration and they encouraged abortion, even as they squandered another 10 Trillion, above all the taxes they forced out of you. Most of these taxes you didn't get to even vote on. Never mind any of this! Just learn the simple to follow *Silver Bullets* and you will begin growing like a sturdy Oak and not be dominated by the Parasital Wasps, Lamprey Eels, and Cuckoo Birds. Instead, become independent and make your own environment. Don't be the Beast of Burden, Pheasants, Ducks, Turkeys, Sunfish, Cicadas, Frogs, and Fish anymore. You don't need to be their laboratory rat on which they experiment with their crazy social tinkering. Never let your guard down or you will suffer the Parasitic consequences!

BEE COLONIES AND SOCIALISM

Bee colonies remind me of countries. As long as there are plenty of available resources (food, raw materials, land, water, jobs, etc.) the individual members of the colonies are able to get along with foreign countries and sometimes cooperate for noble causes.

When resources such as land and food, etc., become scarce within the hive, there is an aggressive outward push for these resources. Any other colony or outsider interfering with this swarming expansion is ruthlessly dealt with. Ant, termite and bee colonies have often clashed and throughout nature this common phenomenon happens, even two different corals fight for limited territory on a sea rock. There are millions of unseen casualties colliding in a fight to the death. I think you know that when our PIPS have finally given away all our jobs, industry and wealth to the foreign Parasites, the foreign appetites will be voracious. At this point, the foreigners will be even more aggressive for markets demanding our wealth at the same time we are in a weakened state from the sell-outs of our jobs and industry. When we have no wealth left to appease these addicted Trade Parasites, then let us see how well they go along with our government agendas. When the shortages occur, watch the feuds explode between the socialized United Nations. I think you see we are letting our intimidated PIPS put us in a very dangerous position with huge National Security risks. Sure, go ahead and falsely believe in the New World Order, United Nation PIP Blue Helmets will save you. The Blue Helmets will be called in by our Socials to stop the rebellion from you as the wealth drain accelerates, destroying our people and especially your children.

Here is another example of a *Silent War* that's growing fast. The beehive colony in Central America is producing too many worker bees for the land to support. They are out of balance with nature. Their surpluses migrate north to find resources. This then results in the "*Crowding Out Theory*" in the U.S. Host country. Once the full effects of wage deflation and shortages of resources are recognized by the Host members, the battle is engaged. The generosity and kindness of the Host has been abused, there are no more surpluses, only a 10 Trillion debt. This may simply be called racism by the PIPS, but the labels will no longer stick as the Host colony sees the long-term genocide of themselves. The Host members will fight for survival with their children in a suffocating struggle against the overly aggressive intruders when the *Silent War* of infiltrating has become unbearable. At this point all will finally realize the PIP Pied Pipers conned us into the wrong direction but it will be too late as our society takes a huge step backwards.

Legal immigration to the best and brightest who will help a colony are welcome if they avoid becoming Locusts and they don't exacerbate the *Crowding Out* of the Hosts own children. Illegal immigration throngs by the millions swamping the system, absorbing Illfare, government services, free healthcare, etc., all ending in higher taxes paid by the Hosts, leading to shortages, riots and anarchy with increased crime and drugs is no way to run a first class country. Four billion people will kill to get in here and Parasite off the wealth you and your forefathers made magnificent sacrifices to build up. What makes you think they won't take everything you got from you and your children if you get in their way? They are starving to death and have absolutely nothing to lose. Do you still want to bestow away our military like our World Order Socialists?

The operation of the hive is kind of what happens with our two-tier educational system. The type of educational nourishment can determine how successful you will be and how far you can go in your career. Many of our public schools are like the ordinary inferior education honey. This is fed to the unprivileged masses of children. They learn how to take orders and become good future worker bees and soldier bees. In public education they increasingly don't teach clear independent thinking, health and nutrition are glossed over and competition is discouraged (except in sports). How to run a small business and Capitalism are last on the list. Only in the private schools do you get the superior educational "royal jelly" to develop into a leader, King or Queen. Socialists believe in extreme interdependence and glory to the State, which is much more important to them than the individual (as long as they get to play the King and Queens). The individual is no more than livestock to be exploited and harvested for their common good. Remember, they are above all the fray and competition of survival, many are the elite Parasites licking their chops, waiting to siphon off the fruits of your labors.

Don't expect under their system to be a King or Queen Bee. The odds are a very, very long shot. If you make it in their elite group, over time you will tend to pick up the smug arrogant attitudes and look down on less worldly educated people. The elite and educated derelicts really believe they are smarter than you are and know what is best for you and especially themselves. Well, maybe some are smarter, but wouldn't you like to find out for yourself? I don't think it is asking too much to give our people school vouchers for their children. Let there be some healthy school competition for students and let the parents have more options and freedom in the rearing of their young so they can give their children a better shot at the American Dream. Fair enough?

A last observation on Honeybees. Our government is like the Beekeeper of the hive. To examine if the extraction is too great, one need only look at crime, Parasitalism, underemployment, slow wage growth, borrowing, inflation, child misery, Balance of Trade Deficits, etc. If any of these are rising, the Government extractions are possibly too high. Normally, 10% of the honey is plenty extraction for a government beekeeper, and that is taxing it once at sale, on the end user, the consumer, not at every exchange. The current 50-75% tax we have today of the gross is robbing the hive and many bees will become stunted or die from the overwork, exhaustion, crime, and hunger.[9] After PIPS take over 50%, that doesn't leave much to live on. If the People in Power want more revenues, I suggest they help our people first by **multiplying the American Pie 4 Times** to increase our standards of living. This way they can suck less but get more. They can do this with the 70% solution. And believe your Uncle Jim they won't learn this in their Political Science classes or JFK government school. They are too busy with Group Think.

Our productive are living a worker bee existence all for the glory of the government beekeeper, which is controlled by the People in Power. Socialism never lasts forever because they won't live in competition producing wealth and there are never enough chairs at the table for the would be Kings and Queens. Most everyone would rather get Welfare than compete and produce. It's easier and, in many of us a sad trait of Human Nature. But you can't avoid competition indefinitely or decay,

---

[9] Taxes are higher than you think and most income is taxed several times. Businesses also pay taxes on everything you buy. There are inflation taxes, inheritance, city, state, federal, property, gas, license fees, franchise, transfer, royalty, dividend, local, excise, tariff, use, personal, sales, Medicare, employer paid FICA, social insecurity, gift, FUTA, capital gains, etc. You can add.

rot and death eventually sets in. Oh, excuse me; there is competition of a destructive sort. They aren't competing to be the best but they are fighting with all their wits to suck off your fruits. Parasitically speaking of course.

THE TAXWORM COMPARISON

Look at the unproductive in our country as tapeworms. Tapeworms take up residence in your stomach, then rob the nourishment from the food you digest for sustaining your very own life. You do the work and swallow as the worms get a free ride and lunch from your efforts to provide food for nutrition. Once you are inflicted, you run faster and faster on the treadmill of life in a deadly struggle, just to survive. This is kind of like when the PIPS prime the money pump causing inflation, raising your taxes so they get more money to spend on themselves and they deflate your wages using Illegal immigration and artificially high interest rates from their obscene borrowing. These are excellent sucking techniques.

Have you ever noticed if you have a good healthy diet the stomach worms, diseases, and other Parasites are dislodged and cannot set up a permanent residence in your body, feasting off your nourishment? As in all of nature's creatures, the weak are susceptible to the Parasites. The strong have defenses they use to eliminate Parasites. So it is with your very own life. You can ward off the pests and be strong with the *6 Simple Habits* in this book. However, if you are living hand to mouth with one paycheck away from ruin, eating junk food as your health deteriorates along with your mind lost in the fog and/or low self-esteem with a lack of faith, you will be exploited. The Parasites will happily direct your life, having you run on their treadmill. Mush, you livestock, or out comes the whip!

So you don't think Parasitalism is growing like cancer? Look how the Parasites are trying to destroy your defenses. They need to weaken you so you are subject to their attacks. Are you beginning to learn or are you oblivious to their orchestrated recessions and now depression? They can stop the suffering today if they really wanted to. You can stop being lunchmeat if you wake-up. Review the following four dimensions of life you must be strong in to avoid the attacks. (In the AMERIPLAN chapter, the 6 Silver Bullets will strengthen you in all areas).

1. **Physical**—They sell you over-rated and over-advertised non-nutritional junk food and often worthless vitamins your body never absorbs. So

much for their Food and Drug Administration. You then get fat and develop diseases as you empty out your wallet for healthcare. Many big hospitals, drug companies, fast food joints, weight loss clinics, big health insurers, exercise equipment salesmen, abortion clinics, suicide doctors, psychiatrists and many others to be extremely wary and careful about. It's still your fault, don't expect fairness and honorable advice as these people are out to make a profit, get prestige, money, power, or whatever and then split. They can't survive in their occupation unless they make money off your labors. If you only knew better, you never would have gotten so screwed up, falling in this awful trap. You need knowledge and stop buying their garbage. If you want to save on all these inflated hospital bills and all the crazy pills they push on you and would like to reduce the colds, diseases, depression and expand your life span by possibly 50 more years, then contact me for a monthly magazine on how you may most likely do this. Maybe this is important to you? I also can recommend an excellent book on healthcare.

2. **Mental**—I've already discussed the two-tier educational system and how the public schools do not teach about self-sufficiency, budgeting, self-reliance and critical thinking. In politics and business, the Parasites have a swarm of spin-doctors on TV to muddy up even their most obvious scams and scandals. Don't count on our media to give you the truth, many are Parasites. (You won't learn the hidden true agendas of the policies unless you listen to foreign broadcasts in Canada or Great Britain). Things are done this way so the Parasites can manage your life without your knowledge and objection. They arrogantly know what is best. Many went to government school to learn how to live off their wits by extracting the fruits of your labors and watch out for their lack of concern over the use of drugs and alcohol. When you fall into the pits of mind numbing drugs, you surely will need to be led around by the nose. Go ahead and make their day as you self-destruct your diminishing brain. Now you are truly under their power and prepped to feed the worms the fruits of your labors as they dictate your entire life. Don't let them berate and verbally abuse you with names like stupid, hater, bigot, polluter, racists, isolationist, uncompassionate, mean spirited, protectionist, cruel, etc. Tell the Parasites their mind control games and labels won't work on you. Tell them to stop being the cruel, haters, racists, jealists, pick pockets and uncompassionate bigots. They can start with 160,000,000 new high

pay American jobs so we won't want their subsistent unemployment benefits, affirmative quota actions and Socialist Illfare. Plus there won't be many poor, homeless, hungry, and insecure people in our country dependant on government, as we stop 75% of our crime rates with a great life for our people for a change.

3. **Financial**—Just look in your tattered wallet. With all the tax appropriations over the years, the Socials have kept your asset base small even as they put you 10 Trillion in debt. This is corruption of the highest magnitude. With all the money they spent, they were supposed to solve crime, illegal immigration, poverty, hunger and many other noble causes. It didn't work as they planned, or did it? 70% of the tax revenues got siphoned off to feed the Parasites as our few poor and downtrodden now makes up a growing army of tens of millions! But besides the extractions from them directly, they have legislated an environment of red tape in this country that has spawned millions of Parasites in the private sector. For example, look how they provided an environment of easy lawsuits for opportunists encouraged by ambulance chasers. Sure some are legitimate but I doubt we need 2/3's of the worlds' liars, oops, I mean, lawyers, lobbyists, and a lot of useless services as we sell out our industries in ridiculous trade deals. We need more people producing something real you can touch and see which is useful. Not more gambling, lotteries, bars, casinos, bureaucracy, welfare, unions, escort services, drug dealers, social workers, adult porno shops, speculators, hedge funds, derivatives, lawsuits, laws, attorneys, lobbyists, massage parlors, hypnotists, mind readers, phone sex, other negative vices and other expensive, useless make work occupations. Oh, and millions of victims.

   If you want a higher quality of life, sure fire businesses to do in your spare time, on your time, as you like, which you can teach your children, make some money, buy products at a reduced rate and obtain tax right-offs, learn about self-sufficiency and independent living, then contact me for a subscription. If getting rich in freedom is your objective, you need the proper philosophical base. I can recommend an especially good book. THIS ONE ALSO! And email me with your great ideas. Help me make this book better. Please give me your opinions and advice so I can improve this book. I thank you for any ideas to help our country.

4. **Spiritual**—Many Socialists and Parasites are hybrid Atheists and worship the government as the divine authority (their idol). They

want to control your spirit and have you pay homage to their false God. They want the State to take over the functions of the Church and absorb this institution within their power (they mostly have). They don't want you to believe there is a higher authority than government. The problem is the people in government have a vested interest, they want to expand their power, pay, and many are selfish with personal agendas. This is why they have no qualms in feeding 70% of your money to their Parasites. These people are not clergy dedicated to a strict set of moral principles, but can be bought. And more and more are buyable as Socialism accelerates. Look what this philosophy did for Russia! Don't believe it? Just wait for the 10 Trillion austerity when the baby boomers retire and you'll feel it. The game won't last forever you know, and you will soon feel the Socialism. The question is . . . will you self-destruct into drugs, alcohol, depression, suicide or crime? Or will you protect yourself with the *Silver Bullets*?

My advice, if you want help with any spiritual problems, don't buy into the idea government, or some other source will solve your problems if you just give them a bunch of money. The social workers, psychiatrists, trial and divorce attorneys, family planners, rehabilitators, and government authorities rarely ever help solve your problems, but will gladly take a lot of your money. You know most divorces and other problems are caused from financial stress. You surely don't need more bills! Get free counseling at a church or from your own support group. You decide how much you want to contribute to these organizations out of the goodness of your heart. Not bullied with intimidation or trickery. Don't be a lazy, lost sheep, your problems are still your problems and only you can solve them. Stop yourself from being raked over the coals by the unlimited Bloodsuckers scavenging with tooth and claw to lay claim to the fruits of your labors. The more they advertise to hook you into their services, the faster you better run away. By now I'm sure you realize even though on the surface Parasites look sincere, sound compassionate, appear nice and caring, but on the inside these city slickers are the most mean spirited, treacherous, two-faced, and cruel people you will ever run across. These are bad, ruthless people. Everyone in this country isn't working together for a common good, making this a better place. The Unproductive have hidden agendas. How could Parasites possibly think and see things the way you do when they are the Parasitic wasp and you are the tasty caterpillar flesh? They only survive in their lifestyle by feasting on the fruits of your labors. Too bad you couldn't secretly tape their conversations and hear what they say to their cronies and associates behind your back. They are having a pretty good laugh! Tell them to get real jobs and you stop buying into their nonsense and get *real* yourself. Don't look for them to be your friend and listen to your mess for free. If you need a pal and someone's shoulder to cry on, buy a dog. You can trust a dog and it will happily eat your leftovers, not your families' dinner.

Now that you clearly understand what is wrong in our society, spawned from the Socialist environment with the by-product of Parasitalism, you can defend yourself and your family. They would never tell you but the AMERIPLAN just did! As it always has been, your life is truly in your own hands. Become a strong sturdy Oak, beyond the clutches of the Purse Snatchers. I cannot stress this enough, if you become mentally mixed-up, sick and tired, hurt from their name calling, broke or emotionally distraught, you are subject to the critical harm of the Parasites. The vultures will be knocking down your door at the first sign of weakness. You will be stunted and never reach your full potential. This is a "*Law of Nature*", which is irrefutable. Truly, the strong get stronger, and the weak get weaker. The simple question is this, do you want to continue in pain and suffering, getting weaker and weaker from a sickness called ***Parasitic Socialism***? Or do you want to grow stronger and stronger as you thrive in this country with unlimited opportunities for growth and expansion in an environment of *real* Capitalism where we have a win-win situation? Not a Parasitic relationship with a win-lose situation and a lose-lose in the long run. Shake off the Parasites, forcing them to hunt for another food source to stick their teeth in. Get back your freedom, man! Come join the Freedom Man.

CHAMELEONS—THE TRANSFORMABLE PARASITE

Watch out for the Chameleons. A parasite can change its colors fast. A parasite isn't necessarily a Parasite at all times. Parasites sometimes are productive and useful when a positive government environment forces this behavior upon them (an example would be the 13 out of 14 people on welfare that can actually work). A Parasite is like an opportunist looking for prey in a weakened state. Speaking of weakened, only one adult in four of us vote, our government is broken, bloated and diseased from Socialism. The Parasites are licking their chops for the feast of your tax dollars! For instance, look at the 10 Trillion debt they spent, the Billions in bank bailouts, the cancerous Illegal immigration to deflate wages, the loopholes, the selling of government land for $5.00 an acre (except to you), subsidies to the elite, regulation favoritism, grants for buddies, government contracts, foreign trade rip-offs, government land confiscations under the excuse of environmental pleas as the value of the remaining land held by the Plutocrats dramatically appreciates, high inflation and interest rates, preventing the use of capital by small businesses so they can't compete with the Parasites, low interest loans for Parasites, enterprise zones for contributors, etc., etc., etc. Now you know why our taxes must be dramatically lowered, to stop all these chameleons from cheating! Sure, the American people should stand up and fix this mess, but they are too busy playing by the rules, working to pay taxes for the Unproductive, and running on the treadmill ("*Containment Theory*"). Another example of a chameleon Parasite is a truck driver from Mexico making a delivery for a very low price putting our honest drivers out of business where the foreign driver is really making his money transporting illegal drugs!

Keep your guard up and be weary, if you desire to obtain a better life for your family. Forget about protesting the dirty tricks and complaining of the abuse. Save yourself. Don't expect the PIPS to understand. Parasites don't understand the critical injury they cause to their Hosts. They are working hard and long hours themselves. They may not produce anything real you can touch, see or use, but nonetheless, they are producing speeches, taxing, regulations, polls covering their backside, expanding government ownership, borrowing and spending with government redistribution as they see fit. Politicians go home tired every night, just like you do. Dialing the telephones, talking, deal making, pushing papers, playing politics and figuring how to extract the fruits of your labors is tiring business. In these trying times, there are a lot of bad people in our country as Socialism has exploded into a sickening disease of spreading Parasitalism. After WWII, when we sacrificed so many of our young people, we had respect for each other, with a feeling of unity. Don't hope for another blood bath; just fix your mess.

Let us end the Parasitic environment and return to a Capitalistic environment of **160,000,000 new high pay American jobs, 75% less crime, pay off the 10 Trillion debt and vastly improve our National Security.** If you can't change the government and the People in Power that are hurting our citizens, then at least change your own environment with the *6 Silver Bullets*.

THE BROWN TROUT

The Brown Trout is one of the most impressive Predators in nature and is my favorite. The Pere Marquette and Manistee Rivers have provided me some excellent observations. When the trout eggs hatch into Frye, they strictly feed on small insects. As the fish grow to fingerlings and adult size, they eat larger insects and worms. Bizarrely, a few trout further grow, provided the environment has plenty of food. Some of the Brown Trout abnormally develop a large lower hooked jaw (a kype), growing 20 times their normal size, turning into super Predators and become Cannibals, strictly eating fish. Because they have grown so big, they cannot live off the natural environment supporting their huge size by eating insects, leeches and crayfish. There just isn't enough time or energy they can afford to expend sustaining themselves at their massive size and bloat. Only by eating their brothers and sisters can they continue to survive. This is like our giant corporations that spend more time eating their competition than they do competing. Oh yeah, I forgot, they need economy of scale to compete, just like GM, AIG, and another hole in your head! I mean hole in your pocket. Too big to fail? Fail they will, the bigger they get, the harder they fall.

Our current economic environment is this phenomenon. Our people are like the tiny Frye working at jobs to provide for their day-to-day needs. Our working men and women will advance to the next stage of growth and open small businesses, provided the external environment is favorable with an abundance of food (incentive). In our case, we need high pay surplus jobs, low interest rates, keeping regulations to a minimum and other factors like available resources, ending wage deflations, stability of the currency, social harmony and much lower taxes. Those laborers who are able to accumulate enough surplus wages will be in a position to advance to the next level and open their own businesses. The obstacles and wasted time in regulation compliance, like now, must be curtailed to the very minimum necessary, so true opportunity exists and the regulations don't restrict participation, or our economic growth will be stymied, as only huge bloated multinational companies can afford to hire the extra paper pushers and spread the cost over thousands of workers. This is how the multinationals like to defeat competition with economy of scale. What a Parasitic waste!

Why do we want to have small businesses? Because they are closest to the consumer with the least amount of bloat and bureaucracy. Small businesses use assets more efficiently. The giant corporations like the big banks, insurance companies and government bureaucracy, are the most inefficient users of capital, labor and resources. Cannibals stifle growth and creativity by sucking up all our capital, labor and resources without a comparable benefit. Big corporations, massive Unions and bureaucracies hoard assets, have dual and redundant uses of labor and cause a shortage of goods, services and capital to the small businesses and consumers. A typical large corporation naturally absorbs all the small business competitors in buyouts and with non-compete clause agreements. Now both the big corporations and the bought out small businessmen can relax for a while, now that they happily don't have to compete! But it is only a Parasitic short-term gain where everybody else loses by paying monopoly prices for these goods and services. (Don't be fooled by a monopoly that claims it is competing because its costs to consumers are going down each year, with real competition the monopolies costs may drop twice as fast).

Unfortunately, all the businesses in other fields are stunted and unable to expand as above market costs of capital, raw materials, energy, supplies, etc., provided by the big corporations and banks will absorb any surplus profits which could be reinvested in the growth of the small businesses. This is one way the big businesses, Socialist government and charities stunt our economy just like they encourage the passage of a lot of crazy regulations which makes the start up costs of competitors too high to enter the market competition. Another problem is the unhealthiness of an economy with a few gigantic corporations with few small businesses in the individual markets. Big corporations are lethargic and are unable to quickly adapt to environmental changes. If these few big corporations become bankrupt the entire industry is lost, as foreign corporations happily fill the void. Plus, with so few corporations there is more specialization of duties, but few who know the business thoroughly and are capable enough to effectively run the business (we need the KISS formula here). This is the Bee Colony example, where the whole hive dies if the Queen dies. I prefer a wide dispersal of knowledge and capital with many small competitors who understand the business and can quickly fill the voids from fallen bankrupt competitors. It is healthy in a decentralized small business environment, as you see costs are held in check by competition with many competitors having the knowledge and ability to take up the slack and react quicker to changing circumstances, with much more creativity, innovation and new technologies, which benefit all, even the rich. With numerous competitions is the only way known to man to morally establish prices. If anyone thinks a monopoly or Socialist Government can, they truly are their fools! And this goes for public utility companies, schools, non-profits, government housing such as HUD and localities getting free tax dollars and to further Parasitize if it wasn't bad enough they don't pay property tax, sales tax or income tax—you pick up their share dummy. This is why capitalism doesn't work; they have you competing against yourself with your own tax dollars, running double time on their treadmill while they live the good life. Your good life!

With many competitors the consumer is the ultimate beneficiary. A further example is the stock market, where it's better to have millions of investors in a liquid market, than having 10 giant pension and hedge funds in an illiquid market with wild, gyrating price swings, where no one can buy or sell if so needed, without large losses or paying inflated prices. If you want more of this let's just open the stock market for one hour a week, charge a 1% transfer fee, and have everybody go get real jobs.

Do you want bloated, over-charging mega corporations and bloated Socialism or do you want them to compete for your dollars, providing you the best products at the best costs? Do you think we have fierce competition in the auto industry? Do they bend over backwards for the consumer? Or do you think we need more competition than three auto companies, with one union is too few for 300,000,000 people? One car company for 100,000,000 people? C'mon, those companies and one Union don't need this much economy of scale size. These problems are solved by the "*Competition Theory*". Our big corporations and multinational businesses are not competing against each other, they don't like competition. They compete like a unified pack of cohesive Parasites to keep competition out with government regulations as their tools. No wonder other companies can't and won't compete in so many business fields. Let us break these Brown Trout blobs into 20 companies each. Protect them from the foreigners but make them compete. The free lunch is over!

Look how the Big Three wipe out the small car repair shops and do it yourself mechanics by complicating car repairs, which need specialist knowledge, expensive equipment and computers to diagnose the repairs along with the high costs of their complicated replacement parts. The Big Three want to eliminate service competition and keep this lucrative business all for themselves, charging windfall profits. This is a Socialism technique, not true Capitalism. These monopolies cause the government to grow bigger to watch dog them. This is the part the Socialists like. The environment doesn't have to be this way. The *Competition Theory* solves this disorder and is most effective in fixing our government systems. The last chapter is based on this powerful theory. The auto companies are just one of a multitude of industries that are broken. Ginormous corporations could never support this much bloat without twisted regulation allowing their windfall profits and unnatural survival.

I understand the fear of competition for these large Predators and our government, but the benefits are worth it, even to themselves and their people as they regain respect, honor and a higher value placed on their jobs and stock prices. When you have the best companies in an industry, which don't compete, it only punishes our consumers. Let us look to the future instead of being satisfied beating Second World foreign economies and continue leading the World. Or give up. Do you want China bossing you around and cornering our bond and treasury markets just like OPEC with their oil prices? How do you like them picking your Presidents? Nice, isn't it? **This is your WAKE-UP CALL PATRIOTS!**

The Brown Trout Phenomenon isn't unique to the auto companies. This is happening in a lot of our major industries. It happened in gasoline. Remember Standard Oil? Once it was broke apart, we had competition again, and gas prices dropped, resulting in a boom in auto sales and new jobs! Do you want this again by busting up EXXON? Remember when their executives said the world was running out of oil? How did you like AIG (American International Group)? Do you think that if our food prices remained high we would have ever found the wealth to industrialize our country? I doubt it. Do you think we would have had the Internet if we didn't have the fierce competition to lower the cost of computers? I doubt it. Do you think we would have had the lively competition in software development if we didn't break up AT&T? Is Microsoft the next Brown Trout controlling the language of computers? What's Intel doing? How about Google, insurance companies or our giant investment banks speculating in our commodities and stocks at 30 to 1 leverage?

As bad as you think the problems with private industry are, the problem is ten times worse with our government monopolies, which give the worst products at the highest costs. Look at the public school Monopoly. The Public Schools have bloated out as they ate up most of the private schools, instead of competing for the benefit of their students.

How could you expect the students to respect the Public School system when our Government servants threaten with strikes for windfall wages and perks? They won't compete with school vouchers, where a student and parents can choose any school including private schools. Oh sure, public school administrators have a million excuses why competition won't work. Do you still buy that bunk? Think how far ahead we could move this country by fixing this big problem.[10] The same goes for the hideous and corrupt returns from the Post Office, HUD, Social Insecurity and Medicare/Medicaid costs. Back to the Trout . . .

Over time, from the Pac-Man feast, there will be few remaining trout in the river. All the smaller trout have been cannibalized with the water soon to be devoid of life because Cannibals can't sustain themselves by going back to eating insects and worms. A disaster sooner or later will strike as always happens in nature, such as a disease, starvation or an otter will eat the few remaining slow reacting trout. How much better for the species with a large productive smaller but scrappier population of Browns!

So it is with our economy. If we continue to play Pac-Man gobble-up, we will have our few giant corporations, but no dispersal of power, knowledge or wealth. When we have a natural disaster in our environment, we will lose everything we have built up. Now what kind of disaster could we possibly have?

What if a rare disease like Legionnaires, Ebola, or a mishandled biological germ escapes from a laboratory where everyone at a company is quarantined and eventually dies where we lose all the knowledge and skills from this specialized segment of our population? How about a suitcase sized neutron bomb or a jar of anthrax targeted at a key computer chip manufacturer? What if a monopoly which produces in a location gets ransacked in a riot from the underclasses when welfare is totally cut? (Prevent this with surplus jobs and the AMERIPLAN, then cutting welfare is a piece of cake). What about a terrorist attack with ransom

---

10 Now you know why they had the book burnings in Germany when Hitler came to power. The citizens had enough. Believing the school unions, administrations and eggheads were Parasitical, gouging the people with a twisted Government environment where they get a great paycheck but won't compete to prove they deserve it like the private sector. If these people are untrue to nature, don't worry, a Velvet Ant will soon pay them a visit. Read on!

demands? A bankruptcy? A tornado? A fire? A war? A hurricane? A crippling lawsuit or trade dispute with sanctions? How about more one-way trade deals for foreigners, using predatory pricing and dumping to idle and eventually cause the bankruptcy of our factories with no sales, ending in unemployment? Do you want all your eggs in one basket? In a few short days we could lose our ability and knowledge to produce for ourselves. We don't become stronger but weaker and poorer when we lose our self-sufficiency. With high unemployment and cheap labor, our industries will never have incentive to robotize and automate. Let's look to the future and become a first class country again, instead of thrashing around in the past with the second and third World Nations, they don't have any of the answers and never did.

Again, I ask you . . . Do you want Capitalism or more Socialism with its by-products, which are Parasites and Predators?

THE_WARPED_ENVIRONMENTALISTS

There are uncountable examples of Parasitalism and I will cover just a few more. To discover if any action or situation is Parasital, just remember the definition of a Parasite "an organism living in dependence on another for its existence without making a useful return."

Of all the despicable and insidious Parasites in humanity, a few of our so-called environmentalists are the worst, deceitful and cruel. They are not really environmentalists in the true sense, but the modern day Communists who want government and quasi-government non-profit organizations to buy up all our lands and resources as they cash in. It sounds noble to preserve land for future generations, but the land is still the land and the Communists are saving nothing, just using regulations and taxes to methodically confiscate it from their own citizens depriving them of Capitalism and freedom.

To understand this Socialist scheme, picture a school of guppies in a fish bowl where the environmental Socialists scoop out half of the water and then as much as they can continually sneak out to shrink the environment. The fish will naturally become unhealthy, susceptible to diseases, and stunted from the *Crowding Out*. It has been shown in laboratory rats that when they are packed tightly together in cages they have behavioral changes. Many become easily agitated, other become homosexual, many grow weak and sick, lose the will to live and become dependent. Could possibly much of the increase in homosexuality be no fault of our people who are gay but our environment of Socialism has caused this phenomenon? This study is beyond the scope of this book and regardless all people have the right to live for their own sake without tax oppression and government tyranny in the privacy of their own homes. Agreed? Let me know your opinion.

The Socialist absorption of our land and resources has many ill side effects on us such as the following:

1. In a Socialist environment, our people are denied the freedom of ownership leading to an increase in dependency and hence prone to *Parasital attacks*.
2. When the Leftys shrink the "American Pie" by accumulating our lands, the rest of us are left with a smaller environment of resources and are subject to the "*Crowding Out Phenomenon*".
3. When government and non-profits absorb our lands and other resources the property *tax burden is further shifted* and increased on those who still have something, causing these citizens to run faster on the treadmill until they exhaust. In other words government and non-profits, etc. are getting a free ride destroying the productive in a Parasitic fashion by not paying income tax, sales tax or property tax. You are their de facto contributor even if you don't believe in their absurd causes! These groups, one way or another, will have to reduce the bloat and start competing. Our productive can't pay these people 500 thousand a year when they don't produce anything of value only spending.
4. As the supply of land and resources diminishes, it becomes artificially more expensive for those wishing to buy it. This *denies access to Capital* by our productive.
5. The remaining resources benefit the wealthy that already own resources even though they did nothing to increase its value through improving it. They get a hidden type of "*Welfare Scarcity Premium*" they didn't earn, as their resources become a rarer commodity. The super wealthy accept Socialism as long as they are benefiting. The wealthy will hold their tongues and say nothing to stop the unscrupulous Socialists as long as the payoff lasts. I think you see after the 10 Trillion borrowing and another 40 Trillion in promises, the house of cards will soon collapse.

6. The best reason to stop Socialism is the pathetic job they are doing as custodians of our resources. For example, look how they let umpteen homes and acres of mature forests go unharvested as they rot in the fields. They don't properly control wildfires and hundreds of thousands of acres burn to ashes. These cause a *great wealth loss* to all of us as lumber prices are artificially increased. Only a rich timber baron could love this Socialist folly! As long as it is someone else's or the baron has a great insurance policy.

   Another huge problem the Socialists can never defend against as they collect and hoard our wealth is the illegal chemical dumping at night on the government lands when the bureaucrats sleep. If individuals owned this land, they would stand watch and prevent a lot of the toxic dumping. As you know, our citizens who spend their own money to acquire land respect it and take care of it better than a bureaucrap paid by the clock to watch it, 9 to 5:00pm.

   Look at the chemical and nuclear waste disposal problem, which the PIPS haven't begun to solve. Look at the toxic landfills, the polluted rivers, chemically tainted foods, and air pollution from allowing burning of chemicals into the atmosphere (with a proper license and fee for the Liberals of course). This surely causes us more health problems and loss of wildlife.

   With all of the problems the noble Incompetent Custodians can't seem to handle, you want them and their Communist Environmentalists to take away more of our land and resources? Go ahead and be their sucker. If you doubt their intention ask yourself why they taxed away all our capital under the guise of Social Security which seems noble, but why did they spend all of it and get this country 10 Trillion in debt? We gave them what they wanted, they got greedy, Parasitalism set in and now they destroyed themselves, and half of us. The foreigners are laughing behind their backs calling them buffoons.

One last observation on Socialism as it relates to humanity. Socialists don't really care for people except their clique and as Socialism further dominates the landscape, our nation and people will stagnate, regress and die. But in an environment of Capitalism and freedom, man will grow, prosper, and thrive. Which do you want?

And don't tell me Capitalism failed us in the Great Depression; the Socialists failed Capitalism which caused the depression and then they prolonged it as *they* did nothing to fix *their* mess!

THE VELVET ANTS TO THE RESCUE! (Last Biology Lesson!)

Velvet Ants are a Super Parasite. They normally directly Parasite only on other Parasites in their environment. The productive are not sought out by Velvet Ants and are only attacked incidentally by mistake. Velvet Ants are the most aggressive Parasites of the bunch, but the environment must be just right for these Parasites to thrive. They need an environment of rampant Parasitalism. After the female Velvet Ant mates with the male, she searches every burrow, nook and cranny for any Parasite nest. She crawls in the nest and her powerful and deadly sting paralyzes the Host Parasite. Then she lays an egg, which soon hatches to devour the Host Parasite. Once her mission is complete, she quickly moves on to the next victim. Strangely, she only attacks other Parasites. Velvet Ants will multiply in numbers until they have consumed most of the Parasites at which point their numbers curtail to balance the availability of the Parasital food source.

Here is an example in humanity of this situation existing today. The Socialists have spawned a Parasitic culture of Illfare dependency where bureaucrats, drug dealers, illegal immigrants, foreign trading partners, big unions, monopolies, foreign lobbyists, rich and poor Welfare recipients feast on the fruits of labors forcibly taken from our productive Hosts. These Parasites are thriving in our culture as proven by their growing numbers. Why are their raw numbers growing? If you have been paying attention you already know. It's the environment we are providing and we can change it today—right now, this minute. It's simple—child's play. But once we exhaust our Hosts, the Parasites themselves are at risk of Parasital attacks. You see, Parasites have no self-sufficiency and their total dependency on you, their meal ticket, is their danger. When our productive Hosts smarten up and cut back on their Parasital offerings and the feasts become leaner, the Parasites are weakened and exposed to Super Parasites (the Velvet Ants). Do you see why and how a dictator could be demanded in this country soon? Do you want to elect the greatest Velvet

Ant [Super Parasite (Demagogue)] into office to punish the PIPS or can we just vote them out before it is too late and they get their just desserts?[11] Parasitalism or **160 Million new high pay surplus jobs**? All we simply have to do is change the current Socialist environment, starting with the Politicians we have in government office.

Velvet Ants can be the saving grace, buying time for the productive Hosts who are victims of the Parasites. However, Super Parasites should never be encouraged. Two wrongs don't make a right. In our environment of Parasitalism, for a long time, it has been ripe for Velvet Ants. We can go three ways with this environment.

1. Keep allowing the Parasites to feast off our fruits of labor as we exhaust and grow a culture of Super Parasites to eat our Parasites. Then finally a dictator will punish them for their atrocities.
2. Shake the Parasites off your back with the AMERIPLAN, eliminating their food source so we don't have any need for Super Parasites to begin with, as you flourish in a life of freedom and prosperity!
3. Have a depression where nobody has any money, which can be Parasitized. The Parasites will automatically be culled from this behavior and with a little luck our honest and productive hosts playing by the rules will eventually put things back together again in a moral non-Parasitic environment, before the Velvet Ant emerges.

The choice is yours. There is only really one smart option. It is yours with the *Silver Bullets* in the AMERIPLAN as you reclaim your American Dream. Now you know why Socialism sooner or later always fails—PARASITALISM! And one day we will defeat Parasitalism. This is the promise of THE AMERIPLAN as nature will be victorious. Socialism is living on borrowed time.

Remember this well: Socialism always works with good people willing to work hard and sacrifice for a common good. But the altruism breaks down over time from those not willing to work hard, as sloth, cheating and Parasitalism manifests in an exploding fesspool.

---

[11] Now you know how Hitler got to be President of Germany.

CONGRATULATIONS! YOU NOW KNOW AS MUCH AS THE LEFTYS. SO FAR, YOU HAVE LEARNED THE PROBLEMS, MOST OF WHICH ARE ONE, IT IS CALLED PARASITALISM! TO SOLVE ONE PROBLEM, IT TAKES ONE SOLUTION—THE 70% SOLUTION.

YOU ARE HALFWAY THERE PATRIOT. SKIP THE NEXT CHAPTER IF YOU WANT BUT DON'T JUMP TO THE LAST CHAPTER. THERE IS MUCH MORE YOU SHOULD REALLY LEARN FIRST! YES, IT'S SICK, REPETITIVE AND DISGUSTING, BUT YOU BETTER READ, APPLY AND PROTECT YOURSELF IF YOU WANT YOUR QUADRUPLE IN YOUR PAYCHECK AND NET WORTH!

4

PROPHECY OF SOCIALISM

Coming up is a potentially gloomy future, with politically incorrect discussion about problems the People in Power have been able to sweep under the carpet and beat into remission. Unfortunately, the problems have become so big, we have to grow up and face them head on, in a search for real solutions and solve the messes or nature with swift cruelty will solve them for us. We have allowed events in our society such as a bloated Socialist Government with extreme Welfare, Confiscatory Taxation, Loopholes for the Elite, Regulation, Illegal Immigration, Free Trade, Crime and Drug Abuse, Nuclear Arms proliferation and other evils to get way out of hand, causing our citizens to become devalued and dehumanized. Based on our current Socialist environment with their 10 Trillion debt and Parasitalist culture, I see intense pressures on our people, resulting in disgust, cruelty, and misery to each other in a struggle to survive. Those freeloaders who are soaking up and wasting all our surpluses without providing a useful return will now be dealt with. Pay they will, one way or another. 40 Trillion in promises and 10 Trillion in debt to buy off votes to stay in office must be paid by someone or accept the dishonor and public disorder by becoming insolvent. Hopefully, the Patriots can fix the mess, but if they fail, read the following to see what could happen out of desperation. Don't be fooled by a seemingly improving economy in the present. This is the calm before the storm. This temporary foothold will collapse with lower and lower bottoms sucking out the lifeblood of the economy. Please understand I began my predictions 18 years ago and here we are now with the baby boomers finally retiring in mass. Some of what follows is already metastasizing. I think it will get much worse with unneeded suffering. Just realize the dismal attempts to solve the mess will bankrupt us Economically, Socially, and Spiritually, unless, of course, we follow the *Ameriplan 70% Solution* real quick.

AUSTERITY

The People in Power are in a pickle and seriously limited in their options. They shouldn't raise *taxes* (income or consumption), as the economy is highly leveraged and teetering on the brink of collapse. They still use inheritance taxes as it is hard for the dead to fight back, but this source is not nearly enough. They shouldn't use *Fiat* or the Money. Managers and foreigners will liquidate financial assets by borrowing all they can to hoard raw materials and hard assets, eventually plunging the economy into depression from escalating product costs and sky high interest rates, leading to product inflation from the shortages, dislocations, fear, unemployment and bankruptcies. *Borrowing* is out as the citizenry sees the crowding out Parasitalism and the eating of our young, harnessing them with $10 Trillion debt enslavement. Only the Chinese will loan, as our berzerk PIPS give away our wealth and jobs for loans, but no one in the world will forever artificially prop up a decadent society living beyond its means. They even messed up signing away our sovereignty with all the Treaties and agreements in NAFTA, U.N., NATO, G.A.T.T., IMF, World Bank, etc. causing the loss of our ability to tax and regulate the foreigners into paying the debt with *Tariffs*. We better get these Politicians out of office before they destroy everything. Vote Patriots in office, not incumbent parasite career politicians.

Whoa, it is a bummer that none of their tools and band-aid gimmicks will work anymore! This time they have to deal with their problems and face their biggest problem—their "Socialism", but they won't and here is the likely scenario, which causes worldwide economic collapse and totally unnecessary abuse placed on our citizens.

As the U.S. short-term debts matured, loans made by foreign bankers and investors were not rolled over into new U.S. bonds. Instead, the holders opted to transfer their wealth into new more profitable opportunities overseas. The safety of holding capital in the U.S. was no longer a concern. Not to mention the fact that the Baby Boom labor force would soon retire leaving a hollowed out U.S. work force to carry the load of government debts, resulting in very little economic growth if any for at least 2 decades; time to plant a new garden.

Another fear causing the shifting of capital out of the U.S. was the massive Socialist government ownership, excessive regulations, Welfare and social spending with growing tax extractions; a sure sign of slow growth with an exploding dysfunctional dependent underclass adding to instability, crime, riots, dependency, and jealousy demanding more freebies.

Finally, after decades, the growing $10,000,000,000,000.00 debt must be paid! Unfortunately, the deficit spending PIPS haven't realized this in time. It is too late and the worldwide economic collapse has been triggered. This disaster could have been prevented with the AMERIPLAN, and even now we can reverse course today with 10% GDP growth rates.

The Politicians still controlling Congress go back to their old irresponsible tricks taking advantage of our Constitution with too many taxes, fiat, borrowing and wasteful Government spending to feed the Parasites. More borrowing is needed. This time the bonds don't sell. Even with higher interest rates, there are not buyers. The baby boomers are now net consumers, not laborers and investors, and are selling off their bonds, stocks and real estate. The generation Xers already are paying a high tax rate and don't have extra money to buy any bonds or pay more taxes. The Federal Reserve has to pay the irresponsible bills with fiat (funny money), by soaking up the theft and parking the funny money in debt instruments until a buyer (sucker) appears or poof . . . . just erasing the debt causing inflation. Sometimes these debts and the nasty consequences of the unwise spending are not felt for years and the con game can go on for decades (but not this time, Interest Rates and commodities soar, plummeting the economy in depression). Often, in the past, when a new administration took office, the Federal Reserve started reducing these overheated economic hangovers during a new party's watch, often making the new policy look bad for a few years. This is why the common man can't figure out good responsible government action and policy from the corrupt or bad policy, which lingers from another era as you experience the whip saw. Also, sometimes a decline in a previous administration happens in anticipation of a change in the political whims of the citizens and the new regime in power falsely blames a past political clique. It is simple to dramatically reduce interest rates, taxes, inflation, and increase economic growth, all with high levels of employment, wages, less civil unrest and normal Government spending! The "70% Solution" is the fuel to stoke our economy and prevent these Government tinkerings producing these recessions. This *tool* can keep a non-Socialist Party in office for 60 years. Socialists will never use the 70% Solution because it totally destroys their idiotology; such is the power of the AMERIPLAN!!!

Much of the money spent by the power drunk Politicians abusing their privileged office is not invested and backed by assets but is created out of air (fiat) and spent (consumption) to feed parasites, raising the price of everything bought, causing shortages and an inflation ripple through the entire economy. Prices escalate with quickening velocity with each new round of fiat fuel (people learn when they get suckered enough). They eventually learn simple supply and demand. When you increase the supply of dollars, it takes more dollars to buy whatever. It all could have been prevented if they would have reduced Parasitic spending which would have reduced both our National Debt and inflation. But, you see this would have meant smaller Government and a reduction in dependant Socialism. They would never do this. We now must do more than reducing spending.

We have the 2 negative factors of large debts and Government revenues drying up. When the baby boomers retire, we need increased expenses to support them and of course pay off the growing Parasites. You can be sure the Politicians will let loose with rivers of fiat money (hyper-inflation) to just get through to the next election, or we have a depression, but either way it will be a disaster, until the Socials fix their messes.

Investors will collapse the financial markets stampeding to liquidate positions at any price to buy inflation hedges or just salvage some cash. The Politicians get some tax money from the few who sold at a profit but not nearly enough. This is the shakeout technique. You pay tax on all your gains but only a small amount of long-term capital losses may be deducted each year.

The inflation continues in a feeding frenzy as everyone stops investing in the U.S. and rushes to get capital out of the country and salvage what they can. The scared, greed mongers and under-capitalized must sell their assets into the hands of the stronger having staying power, who didn't lose their heads. As in nature, the strong get stronger, the weak get weaker, the rich get richer and the poor get poorer. But not this time! The crash engulfs the rich too! This is a monumental sea change in the environment where all the bubbles are out of alignment with nature. Band-aids won't work on these not so tiny bubbles. This is the reversal in a Super Cycle. This will be the birth of a new economic era in about 20 years once the old is destroyed and erased (become self-sufficient to survive this mess; for 95% of us it is the only way).

Where does it end? History repeats itself. With the usual crash into bankruptcies, sky rocketing unemployment, smaller markets, asset devaluations with shortages and a depression which lasts an entire generation as the 10 Trillion plus the other 40 Trillion in promises must be paid off. We will see huge cuts and elimination of Government programs, anarchy explodes from the dysfunctional, and the productive bled dry and unable to sustain families for future markets. All which will further shrink industries and jolt our depressed cities into cesspools of crime, drugs and riots. No longer is our country rich in heritage, spirit and self-sufficiency, only decay, weakness, hunger, rot, victims, and pathetic dependency. Of course, the dollar crashes forcing foreigners to protect their markets with even higher tariffs and currency devaluations. A trade war dominos depressions the world over. The trade surplus countries are hooked like heroin on their trade surpluses which vanish. Their industry withdrawal and losses in employment cause violent riots and civil unrest in their own countries. The extremist all over the world falsely blame U.S. Capitalism for causing the international economic crises as the U.S. leads us into the worldwide depression. Terrorists can't attack the U.S. Government, so they increasingly take to killing innocent American tourists and diplomats. This further increases tensions between nations causing countries to refuse to work together, prolonging the misery. Of course, we all know the problem is Socialism and Neo-Liberalism[12]—not Capitalism.

In the meantime, gold and silver skyrocket. The stock markets plummet in value, leading to margin calls and more liquidations. The greedy OPEC oil sheiks collude to raise their prices on oil, seeing the weakness in the western democracies. To enhance their wealth, the Parasital attack seems a good move, but this angers the western countries. The western leaders always felt second-class to the royalty of the Middle East and are quite jealous of their divine lucky circumstances of sitting on all that Black Gold. The West finds an excuse over nuclear weapons to go to war with the Arabs justifying this. The West is professing they discovered and developed the oil industry so they deserve some of the spoils. The West wins the war taking this booty freely and using it to help their suffering economies and ends the evil OPEC Monopoly. According to the "*E.&S.P.T.I.T.*", the West solves some of its problems but there are

---

12 Neo-Liberalism is a new form of Liberalism which is not based on freedoms for individuals in a Limited Government environment. Neo-Liberalism is a form of Socialism with greater power and freedom for the Government to secure its objectives (be they right or wrong). More freedom for Government causes a sacrifice in individual Liberty. Today's use of the word Liberal is a contradiction and an opposite to the original meaning of our Founding Fathers. Today's Liberals are Socialistic. In this book, Neo-Liberalism, Socialism, and Liberalism along with Liberals, *(dis)Liberals*, Statests, Progressives Leftys and Collectivists are used interchangeably and have similar meanings.

so many more problems that need solving and this is just a drop in the bucket and a temporary fix.

The great shortages occur not from a multitude of willing consumers or producers but Government is sucking everything into a Black Hole to pay off its debt crisis. Those people who have avoided the over taxation and still have cash, scoop up anything they can get before further price increases. Spend thrift and selfishness excels, nothing is stable or predictable. It's a live for today, to heck with tomorrow, attitude with no decency or respect for other people as proven by the "*Loose Money Equals Loose Morality Principle*."

Further shortages occur as producers stop selling and start hoarding, waiting for higher prices. Unfortunately, looting and ransacking of production plants foils their plans. A few commodity speculators become filthy rich overnight with prices of necessities unreachable to the middle and lower classes as price pressures artificially inflate the costs. Class warfare is at a peak from hardships such as hunger, loss of shelter and riots from the underemployed and jobless. These wretched soles are freaking out, just trying to survive. The Socialist system is cracking up in a million pieces. Implosion is eminent with civil disorder, massive labor strikes, bankruptcy, tax evasion, gang wars, and property destruction from the squalid conditions. The Government increases the use of the "*Containment Theory*" coupled with extreme oppression, but the country still caves into Economic and Social Depression.

Frantically our World Order Socialists call in the Blue Helmets to put down the rebellion. Now the patriots believe the real mission of the United Nations is to cripple our people so we can be managed and kicked into place, at our weakest stage, as the U.N. Socialists end our National Sovereignty. The timing couldn't be better for these Parasites as we have little strength to combat the assault. The U.N. will cruelly dominate the U.S. with support from 50 million World Order Chinese soldiers. Even if our patriots defeat the Red Army invasions, another billion stand ready to ravage our homeland and kill all resisters. Many now agonize in fear wishing they had kept their guns.

Over the decades the Politicians In Power have been destroying our self-sufficiency, hoarding our assets, massively pillaging away Trillions to the foreigners filling their treasuries, putting us 10 Trillion in debt, and have secretly sold us out to the New World Order. The World Order U.N. Socialists and our PIPS march arm and arm with a vengeance, imprisoning and murdering millions of our people, strickening us with fear, getting their mitts on our Government, destroying our Constitution, Bill of Rights and Freedom. This will be a cakewalk for them after they finally have conned you to give up your gun rights. You'll see, then watch a New World Order Hitler takeover our country with the backing of the New World Order Socialists and rip us 'mieces to pieces'. The foolish believe a Collectivist Government with group behavior will prevent the massacres and killings, but it only makes it easier.

When the riots start, this country will be placed under U.N. control with curfews and martial law. Our forefathers turn in their graves as their gift and promise of freedom has been sold out to the World Order by a few Politicians in high U.S. Government positions; the death of our Limited Republic. Now watch the cruelty of the New World Order Zealots crush the spirit of humanity. Never before have so few dominated and enslaved so many. What a holocaust World, since even the mighty Patriots in the lands of the free and the brave have been defeated. This invasion destroys the hope for Limited Government the world over. Only if the present course is altered before most of the Baby Boomers retire, do I see this doomsday stopped? Those of us Freedom Fighters must now engage our people intellectually and teach them the great blessing of a Limited Republic before it is too late. Don't give up! Your Patriot Uncle Jim is with you.

HERE IS THE RIDDLE THE POLITICIANS MUST SOON FACE

Why will we eventually have huge inflation and higher interest rates as they balance the budget and pay off their 10 Trillion debt? If they don't want inflation, how do they do it without a depression, unemployment, a crime wave and preventing the collapse of foreign economies? We are already experiencing cracks in the Global Economy. This is nothing yet! I don't think the Humpty Dumptys can put it back together again, do you? Their philosophy disallows them the ability to ever figure out how to admirably pay off their 10,000,000,000,000.00 debt and you can bet on it. Behind the scenes they are panic stricken over this debt and their other 40 Trillion Ponzi promises. This is their Achilles heel. They got fat and too big for their britches. The truth is coming out how they bought their way into power with your money over the last 80 years. You'll know it from the Austerity, Sacrifice and Hardships which will get worse each year. This is the coming dark age of Socialism—the Parasitic Nightmare.

Just watch the cruelty and oppression as they beat your money out of you to pay their bills. Hint—don't give up your guns until after they pay off their 10 Trillion and their other 40 Trillion promises! And if they ever go back on a borrowing binge like drunken sailors, then get some more guns for defense.

THEY PAY OFF THE 10,000,000,000,000.00

The Politicians go to their old tricks. The fiat money used to pay off the 10 Trillion U.S. debt travels to any investors and foreign countries having loan investments. The fiat weapon can be used by any country to gain an advantage on foreigners who have enough exposure. The whole international floating currency system is open to abuse. A debtor nation like the U.S. can inflate the entire debt away. Poof, so much for "In God We Trust" printed on the money. The U.S. unproductive get a free ride but they destroy millions of untold peoples' lives and rip off our investors, families and foreign creditors. This is like bank robbery but what do they care? It's just another tax and an assault on capitalism. These Parasites should bow their heads in shame but they're too busy snickering about the sneaky trick.

Let's not forget the aggressive trading partners who have built their economies on anticipating a further trade surplus position (mercantilism). They have a part to play as the pass through fiat assault works its way proportionately to any country having exposure to the originator. To the slick foreign trade nations, they get their medicine of choice. The mercantilist countries have plenty of tools like tariffs, taxes, borrowing, currency controls, fiat, etc., but it still comes down to lost wealth or lost markets and jobs. They won't get it until the music stops and the consumption binge ends and the debts must be paid off. They get stuck holding the fiat bag unless they plan in advance to internalize their economies. The longer the U.S. and other borrowing nations wait to pay their debts, the more dangerous and precarious the situation for the 2nd Tier Nations to deal with. 10 Trillion is massive and the 600 Billion Balance of Trade deficit is a Welfare whopper. I pray we pay off this debt honorably and not with Parasitic Fiat fuel. The Mercantile countries need to pay attention and keep their money stable with plenty of employment opportunities or they will tear up their middle and lower classes like Mexico did. Inflation puts hardships on productive classes by making them run harder on the treadmill. High inflation manifests in shortages and high interest rates where workers can't borrow capital to produce goods and services. Without access to capital, the productive and lower classes have no stake or desire for a Capitalist environment. "The Socialists love this as they suck in more followers to their degenerative philosophy." Do you think they give you Welfare with one hand and siphon off (for themselves) up to 75% of your wages with the other because they like Capitalism and surplus jobs, or Socialism and Government dependency? Paradoxically the poor and middle class get fleeced the most even as the Socialists profess how much they are helping the poor! Will you believe them to your own peril?

The deficit trader and indebted nations have some major advantages and leverage the surplus nations do not possess, such as a leaner economy from deficits, heritage, faith and ingenuity of the people. A good military might become important but these trade agreements are all made willingly and should be outside of military concerns, but don't bet on it! There is one more monumental economic advantage in the U.S., which will be discussed later in the book! Maybe.

The economies of Europe, Great Britain, Canada, U.S. and Australia have been hardened with over 40 years of economic stress as they built up the rest of the World's economies. The tension becomes unbearable causing Western societies to demand parity in the trading rules to help pay down the debts and repair the Parasitic sickness in their own economies.

The mercantilist countries are over leveraged and when our baby boomers retire and the global trade starts to dry up, these countries come under extreme pressure. The trade surplus countries are forced to cut jobs and their austerity increases, putting their economies in deeper recession where they buy even less from us but want to sell even more to us. So much for ending the trade deficits and the free trade myth. There will never be free trade as long as there is Socialism somewhere.[13] In the meantime, the worldwide depression will snowball until each country develops self-sufficiency, regaining economic independence, at which point the Parasitalism evaporates. After the shake out, global trade can start anew on a stronger foundation.

---

[13] Socialism is a group or clique concerned about themselves. They don't care about the rights of men and women or an individual right to live for their own sake. Socialism is about control. Freedom will never happen under their system, except for their clique.

THE BREAKDOWN OF G.A.T.T. FROM FIAT

The U.S. taxpayers have a 10 Trillion debt and tire of the lopsided trade deals when no one will loan the U.S. Government money to keep the game going. Our PIPS break loose with rivers of Fiat to pay down their bills. The U.S. people have demanded relief as negative population growth (except from the unproductive and illegal aliens), Parasitic Socialism, and financial stress from job depletion and wage deflation has toughened the people. World trade collapses as the dollar plummets, with most countries violating GATT rules, raising tariffs to protect their markets and refusing to buy our products.[14] The problems compound with foreign countries raising taxes at home and cutting social services leading the world in a harsh and competitive existence for the weak. This is the beginning of a great deflationary cycle worldwide; the shakeout with the Humpty-Dumpty fell of the wall calamity. Hint . . . . **Get Self-Sufficient!**

In the U.S., rampant unchecked immigration is totally eliminated to help reduce the Economic and Social depression, only the wealthy and productive get in. Aliens and Welfarians are expected to contribute in the unifying hardships. Many aliens scoot for the border. Welfare is eliminated. Trade wars develop as 2nd tier surplus nations try to maintain their unnatural trade advantage. The strategies of the surplus nations don't work as the 1st world nations implement their strategies and become self-sufficient in a few years. This leaves the 2nd tier nations with massive unemployment, idle factories, deflated assets and social upheaval all at once. At this time, abusive dictators and Communists seize control of weaker democracies as in the past where the people are unable to cope with self-sufficiency and adapting to new trade realities. This is the dark side and consequences of bad social policies and the total Government World Order domination over people. Hopefully, we end the foolish trade deals, Welfare spending, crippling taxes and fiat to eliminate debt, but for the new communist countries it is reasoned by our Patriots, the foreign people in many countries really weren't interested in capitalism, freedom and

---

14 GATT—(Government Agreement on Tariffs and Trade). This Socialist deal making allows them to play the Dictator with your jobs and businesses. They can break you in a heartbeat.

democracy. They only did it while we kept buying them off with "Most Favored Nation" trade charity and other Foreign Aid bribery.

THE NOT SO TINY BUBBLES

The reason the our Politicians are on edge is not because of one big problem, but because they have a bunch of enormous problems and any problem could reach the threshold, causing a snow ball effect compounding and exploding us into Anarchy. The next depression will be caused by a Government breakdown where in a different way it will be the cause again as in the 1930's. Now it is truly every man for himself. Watch the big spenders and socialists take a big fall from the simultaneous asset devaluations, product hyperinflation, Free Trade Bubble, Unemployment Bubble, Immigration Bubble, Victim Bubble, Growing Ghetto Bubbles, Welfare Bubble, the culture of Parasitalism, Tax Bubble, Illegal Drug Trade Bubble, Stock Market Bubble, R.E. Bubble, increasing AIDS and other diseases, education deficit, taxation money pit, Social Security and Healthcare Bubbles, baby boom retirement bubble, a lack of self-sufficiency, company buyouts with further corporate downsizing, shipping jobs overseas, regulation O.D., Overcrowded Prisons Bubble, Government Bloat Bubble, the ripping apart of American families, Liberal loose money, and of course, the 10,000,000,000,000.00 DEBT BUBBLE; with all this going on its . . . Ring a Round the Rosy, a pocket full of posy, ashes, ashes, we all fall down!

Or . . . Pop, goes the Socialist Weasel!

THE DUMBING DOWN OF AMERICA

Because of the politician's desire for greater and greater tax revenues from the productive middle class, the productive are forced to work long hours, neglecting our problems and violating the *Cycle of Democracy*. These taxes cause our productive to have small families which are poorly supervised, taught feel good information at uncompetitive unionized schools and brainwashed with nonsense on T.V. To prevent riots from the illiterate, illegal immigrants, the unemployed, lethargic, teen mothers, criminals, unhealthy and drug junkies, and to keep them busy, they get more Illfare to buy food and mostly drugs and alcohol (horrific!). This extra subsidization unfortunately gives them breeding rights to reproduce a future dysfunctional surplus labor pool. This Illfare will keep riot costs down, but the taxes to support Illfare prevent the middle class from earning high pay market wages to invest in our children for the future. This is good for Parasites in the short run, but as the dysfunctional class grows in raw numbers they become a huge liability, sucking the life's blood out of the economy and virtuous productive classes. This is the Dumbing down of America as we squander our human capital from the Politicians over tax extraction coupled with Illfare Breeding; a disastrous violation of Nature. Lefty tax policies reduce producers and expand dependents. This increases the need for more government domination—the Socialists' secret plot.

THE SOCIALIST ENVIRONMENT COMES HOME TO ROOST

The PIPS wouldn't ever live next door to their failed policies with side effects hooking people on Illfare, dope, illegal aliens and early paroled criminals. But alas, there is now so much dysfunctional humanity, the numbers spill over and expand into their neighborhoods, bringing an explosion of perversion and random crime. Now the charity hits home. The dismal policy failures and foolish ways are quickly abolished. Unfortunately, it is too late with our offspring already engulfed in drugs, gangs, disease, crime and rot.

Now the Politicians discover something everybody else already knows . . . the environment is critical and must be in alignment with Nature. Real Compassion and Charity—Yes. But the wrong kind of Compassion and Charity can be very cruel and disastrous.

With the 10 Trillion Debt, the PIPS are forced to chop the head off the Welfare beast they created. A crocodile tear comes in their eyes. They were so smart and had all the grand ideals and hopes for a better world, full of peace, community and altruism. The overpaid Socialists were stripped of their dreams and blindsided by the Parasites they spawned. I guess we just had to give them a fair shot at their Government philosophy. But finally the citizens realize that things used to work in this country until the Socials, on the take, went and fixed it (for themselves anyway). Now the people must unfix it so things work again ("*Cycle of Democracy*").

MIDDLECLASS PARANOIA—THE ENDANGERED SPECIES

The World Order Socialists in Washington are claimed to orchestrate the methodical genocide of the productive middleclass citizens in the U.S. There is a fear and paranoia the PIPS meet with the foreign PIPS and these Socialists surmise the American productive are too wealthy, independent, aggressive and intelligently dangerous to the New World Order (as if the Socials knew anything!) "This breed must be culled", they secretly plot. Although the middle class creativity and intelligence is unmatched along with incredible energy and drive, the cunning warrior and independent side makes them a threat and an obstacle to the Socialist policies. Patriots thrive in freedom, but the World Order Groupies don't want this. They want to manage and dominate everybody and will do any unsavory act to get total control, including annihilation of dissenters, for their greater pragmatic good. You could say they hate you at the worst and fear you on a good day.

Some of the devious pressures and stress placed on the productive under the environment of World Order Socialism are as follows. The middleclass will be broken by continuing to throw their jobs to the foreign Parasites in twisted trade deals. The productive will have the fruits of their labors heavily taxed forcing them to reduce their offspring. They will be discouraged from raising children with the high marriage taxes, above market healthcare costs, loose and easy divorce laws, both sexes condoned by Lefty Government policy and public schools into homosexual relationships with same sex marriages. To weaken the breed, rampant unchecked immigration will be forced upon them. The People in Power say the illegal immigrants are an economic benefit, studies refute this by showing illegals with their high crime, and free government services cost plenty apiece, and with cheap labor, we will never automate our industries. With suffocating regulation and lawsuits, the middleclass will lose their capital with regulations enforced by the legal system and be forced to sell their property to multinational businesses, the government on the cheap and charities who avoid taxation. Inheritance taxes will prevent the torch being passed to their offspring. The productive will have their churches critically wounded and seriously weakened with Lefty Government Atheists usurping church functions, such as with Welfare policy and holidays like Earth day, instead of Easter. Prayer will be kept out of the schools to break the will of the children. Schools will preach how awful our citizens have been throughout history to destroy their spirits and demoralize the young. Schools won't teach Capitalism or right and wrongs, but more on world diversity, dependency, evolution, collective obedience and Group Think Socialism. Abortions will continue to be strongly encouraged (so far possibly over 200 million). The Socials don't want many American babies from the productive class because they grow into strong competitive dominant adults. The young productive will be funneled into jobs which demand a lot of their time away from their families, so the family unit is destroyed or at least greatly weakened. Dislocations from free trade causing job transfers and forcing families to regularly uproot will break the social bonds between the people, keeping them in flux and distanced from their extended families and communities. With our tax Parasitalism on the family and feminist Cuckoo Bird propaganda, women will be brainwashed into becoming career bound, running on their treadmill doing day care for paltry pay instead of raising a family of their own (children suffer). To keep the productive under Government's thumb, huge taxes are extracted for Social Security. This keeps the people dependent on Government. Without capital, our people are easy pickings for the Socialists. Look how the disingenuous PIPS have exploited the fear of penniless old age with misinformation that capital accumulations are unimportant and Social (In)Security will protect us in the older years even as they already spent these funds placed in their trust! Want more sacrifice and altruism for their Parasites? A lot of aggressive adults will be thinned out in the military by participation in troubled areas like North Korea, Bosnia, and Somalia or warehoused over in Japan, Iraq, Afghanistan or Germany. Keeping a lot of soldiers overseas keeps them unavailable for marriage, hence not families and children. To reduce family size, especially in this country, our productive have been successfully taxed off the self-sufficient farms. Pressures still remain to keep the productive off the land with Government takings and destroying property rights while rewarding giant Corporate farms with special tax breaks, loopholes, regulations and incentives which a small farmer cannot use but has to compete against. This is the plot of the Socialists who want parents defenseless so they can be Parasitic food. Government uses special interest Parasites encouraging them to blood suck on the productive (Parasitation). The middleclass trying to keep the country as one nation are penalized for silly Nationalist views because our Socialists want a one-world government. To satisfy the proponents of Z.P.G. (Zero Population Growth), drugs are very useful in destroying the productive breed along with AIDS and prisons. Freedom of association for community groups will be discouraged. Even if peaceful, organized militias, nationalists, anti tax groups, those stopping illegal immigration, and other groups will be arrested and diffused with massive force at every instance. These fringe and accused separatist groups without any clout will secretly have the pressure kept on them until they are broken. They are the greatest threat to Socialism and the New World Order. Anyone wanting to live in freedom for their own sake is an obstacle, and must be watched.

The PIPS best situation will be to make all productive dependent, poor and a weak majority in the U.S. This must be done before Socialism and the New World Order can totally take over. The assault intensifies as the productive are attacked on all fronts: church, family, school, community, de-based currency, heritage, health and nutrition, population control with drugs, crime, transient home life, abortion, wars, immigration, the assault on marriage, taxing the fruits of the productives' labors, government takings, easy lawsuits, more regulations and most important, violating their freedom and destroying their self-sufficiency with Welfare and socialist bloat. If you ever talk about these atrocities, they call you a hater. Never will they discuss these realities and their diabolical plot of productive genocide. Why should scientists wonder why productive populations the world over are declining, while the populations of the dependant dysfunctional are exploding? It's the engineered environment of Parasitalism chewing on the productive, produced by Socialist Government. Get away from these evil parasites, they don't care about you with those sly smiles, phony words and disingenuous handshakes. Just like crackheads, they can keep a straight face but they are laughing behind your back, again!

The middleclass will finally learn and believe the ultimate objective of the New World Order is to destroy freedom and Capitalism, enslaving all to nothing more than a resource to be harvested at will by the PIPS. Some life! So much for self-determination and living in the land of the free and the brave; Wooosies, soon China will run your life for you.

Don't destroy yourself and your family by following the Socialist Pied Pipers, making their day in their twisted environment which is immoral according to the "*Laws of Nature*". The PIPS will happily recruit illegal immigrants to take your heritage, birth right, and the place of the children you never had. You are expendable. They ate your young with the *cuckoo bird* trick and force you to raise their Parasites. Then after you are old, lonely, fall off their treadmill, and no longer exploitable, go ahead and pay a visit to their euthanasian doctor. No use in you taking up space anymore if you can't be exploited and milked for the benefit of the Parasites. What a wasted life!

AIDS

If we don't get a grip and control the spread of HIV, a new mutated AIDS virus will develop, probably attacking mostly women reducing their numbers drastically. Healthy females will need to be protected. Feminism will fade as chivalry returns. As more women become carriers, spreading the disease, sexual responsibility returns. Gays, prostitutes and drug addicts will be tested at police discretion. The religious right will be voted in by the public, demanding a stop to the AIDS epidemic, being spread everywhere. They will pass a law demanding all HIV and full blown AIDS patients be branded like cattle and have a permanent mandatory one inch red tattoo placed on their right shoulder. This is to prevent the sick from desperately and secretly infecting as many innocents as they can to get the Government to increase funding for a cure and more Illfare.

With all the human interaction and contact with AIDS, I see it mutating where it can live a period of time in the atmosphere outside of a human body. Because of the contagious nature of the AIDS virus and the ease of contracting it from air vapors of an infected's lungs, the citizens will avoid large crowds and over exposure to masses of people. The smart avoid worship services at stadiums, rallies and sporting events. Professional sport teams plummet in value. Rock concerts become an era of the past. Large factories with masses of workers have epidemics which shut down assembly line productions except in very poor countries with surplus labor willing to take a chance of probable infection. Public buses are full of people wearing gas masks to prevent catching AIDS and other deadly diseases.

Often in fast food restaurants, diseased workers accidentally drool or sweat on peoples' food, causing rampant infections. Most fast food companies go bankrupt. The cautious smartly pack a lunch for work. Sadly, the mutated virus is so infectious, just breathing a particle of a contaminated person's breath is a guarantee of catching an AIDS derivative. Anyone working in the food industry must be tested for public protection from AIDS. The smart cook at home and boil their food first. Malls are also dangerous and the smart shop through the internet and mail order catalogs to avoid excessive human exposure.

The *(dis)Liberals* opened Pandora's Box with foolish policies and acceptance of illegal transient immigration, illegitimacy, the blame game, lack of oversight by the Food and Drug Administration and other bureaucracies, poor healthcare policies, avoidance of responsibility, soft on crime, permissibility of drug use, teen sex, the pill, prostitution, free drug needles, pornography, free condoms and of course the breeding of a dysfunctional underclass with welfare fuel. On top of it, we owe 10 Trillion. Now the pendulum reverses from *(dis)Liberalism* to Darwinism. We wallowed in the *(dis)Liberal* Disease. It's always something, once again caution and responsibility for ones behaviors and actions proves the better lifestyle. Time to close Pandora's Box. They never get it, till they got it!

The under classes revolt demanding a cure to AIDS, believing government developed this disease in a laboratory. Unfortunately, rallies, marches and riots further bring clean people together with the infected in close contact, resulting in an explosion of infections. The deaths from AIDS worldwide approach billion. World population deflates with shrinking markets in a deflationary cycle. Scientists who study population cycles down play the severity and pragmatically state, "Our population has increased for 5,000 years or so, and the increasing deaths are a dip, a natural sharp spike in human population. Before we had the Bubonic Plague, Black Plague, potato famine, polio, measles, malaria, small pox, typhoid fever and other diseases, which from time to time flare up. Other disasters have been starvation and a lack of resources which lead to WWI and WWII. Civil wars are partly due to population excesses" as they profess in a calming tone.

The world health organization doesn't want the people to panic so they claim there are 40 million worldwide carriers of HIV, a gross underestimation as history eventually shows the numbers were more like 500 million and rapidly climbing. In the U.S., Politicians claim ½ million are infected with HIV but the truth is much higher.

To avoid catching the disease from air vapors the intelligent, besides avoiding events with large crowds and restaurants, avoid many other activities such as going to swimming pools, movie theaters, health clubs, living in college dormitories, stay-over in hotels, airplane and bus travel, car rentals, tuxedo rentals, auctions, public school activities, promiscuous sex, drug use, bars, public toilets, drinking fountains, living in big cities and working in crowded offices. Hand shaking is now considered a barbarian ritual, along with public hugging and kissing strangers. Even large hospitals cannot control the spread of the disease as the public opts for more home healthcare with doctor visitations and operations at the customers' home and convenience to be free of these cesspools of disease. Dentists and doctors' needles along with all hospitals, scare many from getting treatment for their ailments. Drinking from another's glass is a risk along with water fountains, handling money, public laundries, pool halls, casinos, living in retirement homes or touching anything an infected person was near within the last few weeks. You can't blame the fear in the people; AIDS is a killer and an early death sentence! When the general public realizes the extent of AIDS, people flee to the country and scoop up farmland as prices explode in value. It's truly every man for himself.

The pharmaceuticals and medical profession develops more drugs and treatments to parasitically profit from this tragedy and keeps the AIDS people alive longer. This increases the germ mutations, AIDS even develops the ability to lay dormant if frozen or dried. The virus is everywhere and comes alive if it is in contact with a drop of water or a thaw. HIV also becomes undetectable until the obvious full-blown AIDS takes hold. Eventually, most of mankind has it and lives with a large part of their humanly existence in therapy and treatments with booster shots and pill cocktails to counteract the viral attacks. Near total contamination from HIV leads mankind in tragic doom and jeopardizes mans long-term existence, possibly sealing our fate with potential extinction.

The drug addicts, homosexuals, prostitutes, Johns, criminals, people on welfare, illegal immigrants, prison inmates, and others getting blood transfusions or accidental group work contamination take it on the chin with most of the AIDS victims coming from these groups. Many believe AIDS is the intellectual and moral cleansing of mankind. Tax revenues and Welfare totally dry up at this point. Not because people refuse to help but because so few can help since the baby boomers are retiring and the Leftys owe 10 Trillion and 40 Trillion in promises that must be paid first.

The survivors will be the sectarian and intelligent making good healthy choices with responsible behaviors. These pick of the litter are independent, cautious, unexploitable and skeptical of TV propaganda from smooth talking Politicians, the New World Order and Free Trade Parasites. Patriotic Politicians enjoy strong popularity with citizens in this era of personal responsibility and consequences for ones actions. To know what is acceptable and how an individual should live his life, one must look to the "Laws of Nature". Perhaps one day I will write a book on the "*Six Absolutes of Nature*" with their relation and ability to define morality, and existence.

WHY WAS WELFARE STARTED?

Under previous U.S. leaders, it was felt we weren't competing and our country was in a drift with stagnant economic growth. The Politicians forgot or didn't care that we were busy trying to raise our children, investing in our human capital, not producing tax revenues, but this is another story. The Politicians' foresaw the inevitable job dislocations which would result from their grand strategies. Their fear and punishment method forced our citizens to upgrade their skills and work harder for the state to survive in the great change they planned. To make this happen without social upheaval, they began Welfare and unemployment benefits to pacify the dis-affected or as I call it, the affected. I think we would have advanced our society twice as far if we had an environment of surplus, incentive and confidence over the last few generations. Hey, how about another generation of shortages, a tax dam and fear? How long do you want their pain of job deficits, high illegal immigration, another trade rip off to keep down wages?

So the next time you hear someone tell you the problem is the economy, tell them

"It's not the economy, it's the Socialism, stupid"!

THE NATURAL RATE OF UNEMPLOYMENT

The natural rate of unemployment is an excuse by the government to make us believe a 4% or 5% unemployment rate is acceptable and normal. Many economists believe that a rate of unemployment any lower will cause inflation from increasing wages. This is sometimes true but doesn't have to be. The real question is "do we want to allocate more of our wealth to our human capital (families) or not"? There are multitudes of macro policies which can prevent inflation but obviously Socialists are more concerned about other things (like Parasites) than our families. To question the legitimacy of their theory of the natural rate, if unemployment keeps inflation down, how come in the late 70's and early 80's we had high unemployment with high inflation? If you answer too quickly, you do not understand. Eventually, people see the sickness that has been so prevalent in our mantras and theories which are like a tired out dog that won't hunt anymore.

Right now, we can end all of this Socialism and have Capitalism **Quadrupling Your Pay,** with **160,000,000 new surplus jobs** and end all these crazy government programs, borrowing and spending it, tax abuse, and inflation. The AMERIPLAN will work for well over 60 years. Join me! Then in 60 years we can do something else. I could tell you what should be next but in 60 years someone else can.

THE EUROPEAN ECONOMIC UNION (EEU)

The European common market participants get off to a good start, but as soon as world trade starts to dry up, it's every country for itself. Rivalries intensify as shrinking markets and resource shortages cause huge disparities, dislocations and unemployment.

Great Britain, at the last moment (hopefully), had the good sense to stay out of the Maastricht Treaty with the single currency called the European Currency Unit (ECU). If Great Britain keeps its sovereignty over its currency it can inflate with fiat or use tariffs, to extinguish its debts if other countries continue to procrastinate on free trade.

The U.S., Great Britain, Canada, and Australia could form their own free trade zone because they are so similar. Mexico can't be included. Probably, the Mexican citizens will overthrow their government in shambles. It should be obvious to all that Mexico could not be assimilated into this type of environment. Wisely, leave Mexico to its own development with other third world countries forming its own trading group in raw materials, basic necessities and cheap labor products.

The (EEU) members have sacrificed their destiny and ability on a national level to control their own economic policies such as unemployment, Welfare spending, taxes, trading matters, monetary policy and many other freedoms. Just wait till the Socialists make their inevitable policy screw-ups, I don't know about you, but I wouldn't want to be punished from a bureaucratic Parasitic action and not be able to correct it.

This Socialist centralized common market idiotology will only work in good economic times. In tough times, old problems resurface such as race, language, culture, competition, pricing, wages, nationalism, religion and philosophy. There will be bitter and violent struggles over the currency in jealousy and greed. This will be exactly the same as in the last several centuries with the feuds and world wars. The only difference will be the battle for the ECU instead of barbaric gold and silver. Oh sure, the fights will be over jobs, food, industry, power, prestige, policy, etc., but all of these can be obtained with enough ECU's.

When the EEU passes out the spoils from their tax Parasitalism some countries will inevitably get the short end of the stick. It will be quite a circus as Germany and France gang up on the other participants to enhance their own positions for wealth, dominance and power like Texas and California. Bet on these two countries to get more than a lion's share of the new industries, government spending and favorable Parasitic regulation, while the other members get the crumbs, as they are Parasitized. There is an 80% chance of the EEU failing.

If you doubt the trouble, restudy the beehive colony and the clashes and casualties whenever there is a shortage of resources. As always in nature, eventually there will be shortages, and printing more ECU's won't do the trick.

DEVALUATION OF PEOPLE CAUSED FROM WELFARE *AND POPULATION EXCESSES*

As foreign populations continue growing unchecked, especially in Africa (thanks to meddling politician attempts to bring them into a civilized culture that they aren't ready to participate in), science will be unable to keep up with the new viruses, bacteria and diseases which mushroom from human over interaction. Contamination and exposure to human body fluids and lung diseases will be major concerns. Resurfacing in Africa, there is this disease called Ebola, which causes human organs to rupture, spilling blood through skin tissues, orifices and other body parts. We don't know where this disease comes from, only that Ebola is very contagious and kills 4 out of 5 who have been exposed to it in a very painful death. The possibilities of a worldwide infection epidemic are increasing. The African people will be quarantined from travel if a major outbreak occurs in their continent.

Since the beginning of time, there have been plagues, famines and wars. Diseases, like AIDS, are nothing new. When population excesses occur, something has to give. Look at all the growing ghettos. What's going to happen there? Riots, diseases, wars and famine? Back in the days of Moses, the King of Egypt had the first-born sons of the slaves exterminated. Between Stalin and Hitler, over 40 million people were killed, even more in Red China. The U.S. has had about 200 million abortions. Look at the massacres, hunger and diseases in Africa. The dangers of overcrowding are real and happening now. Welfare is not a solution but a crowding out violation which will cause a solution such as the above. When extreme policy conditions exist, you get extreme actions.

In China, any female having a second pregnancy is greeted with an immediate abortion. But over in the U.S., we encourage illegal immigration and we give welfare, free health care and breeding rights at the expense of our own children. Kind of bizarre, don't you agree? If the underclass becomes too big a threat, besides cutting off all Welfare, there is the potential for all unwed procreating females caught to be fined or thrown in jail for five years with a mandatory tubal ligation to reduce the higher taxes, welfare, future crime, dysgenics and potential disease. This will be done to reduce future abortion, end the "*Crowding Out*" and reduce pollution like some environmental groups want. This will be a mandatory operation for all criminals and welfare recipients before they get any welfare.

Because of the dysfunctional behavior and attitudes in the District of Columbia, we may see our government relocating all operations out of Washington, D.C. to desolate desert areas away from the riots, ransacking, panhandlers and looting from the under classes as Welfare is eliminated out of necessity. The poor need to reduce their procreations. It doesn't work in nature surviving with unchecked and irresponsible procreation to increase offspring with Welfare. It is better for the dysfunctional to only breed one or two offspring and concentrate all their time and energy developing and nurturing these children. Better one success than eight failures according to the "Laws of Nature". With a large class of dysfunctional feasting off the productive with such intensity, there will be little compassion, hence a devaluation of life in general. The Politicians in fear of the growing violence will give up their feeble attempts to help these lost souls who can't responsively control their primitive urges. Hint . . . . Get rid of the welfare Abomination of Nature, but supply surplus jobs with compassion for those who want to better themselves. If they need welfare give tubal ligation and when the Welfarians pay back the Government welfare plus costs and interest they can reverse the operation and have a family. Fair enough?

Our dysfunctional stock grows, "*Crowding Out*" all of us, forcing all of us to forego more freedoms. Did you ever notice the correlation between Welfare increases and freedom decreases? The unmanageable and undependable cannot be expected to have high ethics and moral behavior, protect themselves or play by the rules in a limited republic based on Capitalism. Thus, more laws to protect these wretched creatures from themselves. The PIPS are destroying everyone's freedoms, leading us down the road to Throngite Communism and eventual doom by encouraging more dysfunctional breeding and illegal immigration with Welfare. Note they are beginning to lick their chops now. Most other countries of the world control immigration to protect the people from the "*Crowding Out*" except our PIPS. Once again, this is bizarre to Parasite one's own people. Billions want in this country, when they all get here with their problems, the country collapses, like the Roman Empire. All our Welfare handouts, playing policeman and Santa Clause to the world is expensive business. This is the "*Super Power Exhaustion Theory*" which ends in a depression from multicultural factious divergences, Parasitic tax policies and destruction of the productive classes. Look for mass migration of the productive in the U.S. to foreign countries that respect individual rights just before this country implodes.

To prove the Politicians have devalued our people and don't truly care, one need only look at their actions. You will know them by their fruits—taken from your labors. The PIPS have spent the baby boomers Social Security money and have caused the young to falsely blame the old. The young look at the elderly disdainfully as pathetic greedy relics of the past soaking up tax revenues propped up beyond their useful years, dragging the whole country down absorbing money. Arrogantly, the Socialists think the Social Insecurity savings should go to their pet projects, and Parasites. The baby boomers will get cut off at the knees as Social Security is insolvent and government refutes the obligations. The PIPS only cozied up to the Baby Boomers promising Social Security to get their mitts on all that money to spend on Parasites. They outsmarted you with your goodness of heart and gullibility just like you bought the welfare con! Thanks, New-Liberals. The boomers now old and unable to continue working are targets of the dysfunctional who victimize them even though boomers kept the government and World Order going for the last 65 years. Unfortunately, most of the boomers figure out the Social Security Ponzi scam when they are weak, demented, penniless and it's too late. This is the *Frog Boil Technique*. A drag! The real estate and stock market crash to 50% of current value, which they had all their retirement savings invested in, didn't help either. Now remember the markets may not crash but inflation may explode where a local phone call or cup of coffee costs 500 bucks which means the assets won't be worth hardly anything in real terms.

Worldwide population will soon be 10 Billion. Elites predict this planet can only sustain 1 billion humans. This means 9 out of every 10 must die so the one may survive. Over population is blamed, by atheists, on the teachings of fundamental religion, which doesn't believe in birth control. Religion is accused of creating its own employment by fighting birth control. Priests are surely needed for the growing criminals, dependent Welfare recipients, prostitutes, addicts, gays, malnourished, sick and dying of AIDS, Ebola and other diseases mutating faster than science can solve them as viruses further change and are quickly transmitted by air vapors. The Socialists see a chance to get some quick cash and will eliminate all Religious tax-free status. You know all charities pay zero property taxes, sales taxes, or income taxes, but they use a lot of free Government Services you pick up the tab on. The public gladly takes to taxing these tax avoiders. Get out of their way. Beat the odds. It is essential for you to have self-sufficiency and independence from the PIPS or you will be one of their sacrificial lambs on their alter of altruism. But don't expect them to sacrifice themselves.

I say you better become self-sufficient. You think taxes are ridiculous now? Wait until the bleeding hearts take 95% of your salary. Heck, they need it. People are dying right? After the 70% cut for the Parasites we need money for the illegal immigrants, food shelters, free health care, and schooling the protected classes, high paid government bureaucrats, illiterates, old, children, murderers, the elite, AIDS victims, poor, drug addicts, lazy, prostitutes, Wall Street Brokers, foreign nations, unemployed, alcoholics or other dysfunctional on Welfare. Don't you feel their pain? Where is your altruism, humanity, sacrifice and selfless Host spirit? Even though you don't know them from Adam, you owe them! They voted! Now get back on that treadmill!

Give the friggin' Parasites your wallet you cad! Let the blood-sucking vampires eat the flesh off your back and stick your children (if you could afford any) with their 10 Trillion Debt waste! Then watch the Parasites explode in raw numbers of illegitimacy—to our ultimate doom; an exploding swarm.

No cure for the continually mutating AIDS will be found until the Politicians change their behaviors and themselves fix their own mess! They have devalued life by allowing illegal drugs, loose irresponsible teen sex, over regulation, and illegal immigration, along with Welfare to violate the "Laws of Nature". Now nature has devalued them. Our citizens shout at Politicians with threats and anger. Politicians become too scared to talk in public and avoid crowds. They caused more misery, than if they just kept their greedy mitts out of the misperceived problems. Don't let them make you pay for their massive 10 Trillion social experimental tinkering scam. They broke the system and good this time! You'll see, it is a 20-year depression but they use a code word called "Austerity". It's every man for himself in this era of gloom.

Soon the *(dis)Liberals* will force you to get a license to have a child (with a big fee for them). But, the dysfunctional living in their ghettos, such as drug addicts or Welfare Queens are safe, the PIPS can't penalize them if they procreate. They don't have any money the *(dis)Liberals* can siphon away as they don't produce a surplus. Now the people realize the *(dis)Liberals* don't really care about our children or the country, they only want *your* wallet.

Get back to that termite colony you grub. Bring the Lefty Kings and Queens their favorite green Parasite dish. No, not leaves, your cash! They cried wolf but they truly need it this time!

There is rejection by Patriots of previous liberal Presidents and Liberal leaders; they are looked on as nothing but power mongering Socialists who sold us out with phony solutions. Our *(dis)Liberals* are accused of prolonging the Great Depression and Cold War to shield their agendas of centralized government control and prestige at the expense of the American people. Finally, the unions and industrialists also reject the government and see the situation as business and labor versus Socialist government domination and oppression. As less and less citizens have a stake in Capitalism, the Socialists take over will be a cake walk as few will have a desire in having a Capitalist environment in this country. Socialists are slowly tightening their diabolical death grip around our necks with the "*Frogboil technique*". Look out people, Cuba, here we come.

As our country implodes our PIPS frantically try to keep power and end the special Free Trade advantages they gave China and other countries. China aggressively bullies and confiscates the wealth of its neighboring countries to keep up its high growth rate so it can be in a position to defeat the United States if necessary and dominate the world. Now our cowardly PIPS run for cover blaming our people. Hey, I'll bet you didn't know your pay and National Security would go down when we did the Free Trade thing. The People in Power promised us our pay would go up, and Free Trade and Illegal Immigration was good for you.

The Socials have stifled economic growth with their ill-concocted environmental policies to legally tax the citizens off the land, eat their capital and destroy their self-sufficiency for the Parasites. Because of the looming bankruptcy of Social Security and the 10 Trillion debt, they will turn a blind eye to the big corporate, multinationals and government polluters. All of a sudden watch how quickly they change their attitudes and could care less about pollution, nuclear and toxic waste. All the environmental gains of the past 40 years will be lost when the austerity becomes unbearable. Just breathe the air, drink the water and eat the vegetables. Eat, drink, and be merry!

There will be pollsters dumbfounded as the people lie or won't respond to polls to baffle the PIP pandering and eventual social plundering. The people refuse to be guinea pigs and sheep any longer. There are many political election upsets and polling becomes a waste of time and energy. Besides the American people only want one thing, their American Dream back!

People in Power demands for tax revenues become more extreme and oppressive. Many of our people are turned into looting criminals because they can't keep up with their tax bills even though they are running on the treadmill with all their might. IRS buildings are ransacked, employees bribed or shot. Even now foreign secret trusts are set-up by the rich to escape taxation and boycotts by the poor, unable to afford their taxes from the PIP arrogance, lack of compassion and fairness.

Voter fraud increases with Parasitic illegal alien immigration registration and computer program techniques. The PIPS use ballot fraud and corrupt legislation to maintain power over the masses. Honesty and justice are some of the first causalities in this era as they are up for sale to the highest bidder. They will do whatever it takes to get elected and that means anything! If our people ever allow the PIPS to tabulate votes by computer without a hard copy ballot count, you can bet somebody will rig elections as they already often have.

Glues have the obnoxious odor removed. This allows the dysfunctional class to freely take to the glue sniffing addiction making them less of a threat with physical violence and rioting as their energy is sapped. This is used in Brazil and it really works. This will be used in other countries that can't afford to purchase illegal drugs but want to keep the underclass in check. Soon the U.S. will use it as a last ditch effort to reduce the outflow of currency for illegal drugs.

All Medicaid and Medicare are dropped as government is broke and the now old baby boomers and underclass must start paying all over again for their fair share. Fewer in the underclass will get free health treatment, as hospitals will move to remote locations, and the dysfunctional end up spreading more diseases to their underclass communities. Charities are dumbfounded as philanthropy recedes and no one will help, as Welfare is believed to have caused all this dysfunction. The poor breed less in their sickened state, and die younger, which eventually lowers the overall "*Crowding Out*". The hospitals stop free treatment so there is a decline in healthcare costs, as the productive no longer have to subsidize the Welfare and alien crowd taking advantage of the American taxpayers.

Currently, to know the whereabouts of criminals, they have tethers attached to their ankles. When technology advances enough, computer chips are surgically implanted in the dysfunctional, illegal immigrants, and criminals' brains. Now they can be tracked and arrested by the police if they leave their designated Welfare Zones. This contains the bulging crime and limits the anarchy to small pockets condensed with the undesirables. Certain death results if the chip is removed as it explodes on contact with air immediately killing the dangerous criminal with an arsenic derivative explosion. Other technologies in these microchips could be a continuous electric shock, a warning bell or the release of a chemical that paralyzes the criminal if he leaves the designated zone.

Biological germs released in the big cities by terrorists are a major concern, and nuclear bombs can be made to fit in a suitcase. As our country further decays and our baby boomers retire, we won't have the wealth to buy off the foreigners or the resources to protect ourselves anymore. With all the bombs and biological weapons spread all over, it is almost a guarantee a major disaster will happen soon.

In the future, the PIPS will use a slick method to round up the dysfunctional and weed them out of working class neighborhoods. There will be no more Welfare, food stamps, ADC, Head Start, etc., unless the recipient lives in a designated welfare zone in a high rise apartment (called warehousing). The dysfunctional will implode as they prey on themselves instead of the productive. Females, to receive welfare, must have mandatory birth control so the bastard illegitimacy recedes. Their Welfare is totally cut-off, they get an immediate abortion and sterilized, with a long jail sentence in self-sufficient prisons if they become pregnant. Procreating males if caught and don't pay child support are given vasectomies and jail terms in profit making prisons. Procreation of a dysfunctional nature must be reduced for reasons of safety, pollution, crime reduction, security, civil rights, disease control, taxes, paying the

40 Trillion promises, etc. In some wealthy but over populated countries, underclass females may be given $40,000.00 grants by age 12 if they are sterilized at birth. Their parents make the decision and are custodians of the money.

Costs increase on food, making it more expensive for the dysfunctional. This results in more hunger in the short-term but less future poverty and hunger as the dysfunctional are unable to successfully breed and over-procreate. Saltpeter is spiked in their water supplies to reduce their sexual urges. Mass male and female sterilizations for free are performed at big parties with plenty of cash, food and alcohol to lure in the homeless, drug addicts, and unemployed who are starving.

All schools are privatized with local funding only. You get what you pay for. Scarce tax dollars siphoned off and spent on the children in far off cities with neglectful parents are considered wasted as it takes more precious money to educate them. The productive pay attention on how their tax dollars are spent. These outstanding parents won't allow parasital waste when they control the purse strings of their own labors.

15,000,000 more government make work jobs are eliminated as these produce nothing of value and are more welfare. For those remaining on the dole, Parasitalism is greatly reduced with salary cuts and elimination of all pensions and health care. Leftys go into government to serve not cash in. Bureaucrats must learn they can't take a government job forever anymore. They mustn't become lobbyists and consultants but get ***REAL JOBS***, ending the sycophant lifestyles off the taxpayers' wealth.

Illegal immigration is finally dealt with. With millions of illegals in the country, *The Silent War* is not so silent. The aliens caught are placed in a working jail for one year, earning the $25,000.00 they owe the state for violating our laws. They are fed low protein diets with high carbohydrates for energy. The foreigner may obtain freedom sooner if someone buys him out. We have $5,000.00 bounties for any American who catches these criminals and turns them in alive. No payments for dead aliens turned in but no questions asked either. These aliens didn't have clean hands and most likely were up to their old tricks of smuggling dope, sexual assaults, spreading diseases like the Swine Flu, looting and sneaking currency out of the country, not to mention deflating our wages as they work for cash and don't pay taxes and they do a lot of shoplifting and petty thievery. The parasites come for money, they trash the place, have their offspring born here at taxpayer cost and then collect welfare and waste government services. Oh sure, the PIPS find a few honest illegal aliens (except for their sneaking over our border) but not many, just some to stick on T.V. But the citizens are in a depression and could care less.

People in Power don't have much tax revenues to spare so tax deductions will be limited for the elite class and they may promulgate a flat tax or a National Consumption tax for extra revenues. Only American married couples earning over 1,000,000 per year will receive tax credits up to 40,000 for each child, up to 2 children. This is the "breeding slot". It is figured one will survive with one catching AIDS or killed by random murder.

Taxes are raised on the poor so they won't over-breed. Tax Theory tells us the more we tax something, the less of it we get. So, poor people will be taxed out of existence, just like our PIPS in government have randomly been doing to the productive middleclass for over 80 years.

Soup kitchens, halfway houses, drug rehabs, and mentally ill group homes will be outlawed from working class neighborhoods with zoning laws. The dysfunctional will be warehoused in giant high-rise slums. The disease, crime, drugs, loose sex, negative behaviors, etc. of the dysfunctional must be kept away from the children. Yes, one bad apple can spoil the whole bunch. Keep the Predators away, the parents cry. HUD and other government housing will no longer be allowed to do block busting—destroying working class neighborhoods by putting the criminals, half-way houses, drug addicts, dangerous and others with special needs in working class single family neighborhoods forcing this Parasitalism on taxpayers. The brutality that HUD has purported on the productive will eventually be exposed as an abomination, which will be aborted and eliminated with an auction on all the assets HUD and all Government municipalities have hoarded from our own citizens. The citizens now believe HUD is responsible for spreading most of the drug, violence and crime of our society by enabling this environment of irresponsibility by those getting freebies with no strings and not having to work 10 hours a day like the rest of us playing by the rules.

Each of the 50 states in a desperate attempt to raise more revenues aggressively gives out tickets for speeding, and anyone with a tinted windshield could be a dangerous drug dealer or crackhead and will be ticketed because the police can't see who is in the vehicle. User fees become ridiculously overpriced. The PIPS pass more regulations, ordinances and laws when the people can't remember and follow the multitude of controls we have already. They will come and single you out, yanking you out of bed at 3:00am when they need to generate more revenues.

Parasitic quotas, set asides, low income housing tax credits and affirmative action are eliminated as these are considered problem transference, phony solutions, and Welfare. With a 10 Trillion debt the needs of the many outweigh the needs of the few. The best man for the job philosophy (Realism) returns. The special interest groups and victims now have to compete in the market place, with no more Socialist handouts which are at the expense of all American producers and their families.

To further straighten up the population excesses our PIPS get government to pass out free birth control pills, implants, abortions, patches, condoms, rings and IUDs and give free tube tying operations to the poor. But because of their twisted free speech stance, the porno shows on cable T.V. are stimulating and encouraging more risky sex by the underclass. Unfortunately, this results in more catching AIDS.

New taxes continue to crop up from the PIPS on every conceivable service including the internet.

We have people borrowing on their home and credit cards to make ends meet from the stress of tax extractions, eventually bankruptcies accelerate deflating our capital stock, dominoing corporations into bankruptcy causing more layoffs and more bankruptcy. It's a vicious downward spiral, which caused the stock market and real estate to crash. To think it all happened just because the PIPS and Parasites wanted to suck some more fruits. This deflationary cycle will hit everybody. What do you think will happen to home values when all the baby boomers retire and try to sell their houses to the Generation "X"ers who will be paying an 85% tax rate and they will already have a home? Real estate again will crash. Once more, the numbers and demographics don't add up. Don't expect inflation to bail you out. We tried that in the 60's and 70's and had a heck of a lot of recessions trying to get interest rates back down. There will be a lot more boarded up homes than you can imagine.

Early paroles by judges have been encouraged because of prison overcrowding and costs. This unfortunately further increases the spread of HIV and more "Black on Black" crime.

Free needles are passed out to the poor at inconsistent intervals, increasing drug use and diseases. Eventually, the government gives up fighting drug abuse and taxes illegal drugs to pay bills!

To help pay the bills (for Parasites) and debts, prostitutes now must get a license and pay the state a big fee. Prostitutes do not have to take an AIDS test because of their Civil Liberties but can do as they wish, often further spreading the virus.

Enterprise zones will be kept, providing low paying jobs to keep the dysfunctional in centralized areas. This is the 21st century version of the Indian reservations and part of the "*Containment Theory*" strategy.

The wealthy and even middle classes will increasingly opt to live in gated communities with top-notch security and high walls. This is their best protection from the dysfunctional and criminal Parasites.

The death penalty is aggressively used and after one appeal, which is decided in one month, the sentence is expeditiously carried out the next day. After the killer is dead, the authorities will work with the dysfunctional relatives to clear their family name or help with relocation, but no money.

Just like China, to make profits, our PIPS will cut out the useful organs of the criminals and sell them for kidney and other transplants. The criminal doesn't get a choice on the matter. We really do need the money and most believe we can't afford to worry about foolish matters like this Civil Right.

Riots are permitted and go unchecked in welfare zones but controlled massacres occur if the boundaries are crossed. It is too expensive to catch all these criminals so a policy of *Containment* is instituted.

U.S. borders are closed to illegal immigrants and repatriation and prison sentences given in earnest. Americans especially fear the radical groups of Iranians and Iraqi Muslim fundamentalists as they have terrorized our citizens in the past. Same for Central Americans with their drug trade.

Indians, with their tax-exempt businesses and reservation casinos (a form of welfare not given to whites, Latinos or blacks) now must be assimilated into the American culture and pay their fair share of property and income taxes. Also, since Indians are using U.S. government roads, military protection, phones, technology, capital, schools, commerce, State and Federal benefits, welfare, etc., they must pay taxes on their land, sales tax and businesses so they don't unfairly bankrupt American businesses, which pay taxes. With money tight and after 100 years, the Parasitic special treatment must end. The PIPS need the money!

Non-profit and charities must now pay taxes as these are often assumed as nothing more than tools of rich people to escape taxes as the elite pull the strings behind the scenes for their hidden agendas and often reward their friends and employees salaries and perks out of these as pay backs. The charities pay no income tax, sales taxes, or property taxes but they get a free ride using all the government services for free as the productive class is paying their share. No Way!

In the Third World, populations get so out of control with the rainforest burnt down and the oceans polluted, it's survival of the fittest in a cruel way. Males do not bear offspring, so the answer is in controlling female reproduction. In poverty stricken countries a lottery is started in which all females participate (9 out of 10 females will have mandatory castration to limit over procreation), thus ending the cycle of poverty, hunger, disease and pollution to solve the "*Crowding Out Theory*". No Way!

The American people demand an end to centralized unionized public education, as they believe the children are being brainwashed and manipulated into mindless sheep programmed to be subservient and not free men and women. The predetermined positioning of the youth and Social teachings, destroy the belief and hope of the American Dream. More parents home school their children because of the low uncompeting public standards and the growing fear of the spreading viruses, drugs, violence, guns, crime, and other mental and physical abuse in the poorly supervised schools increasing with unionized teachers without being challenged with competition to be the best, only looking for a fat paycheck. No Way!

With the 10 Trillion austerity, the competition becomes fierce in the government bureaucracies for the smaller pie of tax dollars. The Alcohol, Tobacco, and Firearms bureaucracy is accused to have picked a fight, attacked and hopefully accidentally killed the Waco Davidian Church members and children to get name recognition and purpose in a diabolical plot just to heighten its need for more tax money. It worked! Other bureaucracies use their own hideous tactics; this further convinces the citizens they need less Socialism. No Way!

Some obnoxious Socialist movie actors, athletes and other entertainers are laughed, boycotted and booed off arenas and stages. They like welfare for the poor, so the money can be spent on their sponsored products and events. It is reasoned instead of the poor people paying homage to these false idols and stars, they need to feed, clothe and shelter their families. The entertainment groups are called hypocrites who want higher taxes. If they make 10 million a year and are taxed 20%, they still make 8 million. But the poor making 20,000 a year may not pay much income tax but after Social Security and Medicare, 2,000 in taxes, is making them destitute. The entertainers want to give the poor a little of Welfare money, sucked from the American tax payer and play holier than thou role but won't take the time to really help the poor by improving our educational system or creating an environment of jobs and businesses that provide the poor with real help which is self-sufficiency and unlimited opportunities for freedom, growth and self worth. The examples of daily living by this star bunch are considered terrible role models and most are looked on as a disgraceful bunch of money hungry vultures. These self-serving creatures have their product endorsements boycotted and returned for refunds. The super rich, foreign lobbyist, entertainers and other Leftys who don't believe in helping families are placed in this group as they have all the time and money to hire people to further their agendas and twist the government in their direction with favorable legislation. The honest, hard working family men and women are too busy, rearing a family to combat these sycophants, sucking off their fruits. No Way!

During the coming depression, the PIPS will pass the blame of their legislative mishaps on global trade, some foreign currency crisis, speculators, or on the Federal Reserve, saying the Feds raised interest rates or cut off the money supply again. The people finally realize this is not true. As long as government policy is really improving the economy, the Feds purpose is inconsequential and 10% growth rates are obtainable without inflation. The problem is the policy from the Politicians, not the Feds. One day the public will grow up and no longer be conned with the blame game. The best approach for the Feds is to keep inflation low so a dollar is a dollar and people will think before they act in a spend thrift manner. This is important to solve the *Loose Money Equals Loose Morality Theory*.

From the increasing austerity to pay off the 10 Trillion, many citizens believe there are more crooks and Parasites in government than in the private sector. The people believe government is worse than organized crime. The government takes over 50% of the workers gross pay. Even the Mafia never took this much with their protection rackets.

When the major austerity starts, bureaucrats will be despised, abused and jealously attacked by the underclass for their higher than market wages, new cars, pensions and easy working conditions and hours. As they suck more out of the retiring productive workforce to pay their expenses and 10 Trillion, they get even less as the remaining productive jump off the treadmill, seeing their rewards confiscated for the glory of PIPS. The Politicians are faced with a no win situation. If they increase government borrowing or taxes the economy will deflate. If they increase fiat funny money, the economy hyper inflates. They are in a pickle and losing ground as the number of retirees swell to massive proportions. One wrong move and their system collapses like a house of cards that it is. They can't fix their mess because that would mean doing the right things (reducing the Socialism), which is the only thing they crave more of. Good luck Politicians! When the citizens tire of the degradation, they will demand the 70% solution to reduce the Socialism in the last chapter—don't jump to it, keep reading!

HOW TO PROFIT FROM NAFTA

NAFTA (North American Free Trade Agreement) is not for job creation, but job switching, with hopefully more wealth for the U.S. Government and Parasites, in a move up to higher pay jobs and industries.

Another purpose of NAFTA is to control populations of Central America and the U.S., but this is too slow and will worsen things before they get better, if they ever get better because when the civil unrest and riots in Mexico start, tens of millions more will run for our border. Warning: eventually NAFTA will end in Mexican overthrow of the government with the multinational businesses kicked out and 36 family ruling class possibly executed!

In Central America the peasants will be enticed to leave the subsistent farms and move to the cities. Government agriculture projects and giant agricultural businesses will buy their lands. After another generation or so, birthing rates should decline from a generation of government family planning and tax extraction preventing large family existence in the cities. The U.S., Japan, and the Mexican 36 family ruling class will provide the low paying jobs for the under classes in Mexico. Labor is cheap and will stay so. (Hint—Buy land surrounding big Mexican cities about a mile out from the growth and build cheap housing shacks to get rich)! Watch the cities double in size in another 30 some years! This should occur even if a cure for AIDS is not found.

Now let us see where the U.S. profits occur. Because our city population growth has already been curtailed, except illegal immigration, our growth will be in other areas such as farmland. As the dollar declines, our farm profits increase along with bigger markets from foreign population gains, plus agricultural property taxes are low encouraging more to move to the country. Big city office buildings and surrounding suburb business/ industrial parks are overtaxed, have too much crime and pollution, these go to seed. With technology like the internet and great product distribution systems, there is less need to be in a skyscraper or expensive office complex. Watch the big Insurance companies, banks, and pension funds take it on the chin in commercial real estate, with both growing vacancies, high utility bills, and municipalities scavenging for every dollar in property taxes they can suck out of these decaying buildings. You can't take your building and move it somewhere else. You can only sell it for a cheaper price than you bought it for. Stay out of these investments or go broke along with the casinos, banks and insurance giants, unless you get this stuff really cheap. These companies will soon be giving away their buildings for free. Cities like Detroit already do, some they just bulldoze. Rental apartment housing will fare better. Money alone will not guarantee success, but those who work hard, are savvy, experienced, good promoters and quick decision makers will do well.

THE TRUTH OF SOCIALISM

It is now figured out there is only one reason why the PIPS raise ridiculously high taxes on production and take all of our land and capital. It's not to solve problems, they create more than they solve. They want your fruits all for themselves. They aren't working for a common good and a better country. They want domination, obedience, totalitarianism, and a cushy life. What Socialist wants to work and compete when the environment enables them to be a Parasite? Parasites are opportunists and quick to take advantage of our dysfunctional Socialist environment. They don't want to work producing something real and useful in a real job—they want to live off their wits and sneaking a share from you. You can count on lawsuits to explode against the government and big charities. Why? Because this is where all the money is hoarded. Now the citizens know why Socialists try to pass laws that prevent you from suing the State! They don't want to be responsible for their actions; they only frantically want your money by whatever means. This eventually is their imploding circus where the Parasites will get eaten up by Super Parasites. Let their feast begin on themselves. Bon Appetite.

Just remember this, anything in this chapter could happen. Maybe some of these actions should be taken, but the longer we let things fester, the more extreme the action the Politicians will have to take to fix their mess according to the *Pendulum Theory*, unless we get rid of the rest of them we still have left when you vote. They don't like it, but you still own the Country. Don't let them take **your** Country away from **your** family! We don't have any more time to waste! Now, let's get to some of my Theories to make you an Economic Genius.

5

ECONOMIC AND SOCIAL PROBLEMS TOTAL INTERRELATION THEORY

The *E.&S.P.T.I.T.* gives us essential understanding and the importance in solving both economic and social problems at the same time. What good is it to solve economic problems such as creating **160,000,000 new jobs,** create more billionaires, reduce bankruptcies, etc. if we cause more social problems such as crime, poverty, substance abuse, pollution, mental and physical disease, child neglect, etc.? And what good is it to solve social problems such as **reducing 75% of our crime** if we cause more economic problems such as stifling growth, unemployment, bankruptcies, shortages, monopolies, welfare, confiscatory taxation, etc.? In actuality, we have solved nothing. All we have done is trade one problem for another set of problems. This is a Parasitical Win-Lose situation and we need to do without this foolish *Problem Transference.*

If we really care about our people, the most compassionate, admirable and virtuous action we can take is to provide a safe environment with surplus opportunities. This most certainly will improve the morality and cooperation of our people as the perverse environment of Parasitalism is diminished. The last two of our four major problems can also be solved by applying the *E.&S.P.T.I.T.* without Parasitic increases in economic or social problems. They are the economic problem of **paying off the 10 Trillion Debt** and the fourth is a social problem of the need to **Vastly Improve our National Security** (including reducing pollution.)

It is so exciting when you finally can see the root of our major problem and confidently know how to fix it. In our case, it is the Root of Socialism with its growing Parasitalism. I hope this chapter helps to cure our ignorance so we can prevent the arrogance of a Socialistic environment and move this country forward in honesty and respect once again as you **Quadruple your Pay and Reduce Crime 75%**, both at the same time!

Most people with a little thought can imagine the devastation when a parent with 2 children loses a job, unable to find comparable work to support and feed the family. Out of necessity, the parent may have to get welfare or take low skill work, leaving the children unsupervised. If a parent cannot properly provide for the children's needs, he or she will be neglectful toward the family spending long hours at low pay, struggling and trying to keep up, instead of supervising the children. The children may resent the parent. An absentee parent is a poor role model, raising the children in poverty (this wasn't a problem when most of our grandparents had small businesses, such as farms and their children worked right alongside them all day and were taught responsibility). But today, the father or mother, filled with the shame and a heavy burden on their heart, may self-destruct in drugs, gambling or divorce if not already. This parent doesn't believe in the American Dream, share love or get any back, doesn't teach honesty, respect, nationalism and guide the children from the pitfalls of crime, dope, gangs, diseases and other rot. This parent has neither the time, money or care to be a positive influence; this spreads a negative ripple throughout society. Are we all not worse off because of this immorality? Do you see how the Socialists are ripping our families apart by not truly investing in our children even though they say and pretend they are? And believe me, welfare is not truly investing in our children but expanding a sickening disease as you are beginning to learn.

Our current *Economic Problem* is a lack of good jobs and the Social Problems will manifest in negative behaviors (social disorders) of the parents and their neglected family in society. If we don't want these Social problems, this Economic problem of a job shortage must be solved, such as creating **160,000,000 new high pay American jobs**, eliminating income taxes and only allowing immigration for the highly deserving, who contribute, not the Parasites! At the same time, we create the jobs; welfare must be eliminated to end the cycle of dependency. All these actions reduce the Parasital rot and the decay from the "*Crowding Out*", as we expand the *American Pie*.

Economic problems will result in an environment where more Social Problems are possible such as a niche for a drug pusher. Maybe this person couldn't find employment or just likes drugs, gets hooked on them and resorts to peddling drugs. Others become addicted, unable to work or don't care about work because Welfare is their safety net, catch diseases, get hurt or commit crimes to support their habits and become a burden on the productive of the State. You know if we didn't have Welfare, we wouldn't have 20% of the drug abuse in our environment we have now. The Social Problem is the proliferation of drugs. The Social Problem manifests in higher security, safety and insurance costs, along with higher taxes for building prisons, rehabilitation, healthcare, etc. If we don't want the inevitable Economic Problems, this Social Problem of drug abuse must be solved, such as protecting our borders from the drug trade, controlling immigration, beefing up custom inspections, eliminating welfare and strong penalties without parole in cost-free prisons for the perpetrators. If the criminals are incarcerated by using tax dollars, this is Parasitalism and punishment on the productive and another Social Problem will occur from this economic rape. The burden of this economic cost, absolutely, 100% must be placed on the criminal (Parasite).

An Economic Problem causes Social Problems and a Social Problem causes Economic Problems. The interrelation and repercussions between Economic and Social Problems are irrefutable.

You may not be able to identify the exact (cause and effect) result of the original problem, but it is inescapable. There will be a cost to bear by someone, one way or another.

With any Social or Economic Problem, you can't ignore an opposite reaction or correlation to the other. You may even wonder how many good Economic or Social events were cancelled out by other negative Economic or Social Problems. Also, understand a chain reaction, like a domino effect, positive or negative, can occur such as an Economic Problem causing a Social Problem causing an Economic Problem causing a Social Problem and continuing until the impact is exhausted. It's just like Fluorocarbons eating up the Ozone Layer or a snowball growing down the mountain. Who knows all the lost opportunities to do the right thing and how many lives the birdbrain do-gooders have destroyed. They forget the 1st rule. DO NO HARM!

To solve Economic Problems, Social Problems can be solved. And to solve Social Problems, Economic Problems can be solved. Both should be solved together to obtain maximum benefits and allow the greatest number of citizens to reach their American Dream.

Our Social Problems are a barometer in measuring the health of our economy. Some of the Social Problems are crime rates, drug use, alcoholism, prison over-crowding, poverty, pollution levels, lawsuits, divorces, illegitimate births, etc. I place more faith in the direction of these simplistic statistics over GNP figures, which include the expenditures in replacing broken windows and rebuilding after riots.

Our Economic Problems are also a barometer in measuring the health of our current and future society. I would look to the trend of taxes, health cost and insurance rates, Nation indebtedness, trade deficits, tax burdens, consumer debts, wealth distribution, inflation, unemployment, etc. Then ask yourself if these Economic Problems are improving to judge our society. Think about it . . . . giving welfare does not solve poverty but grows the sickness with more future problems.

To put this Theory simply, every Social Problem solved makes the country a little richer and every Economic Problem solved makes the country a little safer and a better place to live. If you think you have solved a Problem of Economics and no Social Problem has improved (or vice versa), then you are only fooling yourself. An example would be shutting down or over-taxing a factory that emits too much pollution. The Social Problem is cured but the factory workers and town are economically hurt. This is Problem *Transference*, a Parasitic Win/Lose situation. Another *Problem Transference* from a Social Problem would be taxing workers to provide welfare for the unemployed. Spending tax dollars and draining our Treasury rarely ever works because the Social Problem is temporarily solved, but the problem comes back to an Economic Problem as the working people are Parasitized and when the money runs out, the problems return. This is where the *(dis)Liberals* have their great failures. Spending for welfare if done by borrowing is doubly the ultimate in Parasitalism. The spending displacements cause inflation and/or high interest rates in the short run. The Welfare debt is transferred to a later generation with no investment and a growing Welfare class that has lost its self-sufficiency and will be a greater burden, suffer even greater pain, Parasitalism and problems in the future. Even worse, the productive will suffer from austerity as the debts are finally paid, with higher taxes than normal. Those playing by the rules get penalized. Crime will increase. Everyone gets the sacrifice and punishment in this era from all that's borrowed. At this stage, no further money can even be taxed without extreme oppression; the tax rates are already at Parasitic levels. With permission, taxing surplus—yes (but never over 10%), but Parasitic taxes—no. Even one precious penny wasted or spent unwisely by our Government is a crime against humanity! The wasted money starts out as an Economic Problem, which manifests into a social disorder. You don't get anything for free or without consequences in life. **I CHALLENGE THE POLITICIANS IN POWER TO SOLVE EVEN ONE PROBLEM WITHOUT SPENDING MONEY. YOU SEE THEY REALLY JUST WANT YOUR CASH! SOLVING PROBLEMS NEVER COSTS MONEY OR YOU ARE CAUSING ANOTHER PROBLEM!**

Another example of *Problem Transference* is solving a Social Problem, but creating a new Social Problem. Affirmative Action quotas and preferences were initiated by the elite to supposedly solve racism. This is no solution because the Parasitalism is switched to all the excluded groups who are now the victims of Government punishment and reverse racism. You don't solve Social Problems by creating another Social Problem. To really reduce racism and jealism, eliminate the Problem Transference . . . end Affirmative Action and create 160 Million new high pay jobs and opportunities, together, which solves the "*Crowding Out Theory*".

But the Socialists won't create surplus jobs because this allows the citizens to be independent, strong and an obstacle in their Government takeover and domination. Socialists hate limited Government and are constantly gnawing away at our Constitution and Bill of Rights.

You know how to tell a Socialist? If a person doesn't want an amendment to abolish the income tax, require a balanced budget and term limits, they are no friend of this country. They will force you to be their Parasitic food for the unproductive.

Socials see you as Beasts of Burden and with their wicked Parasitic arrogance; they want to order you around to reach their hidden Government agenda. They don't believe in free markets or personal freedoms. These are expendable in their pragmatic logic to reach some common good and impossible utopia. Socialists for 80 years promised so much in the future, but deliver so little in the present. Have you had enough sacrifice yet?

PIPS have a vested interest and if they reduce Government ownership, spending and solve our societal problems, we won't need them. They won't get their huge salaries, prestige, perks, book deals and pensions! Get it? And don't tell me you can't see the growing Socialism and Parasitalism over the last 60 some years! Where do you think the 10 Trillion Debt came from? It wasn't run up by the Patriots! The Exploiters and Parasites—Yes! The number of hungry Parasites in our country is the Social Problem. To solve it, we need to solve Economic Problems by cutting taxes, reducing Socialist spending, asset hoarding, counterfiating, demanding a Balanced Budget and creating **160 Million jobs**. And with the jobs, all the businesses will cherish their workers or go broke as everyone quits the racist or exploitive businesses to go work down the street for the good businesses! Got it people? Surplus jobs solve all the capital exploitation problems according to the *E.&S.P.T.I.T.* It's simple.

Our citizens need purpose for being here. Their purpose could be developing and running a large company, becoming a world leader, spreading the word of God, excelling in sports, an entertainer, a journalist, solving 70% of our problems, inventing new technologies, creating a fortune, etc. But, for 90% of us, our greatest ambition and purpose is to raise a good family. Good people will follow and allow any Government system to work if they believe the system can provide an environment in which raising a family is possible, including Communism, Dictatorship, and Fascism for a short while. To desire a family is the greatest human instinct after self-preservation. Otherwise, we wouldn't be here.

Socialism has been temporarily able to flourish in our society by using some slick techniques. They are borrowing, spending counterfiat money, over-taxing our producers, encouraging abortions as they entice illegal immigration and then taking these short-term gains to buy-off people with Welfare, buy products from favored businesses, cash pay-offs and giving Government jobs. These are all Parasitic violations of a market economy which eventually exhausts in failure. Unfortunately, for the People in Power, the citizens have finally discovered this immature degenerative philosophy of centralized planning is out of alignment with the free market. The Socialists have had a pretty good run at masking their flaws, as they ate our capital. But it has come to an end by not providing surplus jobs. Everybody can't work for the Government, somebody still has to produce something they can consume and pay interest on their 10 Trillion Debt and 40 Trillion other promises, which have placed our families in debt bondage. Now the pendulum must reverse from Socialism to every man for himself. Government has squandered our resources with foolish Parasitic giveaways and the more it taxes, borrows, takes our businesses and tries to run rental property, inflates and spends, the worse the economy gets, making their wacky philosophy all that more oppressive and corrupt as time goes on.

Our families come first, but our jobs control our time, providing the money to support our existence. We are now a very specialized society in which few of us are islands, able to live off the land, independently and decently feed, clothe, protect and house our families. With a job deficit, a lost job means big trouble because our people have given up their self-sufficiency and cannot produce the daily necessities to keep a family going. With a job shortage, our people are backed into a corner and subject to Parasitalism. Just the way the Parasites like it! And if you play their game and even have reserves they will steal what you have. Oh? You trust them? *Save* money in a bank account and watch them inflate the value away while they spend on themselves. Go *borrow* money for a business as they crowd out the capital markets with their Parasitic borrowing forcing you to pay grossly high interest as thet selfishly spend on themselves.

Oh? Don't need to work, got yours already? Great. Watch them shut off all the valves where you get 1% interest on CDs. They bankrupt you in the Real Estate markets. They take *your* money to pay *their* tenants' rent which then goes to *themselves*. Then *their* criminals, drug abusers, etc. spill over into *your* place. Now you get to solve more Socialists problems for them, but you don't get paid. You keep paying their increasing property tax, sales tax, and income tax. They get free police, fire and government services (you pay their share). They pay none of this but get your money for free. Oh? Put your money in stocks? Watch them force out capital gains taxes as they suck in more money and they scoop up your lands, businesses and assets on the cheap with their orchestrated Boom then Bear Markets. Wake up! You still believe in the tooth fairy? And if you don't have a pot to piss in, they will make sure you never get one! You think you got nothing now? It will be harder to get anything in the future.

Did you ever notice when unemployment is high, there generally seems to be more riots and crime? And didn't it seem there was less crime when unemployment was low with most of us working in high pay jobs? Doesn't it make sense to have surplus high pay jobs and opportunities to reduce stress, loss of hope, loss of faith, and loss of love for our family, friends, and country? Won't the inclination and propensity to commit or allow crimes to go unpunished in our communities curtail when our citizens have a stake in the system? And with more taxpayers producing wealth and less needed expenditures on crime control, won't our National Wealth increase? Would it not be safe to say that if all of our citizens found abundant opportunity wouldn't their hope, faith and love improve as they become better citizens and stay away from crime? And why? Because they have a better life worth keeping and they don't want to lose it! If we fix this, we are well on our way to reducing 75% of our crime! At the risk of being too complicated (sarcastic) the E.&S.P.T.I.T. tells us . . .

↑ Jobs = Crime ↓ and National Wealth ↑
↓ Jobs = Crime ↑ and National Wealth ↓

In place of the word Crime, you could insert Parasitalism.

Fill in the blanks: ↓ Crime = Jobs __ and National Wealth __

If you answered Jobs ↑ and National Wealth ↑, congratulations! You earned a masters degree in government economics.

We don't need to waste any more money on complicated, meaningless studies. Let's just get everybody fully employed. At the very least, this will be 9 hours a day people can't steal or commit crimes. I know, you're thinking many people just don't want to work, will waste their money on drugs, commit crimes anyway and we have the jobs, but the potential employees don't have the skills. All of this is true to an extent. *First*, for those who don't want to work . . . eliminate Welfare and stop allowing the Government to be an enabler. In other words, PIPS are creating the very unemployment that they pretend they want to solve. This is their Parasitic job security. *Second*, for those who waste money on drugs and *third*, who commit crimes, stop the drug trade and illegal immigration, by protecting our borders, reducing Welfare, along with ending the Socialists soft posture on crime. Make criminals pay society for their dastardly deeds without early parolees, in self-sufficient prisons, instead of making the productive families playing by the rules, pay the prisoners' rehabilitation, gymnasiums, education, libraries, free legal, entertainment, food, clothing, TVs, and air conditioned housing. We don't need illegal immigrants to pick our tomatoes, cucumbers and apples; we have criminals in jail, living off our families' blood, sweat, tears and labors. This is Parasitalism at its worst. Oh sure, the Socialists cry the convicts won't work. That's fine, of course a few of the antisocialists can stay in their 4'x8' solid block walled cell in solitary confinement. Again, let us stop the Welfare system from being the Parasitic Enabler.

Fourth, for those of our people who don't possess the skills, create the 160,000,000 new jobs. Then businesses will be happy to provide on the job training. Businesses will take anybody they can get! Businesses will give signing bonuses and treat their employees with respect again. Businesses will have to or they won't have a work force! Now some say the workers will get greedy and form stronger unions and strike to get more goodies. I don't think so. Remember that a greedy workforce will cause its company to close up shop. Not out of punishment but from necessity. So workers cut their own throats on this one. If these businesses and jobs are worth keeping, assuming we have competition from other unions and companies in that field, instead of a bloated Union monopoly (like the UAW), the remaining companies and their workers will fill the production vacancies opened by striking unions.[14a] If we can get the PIPS to stop foolish regulations on businesses, we will have the essential competition we need. Now labor markets can morally find their own wage levels without inflation and Socialist Government tinkering. This is all solved with the "*Competition Theory*", which dismantles Monopolies and bloated Unions won't be needed or able to survive. With surplus jobs, our people will happily find better jobs, which they deserved anyway and by our citizens, with incentive, upgrading to higher paying industries, we all benefit. We don't have to improve our economy with pain, fear and oppression. Let's have incentive, opportunity, and freedom. All we need do is provide the proper environment.

Because our businesses will want to properly train our people, we won't need to waste as much tax money in public schools that are ill-equipped with too many Socialists who never had a real job or a clue about self-reliance, critical thinking, Capitalist markets and how to prepare students to participate in Capitalism, instead of being Parasitic food. How could uncompeting, tenured, unionized Government Bureaucrats and unionized public school teachers have the skills necessary to name their own pays, regulate our economy and educate our children, without having spent 15 or 20 years working in the private sector, experiencing all facets of small business? Maybe 20 years of work in the private sector should be required of all politicians, social workers, teachers and bureaucrats. And I don't mean working as a lawyer, pollster, running a campaign, a Lobbyist, producing regulation, a politician giving speeches or somebody who ten years ago held some job that was in some compliance or paper pushing with a lot of fast talking services that don't produce anything real that you can see or touch that has some permanence or is useful in helping our daily lives. Any job dividing up the spoils or Parasiting off others without an equal return, breeds arrogance along with ignorance. These are activities that might fill up a page on a resume, but are not the kind of experiences, which help in running a business, country or a classroom. We need people who have had a real job, producing, not city slickers consuming and Parasiting.

Each person knows in their heart that it is a long shot they will ever drive an expensive car, live in a mansion, travel around the world, or quit

---

[14a] The UAW and other unions must end their parasitalism also, and compete by splitting up these monopolies where the pieces are no bigger than the company each union is involved with.

work like the rich drinking fine wines and dining in fancy clubs. They know they are stuck in their environment without a pile of cash, but at least these people believe if they work long and hard in sacrifice, they could be just like the rich man. But they can't as long as we have an environment of Parasitalism, which punishes the productive. **SURPLUS JOBS ARE A POWERFUL TONIC GIVING OUR MEN AND WOMEN HOPE, A PURPOSE AND THE MEANS TO RAISE A FAMILY IN A CRIME FREE ENVIRONMENT.**

I know, you think some people will abuse society by breeding their 15 children. It won't happen if they can't afford them and Government is prevented from being their enabler with Welfare. Let the non-profits fix this "Crowding Out" misery; it's their problem, not the Governments. They don't want abortion so let them do this. Many non-profits are hung up on money. They are afraid to lose their tax-free charitable status and have been bought off with the hush money hook line and sinker. They won't speak up to the People in Power and help fix anything as long as they don't have to pay a fair share of property taxes and income and sales taxes. They have a twisted environment and their leaders have let us down by not speaking up about doing what is right. You'd slit your wrists if you really knew how much some of them make!

With high pay jobs, I think we find a lot of our parents leaving the bread earning to one spouse. With surplus jobs, one parent will be able to stay at home, fix our nations' problems and properly raise our children instead of working on the treadmill to pay taxes and daycare. What a waste.

With a little less taxes killing off jobs and Welfare enabling irresponsibility, social problems will decrease. How many divorces in this country were really caused by incompatibility and how many are the result of financial and economic problems which manifested in social problems? They'll never tell. But just look at the divorce rates, drug abuse, abortion, suicides, unemployment, child neglect, job pressures, and other crimes before the Socialist philosophy came into power and how problems have mushroomed today. These are their byproducts, their waste as our Socialist big spenders destroy our families.

An unfortunate misunderstanding poor people have is thinking they can't get jobs because the businesses are prejudiced and want to exploit people. The real problem is much subtler. A business is always looking for a good deal and interested in making money. A possible employee is judged for this alone. Qualities which help an individual contribute to the organization are dress, cleanliness, manners, ability to communicate and work with others, salesmanship, punctuality, stability, organization, health, energy, alertness, creativity, ability to make quick and correct decisions, references, other habits, skills, interest in job, education experience and speech. As important as all these factors are, there must be real opportunities for growth and profits in the environment. Currently, our Socialists have constricted our economy to less than a "Zero Sum Game" with their policies of 90 or 95% employment. There are great risks to consider whenever offering an applicant a job, such as lawsuits, crime and drama. This accounts for the unwillingness of companies to hire new people even though they interview hundreds of people to find the one needle in the haystack that will make them rich. The Socialist environment forces these businesses to treat you as another number or piece of meat. In other words Socialism is about controlling, especially your life and wallet. Hint . . . . create 160 million jobs and no one will care about racism or eliminating welfare.

But don't get down and blame your problems on the environment using this as an excuse for selling drugs, staying on Welfare or stealing, and don't think your low intelligence or dropping out of school is your excuse for failure. You can start your own business with a little creativity and without money. It won't be easy, but you'll get there quickly by keeping the fruits or your labors and avoiding all the Parasitalism. The average person uses 10% of their brain. Use 10% more and you can with *Six Secret and Simple Habits* in this book! And remember, even in this era of Parasitalism you can prosper by obtaining your self-sufficiency, which is covered in the Freedom Chapter. You won't learn this information from the Statests and PIPS, because once you fix your mess, they have to give up their Parasitic lifestyle and get a real job, producing something of value, like you.

6

AMERICAN PIE THEORY

Most of us are producing a certain amount of wealth. Depending on what we produce and its value to society should determine the amount of money we earn. The amount of money we make is a portion of the total of all peoples' efforts. Look at each person's efforts as a slice of the total pie. If we grow the pie evenly with each person still doing the same level of productivity, each person's slice and return is bigger proportionately. A bigger pie results from diminishing the rotten blob called Socialism in our country.

One technique in the AMERIPLAN by itself will quadruple the size of your slice.

When we regulate and frustrate the leveling effect and balance of competition in a free market, the slices become distorted. With Socialist policy, some receive larger shares than are deserved such as non-competing unions, multinationals, the Government Bureaucracy, rich elites and monopolies. This is at the expense of others who compete at a Parasitic disadvantage and are prevented from getting fair slices as their spoils go to the anointed classes. A just Government's purpose is to be a referee, not an activist for the Parasites.

A large share of our workers' and business' slices are eaten by our lopsided trade deals. If we have a 600 Billion trade deficit, the *American Pie* will shrink approximately this amount with ripples up to times 10 from devaluations on our businesses and less savings as jobs become scarce. Trade imbalances are a Global Parasitic phenomenon that deflates the "*American Pie*." Some in our country will do better but most will do worse. On balance our country loses if these deficits accumulate over more than a year or two as our companies exhaust and close-up shop. This results in less competition where foreigners can raise prices for monopoly profits. This is *International Parasitalism,* not Capitalism.

An encompassing share of the pie slice is cut around the outside with *taxes* for Government. Some pay more in taxes, some pay fewer taxes, depending on who the People in Power favorites of the day are. If taxes are cut evenly from the current level, everyone will benefit, especially those who are currently being punished the most.

According to the "*Crowding Out Theory*," the amount of illegal immigration has an effect on the pie. With more illegal immigration, each slice will shrink. The few able to exploit the cheap labor may not lose, but families lose with wage deflation from the increased participants in certain industries. Plus with new people, existing Government services are spread thinner amongst the increased population causing tax increases on the already oppressed segment of citizens. This causes disgust, jealousy and hatred as we get more Parasitalism from the illegals.

A shrinking population would normally reduce pressures and expand the slices for those still around. The echo boomers are having fewer children from this Socialist illegal immigration "*Crowding Out*" environment, but the problem is we are reducing our most productive and Crowding them out with unskilled dependent labor from illegal immigration. These criminals won't grow the Pie. Beside Government's increasing costs for services and taxes for illegal immigration, there are social costs, such as pollution, transient behavior, crime, disease, illegal drugs, safety concerns, etc., as Parasitalism sets in. This is all according to the "*Crowding Out Theory*" and these social problems manifest in more economic problems, which further reduce each slice and a good life for the Hosts. Parasitalism is no way for a 1st class nation to operate.

Government also adds back to each individuals slice with subsidies, entitlements and Welfare from what it takes in (about 30% back.) This also distorts the pie with favoritism for some and punishment for most. They never can be fair as they try to pick winners and losers mostly based on politics and paybacks, not economics.

More cruel than the political siphoning and then rationing of the fruits of your labors is the Socialists' agenda to totally dominate our economy where they control all the tools of production, where you will have no control over your wages, no ownership and no freedom. You become a slave and won't have any stake. And how will they accomplish this immoral deed? They will take our wealth by brainwashing you into believing it is your duty and obligation to the community. If Altruism, self-sacrifice and generosity to the Government are not your choice, they will try to shame you into it by calling you names, such as selfish, racist and bigot. Another technique to encourage you to donate to their Socialist cause is to entice you such as with tax write-offs. To further exploit the fruits of your labors and to takeover your assets and lands, they created the endangered species act, raised your property and other taxes to confiscatory levels. They told you the sky is falling with catastrophes, passed restrictions on your property and when the greed of the Socialists swells, they will just step on you and grab it just like the banks, car and insurance companies. If you doubt this, just look how they forced you to pay Social Security Ponzi taxes and spent the money already! Once the Socialists grab everything, like healthcare, you will be weak and Parasited like you couldn't imagine. Remember the Socialists are like a crackhead. They become very good when they have a $400.00 a day habit and addiction craving your cash. You can't beat them; just get away. Produce for yourself and . . . . **become self-sufficient. Use the *6 Silver Bullets* and stay forever vigilant and on guard.**

All the above are Socialist distortions on the honest value of work according to the free markets ability to set prices. Any tinkering into markets by a plundering Government often leads to Parasitic immorality. A sickening disease.

Let it not be forgotten, any Socialist Government losing jobs has caused the American Pie to shrink. These losing individuals may aggressively, maybe even illegally, compete to get a piece of somebody else's slice. Like the water being sucked out of a fishbowl. If a job is hard to come by, this person will want more Socialism and Government jobs with Government distribution for himself. It's the lazy, fearful or jealous mans' way. This is Parasitalist behavior. Don't expect this person to appreciate Capitalism and don't expect the Socialists to create abundant opportunities or grow the American Pie! Wake up—get the fog out! Do you remember when we had that Yankee Doodle can-do confidence? Fire the Socialists and get your life back.

Inflation is a sneaky trick and a tax on the productive, as well as the savers, distorting their slices. The borrowers are rewarded in this environment. The richer one is the better, as they can borrow, leverage their assets and get more inflation wealth without producing a darn thing. This is how great fortunes can be amassed off the productive classes in a very short time. The productive are robbed and decimated in this environment and stay stuck on the treadmill of life, running faster like rats for nothing, only lining the pockets of the elite speculators and enhancing Socialist Government power. This high inflation technique is used in Mexico to artificially prop up the 36 family ruling class (or is it 24 families now?)

Some in the PIP camp do have honorable intentions, but you see the cruel distortions from Social meddling with regulation, inflation, taxes, borrowing, illegal immigration and Welfare for rich and poor. They can never be fair and compassionate, even though these leaders claim how much they care for you when they raise taxes and eat your spoils. Whether they know it or not, they are hypocrites! There is honesty and fairness in only one way. It is done through our markets where wages and prices reach their real level and fair value with numerous competitions, and not by a paid bureaucrap pretending to be impartial.

A good way to stop the unfairness and perversion by the Socialists is to do the thing they don't want to. Which is to shrink the size and influence of Big Businesses, Public Utilities, Multi National Companies, Healthcare, Bureaucracy, Regulation, Bloated Unions and Government. This will reduce the cheating, corruption and Parasitalism. This will allow the free market to morally seek the level of prices, wages and wealth. Only at this point will a worker or business get an honest days pay for an honest days work. This is true Capitalism in a Win-Win situation based on respect.

One day when we return our society away from the Socialism and Parasiting on the productive, we will see an incredible change in our society. When our people have the freedom to keep their earnings with unlimited opportunities, they ***will*** be better citizens. They ***will*** willingly pay their debts (including paying off the 40 Trillion PIP promises.) They ***will*** be self-sufficient and able to care for their families (and want to!), they ***will*** donate time and money to just causes, have more leisure time to supervise their children, time for their communities and time to create technology to benefit all mankind. This powerful tonic of freedom from the shackles of Socialism will revalue humanity. With the higher quality of life, our people will avoid the risks of drug dealing, prostitution, crime and other negative behaviors. With a prosperous life too good to lose, there is real value and every citizen will want to protect his or her good standing in the community. The *American Pie Theory* is the second greatest theory in economics.

After creating **160,000,000 high pay jobs** to provide our opportunity and by growing the "*American Pie*" **Four Times Bigger** to provide incentives, we will have a society with less crime based on True Moral Capitalism. Now welfare and most taxes can be eliminated solving the "*Crowding Out Theory*" and ending the *Breeding Rights* violations. This can be accomplished compassionately.

HURRRRRAY!!!!!

7

4X JOB THEORY

The premise is that each new primary job we create causes a combination of at least three more new opportunities to be created in Primary and Secondary jobs. Primary jobs are most desirable to create and are the Basic Building Blocks of great wealth in a society. They consist of direct production jobs such as in farming, textiles, shelter, infrastructure, manufactured goods and energy. Lesser important Secondary jobs or services play a supportive role such as in distribution, education, accounting, healthcare, government, banking, food service, computer services, etc. The worst types of jobs may cost us 4 or more jobs apiece, are destructive and counter-productive. These are Parasitical jobs, which reduce the Primary and Secondary jobs. These negative low productivity or non-productive endeavors would consist of crime, monopolies, excessive government bureaucracy, regulatory and compliance, pornography, gambling, illegal drug pushing, lobbying, influence peddlers, special interest groups, tobacco marketing, some trial attorneys, some big union bosses, speculation, etc. Socialistic Government over time breaks down, enabling an environment for Parasital occupations. A successful Government will prevent this stunting of society with proper management.

There are ten major areas I have identified where we can improve our society by reducing the Parasitalism and create surplus jobs. If we greatly improve in these ten areas, the Job Growth Factor may be 10. I believe if we create surplus jobs, most of our people with confidence will gravitate to the highest pay jobs. Our people will have more leisure time and wealth to supervise our children, avoid Parasitic and criminal behaviors, create more technologies to advance our society, automate most routine jobs, fully embrace Capitalism and take the time to fix a lot of the broken institutions in this country, and repair our Government, which is burdened with ugly Parasitalism. I think 10% yearly GDP growth rates and 160 million surplus jobs is probable by improving and solving 10 Economic and Social Problems. Obviously, we don't need 160,000,000 surplus jobs but this allows our people to choose the job they can do best. If in trying to better oneself, a worker stumbles or falls, there are plenty of other high pay opportunities to fall back on and regroup. Let's take the fear of job loss out of our system so our people won't be afraid to start small businesses, create jobs, and take the risks in gaining success in a Capitalist environment. In other words get rid of the pain and punishment; let's have confidence with reward and incentive!

1.) *Reduce and Simplify All Regulation*—Look at most regulations as pills to prevent disease. It works until the disease builds resistance or another disease develops. Then you need another pill for a new disease. Soon you are swallowing so many pills the medicine kills you. The best solution would have been to let our economy build immunities to most of the diseases and forget the foolish short sighted regulations and let the free market make adjustments.[15]

As a goal, I suggest we fit all Federal Laws on 100 pages. If they can't fit, then we probably don't need them. This is the K.I.S.S. Formula (keep it simple, stupid) in action. What came first? 2/3's of the worlds' lawyers or all these crazy laws? Do you want to understand the Law and hope your lawyer can? How many businesses never got started because of arcane regulations? How many lawsuits were feared from inconsistent legislation? How many years of our peoples' lives are wasted, documenting their steps, trying to get through lines and Red Tape? It would take your entire lifetime to read every law, but would you be able to remember them or even understand them? Ignorance of the law is no excuse they say. The Arrogant Parasites have made you into a criminal. You don't know what laws you are breaking, but they will come and get you when they want to get you out of their way. Today, the laws are so complicated and confusing to our people that the whole system is breaking down. Think

---

15 When I talk about the free market, I mean in the U.S. not the entire 2nd and 3rd world countries. This country is set up to protect our own, not foolishly languish with the 2nd and 3rd world countries. We need to solve our own mess. There will always be some country that can make something cheaper and worse. We will never advance our robotics industry if we base our economy on 3rd World cheap labor.

of all the hours in regulatory compliance instead of spent being productive, building new businesses. Fortunately, the good Lord had the divine wisdom to give people only ten simple Commandments. The people understood these rules and could follow them. If things are too complicated, and even if you want to play by the rules, you can't, so you often sit things out, doing nothing. Another major problem with Federal Legislation is when the Socialists try to micro manage our daily affairs. This becomes too inefficient with trade-offs and sacrifices, which stunt and cripple all the people who must change for the special interest beneficiaries. **"One macro-law can lead 350,000,000 people, but one micro-law can destroy 349,999,999 lives."** Regulation based on simplicity, clarity, and efficiency for the users provides the environment where millions of new jobs can be created. You can take this to the job bank!

2.) *Incentive by Eliminating Taxes*—One of the worst disincentives and Regulatory Parasitalisms is our current Tax Code. Only the Special Interests Parasiting on the Productive have the wealth to weed through the legislation to benefit from the loopholes. The super rich get richer and the productive get more productive until depression, when we have exhaust, falling off the treadmill in penniless old age. A better thing we can do is to have a 5% consumption or flat tax, with no loopholes. The best thing we should do is to eliminate all taxes on Income and Consumption. We can, by cutting the size and scope of Government spending. We can live off the fat of the land for 60 years, or longer.

Remember, the Super Rich and Monopolies don't pay taxes on their businesses and production. If the Socialists raise taxes, the cost is totally passed on by businesses to the consumer because you don't get a free lunch. Since prices will be raised, less people can afford the product, production will be cut and you can kiss your job goodbye.

We already tried this. It's called inflation and unemployment (stagflation)! So by cutting taxes, prices can be lowered (assuming we have competition), production and jobs will increase because more consumers can afford the product. This is not rocket science you know.

When we send our hard-earned money to Washington, how much do you or any of our citizens get back? Some say 30% gets back to our needy people, the rest is Parasitized. Wouldn't you like a huge tax cut and use this money for your charities of choice and expand your business and help our unfortunate with a great job? With powerful incentives from tax decreases, our businesses will create millions of jobs and even train our workers to succeed in the highest pay jobs. If you need any services the Government has tried to supply in the past, forget it, you buy them on your own at 30¢ on the dollar.

Just think of all the time you will save by not having to keep all those receipts, documentation and log journals. You won't have all that organizing, filing, computation, and precious time and money wasted trying to figure out how to fill out all those crazy forms. You won't have to worry about audits or if the IRS will put you out of business, even though you made an honest mistake. You might save 400 or more hours a year. Now you can open a business and create jobs without fear. Don't worry about your poor accountant, attorney and the IRS; the AMERIPLAN has plenty of new jobs for them. But start worrying about your children and use this spare time to raise your family. If you are broke, use some of these tax savings to pay off all of your credit cards and back tax penalties. These are extreme Parasitalisms you better escape. And these Parasites have the nerve to say you aren't competing enough? Don't make Uncle Jim laugh!

We need to get back to the philosophy that made this country great . . .
"To Reward Those Who Produce"[16]
I have just the Rewards we need coming up!

3.) *Debt Transfers*—"**Man thrives in an environment of abundant Resources and Freedom or man regresses in an**

[16] Many years ago I heard a wonderful motivational speech by Rich DeVoss, co-founder of Amway. May we never forget these basic words of Capitalism.

environment of shortages and oppression from Socialist Parasitalism".

As proved by the 10 Trillion Debt, our Bureaucracy is incapable and incompetent in managing our assets. If you doubt, look at their custodianship over our thousands of valuable timber tracks they let go up in smoke or just let rot. The mismanagement is seen in excessive and destructive regulation, lawsuits, debts, crime, poverty, bankruptcy, alcohol and drug abuse, etc. With all the money the Bureaucracy has taxed and put us in debt with, you would think these problems would have been solved by now. What about the poverty, ghettos and decaying housing stock? Look at the polluted rivers and lakes, toxic waste dumps and habitat destruction our Government wanted to be in charge of preventing. PIPS have commingled the Social Security and Medicare funds into the General Fund and then spent it. We get all this and more with slow growth, deflated wages, inflation and huge taxes. The Socialists say we have a mature economy and the growth rates of 10% are impossible, only the immature economies of the Second and Third World can have impressive growth rates. I say this is garbage and just their excuse for failure. We better sell the Government assets back to our people and end this Parasitic Socialism if we ever hope to find the incentive and raise the capital to create a positive environment with 10% GDP growth, unlimited opportunity and surplus jobs. I don't know about you, but I'm sick of the oppression from the Socialists, Plutocrats, Predators and Welfare Parasites. If these people won't fix the mess and honorably, don't worry, you don't have to keep getting abused, smarten up and use the *Silver Bullets*.

You ought to realize any country that can easily feed, clothe, and shelter its citizens and has all the timber, farmland, fresh water, iron ore, coal, gas and oil, seaports, it could possibly use, is destined to be a very rich country. We can be at least four times as financially secure right now without a 10 Trillion Debt and have a much higher Standard of Living in which to reach your American Dream. We can do so much better if we get rid of our Socialist mentality and tell the Government to get off our Assets (and sell them). Only to us because . . . it's our land and bounty we built and sacrificed for, not the foreigners. The foreigners have their own lands.

With rising wages from all the new high pay jobs, how do we prevent inflation? Our Congress controls the amount of asset sales and can accelerate these if necessary to lower inflation and increase the capital requirements without resorting to the immorality of the past with opening up the Fiat Money Spigot. The Federal Reserve can take a hiatus, for 60 years!

These Government asset sales more appropriately should be called Debt Transfers. When Government sells intellectual property, buildings, technology, timber, land, oil and gas leases, mining rights, etc., etc., etc., the money received can be used to reduce the National Debt and pay off the investors and foreigners, especially the Chinese. The investors now need a new investment to park their funds in. some of these funds may be spent on consumption. It really doesn't matter because consumption will cause future investment from the "*Demand Pull*". But most funds will go directly into business loans and venture capital for new business expansion. This causes a "*Supply Push*" which further lowers inflation. In essence, public debt is transformed into private debt. This is a Debt Transfer where Government has shed debt off its books to the private sector. I think it is safe to say the private sector, which produces wealth and has pride of ownership can pay back the debts much better than Government, which must oppress and tax productive wealth to pay its 70% Parasite consumption obligations first. What do you think?

Don't fall for the PIPS phony excuses for maintaining the National Debt. In a nutshell, the Socialists don't want to shrink the Power, Size and Spending of Government, the Multi Nationals and Super Wealthy don't want to compete in production and love the high interest rate payments, and the poor have been hooked on Welfare like dope. If spending is cut, Parasites will have to get jobs (REAL JOBS!) and compete.

Here are the Socialists phony reasons for the 10 Trillion Debt and why they say it is good for you:

A.) We need Government Debt and the issuance of Treasury Bonds so we can have a vehicle to invest the Social Security Surplus in. (Sorry, they unethically commingled the funds and Parasitically spent the surplus, there is nothing to invest).

B.) The 10 Trillion Debt stabilizes the economy. (Again, sorry, this debt creates a distortion by rewarding the Super Wealthy investors with Trickle Down. It robs the productive in this country by artificially propping up interest rates, which kills good jobs, stunts economic growth, and keeps wages low.) Instead of Trickle Down, Congress can stabilize the economy by controlling asset sales, lowering interest rates for businesses to 2% and eliminating taxes. There won't be much need for taxes if we get the Government to do its job by just encouraging competition and protecting us from Predators and Parasites.

Why won't the PIPS implement Debt Transfers? Because they want you weak and susceptible to their Parasitical attacks. It is much easier to suck on your fruits, than them earning a living producing something of value. They won't free you if they have anything to say about it. You are their meal ticket; don't expect them to tell you this, you Unsymbiotic Life Support Enabler.

An important side benefit of returning our Capital back to our citizens is to give them a bigger stake in this country and make them strong so they will be a check and balance to the Socialist Zealots driving this country in the directions of Fascism and Communism. Only a free strong citizenry not dependent on Government can defeat the evils of Socialism.

Finally, it's great to have National Parks, Nature Preserves, National and State Forests, Reservations, and other vast tracts of land set aside, but these prevent the use of capital and hurt our people (along with all the other Socialist confiscations). I don't know about you, but I believe land is here for the living. It's hypocritical to hear the people with power and money say they are saving our lands for our children. Right, just like they're not saving children the 10 Trillion Debt and 40 Trillion other promises.

4.) *Reduce Business Risks by Reducing Crime*. Before a new business is formed, there must be a sense of security within the environment. It's great to make money but it's more important not to lose what you already have (or your life)! For example, a beautiful apartment complex in a slum is still worth a fifth of a comparable property in a safe area. The "Economic and Social Problems Total Interrelation Theory" tells us the more jobs we create the less crime we will have and the more we lower crime the more jobs and wealth we will have. If we want to reduce crime we have to solve the "*Crowding Out Theory*" and stop the "*Breeding Rights*" violations; it is essential to an everlasting strong economy or eventually things blow up in your face. By solving these, we also take the pressures off of over-consumption with low productivity. The chapters on **Reducing Crime 75%** and **Improving National Security**, cover more methods and further details how we can reduce crime in a non-Parasitical fashion. The following short list will help us respect one another and end the dysfunctionality in our society, which often are catalysts for crime.

A.) Self-sufficient Prisons With No Early Parolees—This will reduce the *Crowding Out* burden placed on our families and end the tax Parasitalism. Also, prisoners should not have conjugal visitation rights. We don't want prisoners accidentally breeding offspring which become a burden on all of us. Statistics have shown offspring of criminals have very high odds of becoming criminals themselves.

B.) End Illegal Immigration—We can't let criminals migrate here if we want a crime-free environment. Let these people stay in their own countries fixing their own problems instead of bringing their problems here, making their problems our problems. Of course, those who are the best and brightest are welcome but we have enough ghettos, crime and poverty to solve, without more Parasites sneaking over the border, causing our taxes to increase for crime control, health and rehab and insurance costs. It is said the average criminal commits 200 crimes before he or she is caught. Let's avoid all 200 crimes by eliminating this first crime!

C.) Amnesty With Deportation—After the illegal aliens and other criminals have worked off their crimes and costs to the State in a tax-free prison, we deport them. If the offense by the criminal is minor, the prisoner may get an early deportation if a fee is paid to the State, but the criminal may never return. This could also be selectively used to buy out American citizen prisoners for the proper fee and if they promise to never return to the United States. It's a privilege to live here, not a guarantee. I'll bet that with a little arm-twisting, our criminals can find a lot of countries to buy their way in to. But let's limit the amount of wealth they can leave with.

D.) Capital Punishment—For horrendous crimes, there is no reason to keep an evil criminal alive. Especially if there will be satisfaction in extermination for those who have been violated. These executions could be shown on late night TV, so would be criminals see the consequences. Crime may go down much from Capital Punishment, and it sure stops repeat offenders and ends Tax Parasitalism. Since we have a lot of late term abortions, very few will have a problem with Capital Punishment.

E.) Shrink the Socialism and its Something for Nothing mentality. The entire book talks about Socialism as the enabler of Parasitalism as it "Crowds Out" a good life for our people with increasing crime, shortages and disincentives.

F.) Birth Control—This is a decision, which should be made on a personal level. But statistics show that the most irresponsible on welfare in this country are the ones producing most of the dysfunctional offspring. A Federal Government 10 Trillion in debt can't remain a strong country if it grows a garden of anarchy. The religious zealots cry for the rights of the unborn, which is honorable. But where are they when it comes to raising and paying for the crack babies, preemies, retarded offspring and unwanted children after they convince ill-equipped females into keeping the pregnancy? If the Pro-lifers want Pro-life, they have to step up to the plate and fix this misery in a Non-Parasitical fashion with their money. This means no tax revenues for these expenses. The zealots must focus their energies on the consequences of their policies and if they can't handle it with their own resources, they must change their position or they are nothing but a Parasite themselves. The Pro-Choicers want Parasitalism themselves by forcing taxpayers to pay for abortions and other birth control for the poor. The Pro-Choicers must also stop lobbying Government for more Parasitic taxes and Welfare to support the dysfunctional unless these procreators have vasectomies and tubal ligation. It is time for our tax free charities, Civil Liberties Lawyers, Political Action Committees, and other interest groups to start solving the problems with all the money we are giving them, instead of paying their employees and bosses fat salaries, perks, pensions, and lobbying Government to spend more of your money to fix problems Government can't fix.

It also amazes me that Pro-Choicers want abortion, but not capital punishment and Pro-lifers want capital punishment but not abortion. These Socialist Hypocrites! Where is the sanctity of life? Birth control and reducing Welfare will cause people to take responsibility for themselves with very little need for abortion or capital punishment. Without Welfare, people will take marriage and birthing more seriously. With Workfare there will be a reduction of the irresponsible pro-creating Government must no longer be their enabler. Morality will escalate as crime plummets. Guaranteed, with your tax money back! Hint: Create the 160 million jobs first. (You don't want their riots.)

G.) Welfare Elimination—Besides what was said above, the costs of Welfare are enormous. The people who get hooked on Welfare soon lose their work skills, good habits and ability to think clearly. Businesses have difficulty employing them. Another problem with Welfare is the dishing out of the spoils with too much Parasitized by administration costs and fraud by greedy individuals. When Welfare is eliminated a wonderful thing happens. People begin to pull together and help their family, friends and neighbors in times of need. Also those who would sell drugs, steal or dump on their neighbors and families will think twice about hurting people because they may need help one day and Government is no longer giving Welfare. You see when Government gives Welfare, it allows the recipients a license to be irresponsible, act any darn way they want and this includes criminal behavior and no desire to improve the community whatsoever. It's a cruel world out there. Let's not let the People in Power make it any crueler. To show compassion all we need to do is create surplus jobs and **Multiply Our Paychecks 4 Times** as we eliminate Welfare. With surplus opportunity the lazy and deadbeats will have no excuses. They will work. If not, they will be compassionately put in a home for the mentally and physically ill so they can't hurt themselves or society. It's their option of course.

5.) *Patent Protection*—When businesses develop new technologies and products, they deserve the right to make a tidy profit. If a foreign country is Parasitically obtaining our technology by theft and copycat, we need to examine the loss to our businesses and factor this in our trade agreements. Another way we lose our technology is by trade restrictions in foreign countries, requiring our teaming up with a foreign business to sell in that country. This is another free trade violation. So in other words, free trade is idiocy and deceit and a form of Parasitalism. Our military should be used to prevent the theft of our technology and nationalization of our wealth by foreign countries. Our Government has the obligation to resist pacifying foreign nations by giving expensive technology away. One day these mistakes will come back to haunt us. Because of our open Patent System, many of our companies won't even record their patents in fear foreign businessmen will look up the patents and freely copy the public information. This system is broke. With our technology in hand, the foreign businesses can Parasitize U.S. businesses by undercutting our price because their cost base is so low without the expenses of R&D. How much we lose in business and jobs is anyone's guess, but it is an important hole we should plug to save millions of jobs.

6.) *Limitation on Liability Lawsuits*—Many businesses won't expand into new fields or hire new employees because of the real fear of lawsuits from disgruntled employees and product liability. Business is risky enough without the potential to be wiped out by a lawsuit or waste valuable time and money defending against some trumped up charges encouraged by an attorney. A lawsuit should not be filed without merit. I suggest a **20% at risk rule**, requiring the Plaintiff to deposit 20% of the lawsuit amount in cash to the court to stop bogus and frivolous lawsuits. Also, this puts a cap on the total costs the Defendant could suffer. If the Plaintiff has no money, he or she may find someone to invest in the case and receive some of the winnings. If the Plaintiff can't find any investors, then it is obvious the lawsuit has no merit in court. The 20% risk rule is a powerful Parasiticide and will encourage the creation of jobs by improving the commercial environment.

7.) *Education Improvements*—If we want the best schools, we need the best system. We have to reward those who produce, instead of Parasites hiding and entrenched in our Unions and Administrative Bureaucracies. The only way we can figure out who is doing a good job and producing is through competition. I think you know we will have to drag the Parasites as they kick and scream every step of the way, fighting competition. It's okay for you to compete for a less than market wage against $7.00 per hour foreign countries, but they want a monopoly wage and easy working conditions, with the use of Socialist Parasitalism. I'll bet if they got paid like the foreigners at $7.00 an hour they would change their tune quick!

A political clique that gets a Government to forcibly tax your fruits of labor and divide the spoils but prevents competition for themselves is an oppressive monopoly or clique, a job killer, and an evil Parasite no matter what spin they use. The following is a short list of systems to improve our schools using competition and common sense.

A.) *Tenure is not a system for winners*. Tenure breeds complacency and Parasitalism through the monopoly of Government job security, which most often provides the worst services for the highest price. I understand some administrators and teachers hate and fear competition. Knowing human nature, most people are lazy and don't want to compete and prove their worth if they can get out of it. One compromise to Tenure would be to allow the worst 10% of the administrators and teachers to be pink slipped each year to weed out the undesirables; with 160 million surplus jobs they can find something else to do. If a school has 5% teachers and administrators who don't cut the mustard, so be it and only fire them. But no absolute tenure to enable Parasites to hide in the system. The rest of us don't get this free ride. If we want to save this country, we have to de-program the Lefty mindset that everything comes from the Government and you can get something for free without Parasitically hurting others. Don't be fooled by those who won't compete. Whether a monopoly, oligopoly, government political clique, bureaucracy, super rich, monopolized labor union, or anyone that doesn't have plenty of competition, can't be trusted. You'd be surprised how many perverts, deadbeats, drug addicts, alcoholics, crooks, predators and parasites can hide in these sanctuaries away from competition and responsibility! In other words alcoholics and drug addicts don't last long in a competitive environment and do you want one teaching your children? And while we're at it each teacher should take a 3-hour competency and psychological test for recertification every 6 months where we weed out the 10% slackers and mentally unbalanced.

B.) *No Teacher Union Strikes*—Let each teacher compete like the rest of us and work their own contract out with the Administration. It is pure insanity to allow monopoly unions in Government and let them strike and lobby Government to pay them more money. People go into Government to serve, not cash in and hold children hostage for higher pay, without positive results. The only honest and moral procedure to set pay, is with Market Competition. Anything else is Parasitic. It should be an honor for our teachers to teach our children. A good step will be to eliminate the National, State and District Unions, allowing each Union to be no bigger than the size of the individual school. And why shouldn't we, I'm showing teachers, like everyone else, how we can **Increase Their Pay 4 Times**, with honesty. Now these people can debate this all they want; but if they don't have competition it is Parasitic, and all Parasites are eventually eliminated with Super Parasites.

C.) To get *accountability* and a judgment of worth from teachers, we need a Statewide and National test at the end of each grade level for students, making a comparison with previous years and all schools. We need competition at all levels because even states will differ and all will want to know how they stack up.

D.) Public Schools are eroding into a disaster. They have eaten up most of the *competition* from Private Schools and did it by forcing Government into giving Public Schools an 8,000.00 a year per pupil advantage over Private Schools! And Private Schools still produce superior results! Is it because only the smart kids go to them? Let's have the money go with the students and let some competition in the market between schools. We will quickly improve public schools and learn who is the best when the consumer isn't Parasited over the coals anymore. Universities compete for students, why should K-12th grade schools live a Parasitic existence at your expense for nothing?

E.) Run the *schools year round* with a break off for Easter, Christmas, Fall and Summer. Teachers can work a full year, like the rest of us. The taxpayers work year round and need a babysitter over the long summers, so why not use the teachers to hopefully teach the kids something and keep them out of trouble? We don't need summers off for farming anymore; we put farmers out of business with the help of property taxes and Parasitic foreign trade deals so we gave all these wonderful jobs and our lands to the conglomerate monopolies, government and multinationals.

F.) *Extend class hours* from 8:00 to 4:30. This will match most of the parents work hours. The parent will be home when the kids get off the bus and with a longer school day, children can get some of their homework done at school. If the parents have to keep working longer and longer hours to pay high administrator and teacher salaries, then I don't think it is too much to have these public servants work a full work week for at least 50 weeks a year, like the parents and help with homework. It's not working for us the way the Unions and Administrators have it set up for themselves.

G.) We need some *Patriotism and Pride* in our daily life. I think we need to fix things so they work again and have the Pledge of Allegiance and National Anthem recited and played daily in school, from Kindergarten through 12th grade.

H.) We have prayer in our congressional sessions but we don't even let our children pray. The children get a different religion called Atheism and humanism based on monkey evolution. This is the religion of choice from the American Civil Liberties Union and the secular society who look at Government as the supreme authority. They enjoy tearing up the Ten Commandments posted in schools and nativity scenes. One must wonder how many of our young might have fought the life of crime, suicide or drug abuse with a few little symbols, such as the Ten Commandments or a little *morality taught* at school. Some unscrupulous lawyers will do anything to create new business. If even one life is saved by a posting of the Ten Commandments, it is worth it! When do you think the powerful lawyers will change "In God We Trust" on our money to "In Government We Trust"? Do you trust it and them?

I.) *Class Curriculum*—From 1st grade through 12th grade, one class each day should be Health. This would emphasize a brief but daily discussion on mental attitude, sleep, hygiene, exercise, nutrition and diet. Other topics would include physical education, healthcare treatment, and at an appropriate age level, teach about sexually transmitted diseases and abstinence from sex. You can bet this Health class taught every day will lower your medical bills enormously! Another class to be taught everyday for 12 years is in Computer use and related technologies to give us a leg up on the high pay jobs of the future. Another everyday topic should be Economics, with an emphasis on Accounting, *self-sufficiency*, household management, running a business, business math, and mechanics of Government and personal finances. Everyone by 12th grade should be able to fill out the IRS forms and know how to balance a checkbook or can't get a diploma. Reading and writing needs to be done daily. This includes Spelling, Grammar, Speech and learning how to use a thesaurus. Something in Science should be taught daily, including Biology, Advanced Mathematics, Chemistry, Physics, etc. The next topic is Ethics. This would include emphasis on Morality, Philosophy, Family Values, Freedom with responsibility, Capitalism, Socialist Parasitalism, Patriotism, Religion, Government, Political Science, History, etc. Finally a class must be chosen from Music and the other Arts. It is true those in Music and in the Arts are on average smarter, happier and better adjusted psychologically. Music and the Arts bring great joy and fun when we all sing together in a group, perform on stage in a band, or see the excitement in a play or go with our family and friends to see a work of art unveiled. Imagine the thrill to the individual when a creative piece is brought to fruition from nothing more than a single thought! This book sure brought me happiness. And I want you to give me your criticisms. With your help I want it to become a MASTERPIECE. Seven topics a day for 12 years. Emphasis could be in different areas for the final four, but Health, Economics, and Computer Usage are so crucial to our children's future they should be non-elective with similar content for all schools and students, at each grade level.

I Health (mandatory)	V Science (elective)
II Computers (mandatory)	VI Ethics (elective)
III Economics (mandatory)	VIIMusic/Arts (elective)
IV Reading & Writing (elective)	

If you don't like my schedule, that's fine, make your own and have your School Board institute it. You pay the taxes, you own the Teacher Unions and School Boards. You are the boss, not the Bureaucrats.

8.) *Increase Competition*—Competition brings us the best products for the least cost, which will free up a lot of our time and money for other important matters. The lower the cost, the more sales, hence more production and more jobs. Monopolies bring us the worst products for the most cost. You don't have many willing buyers when Monopolies and other Parasites bloat out. Look at a lot of our wasteful Government services, such as Welfare, Medicare, Social Security, the IRS, Dept. of Energy, the Post Office, Dept. of Education, HUD, etc. Most of Government services are so bad they force you to pay for it! Just look how they take and promise so much, but deliver so little. Stop being duped. The Government, so they stop killing jobs, needs Competition like business. Your first silver bullet makes our politicians compete for your interests by firing the career politicians in power. In the last chapter is a fun idea to encourage our elected officials to compete for our interests in a positive environment.

Monopolies should always have competition and need dissecting in most all cases. An Oligopoly is a group of competitors who turn predatory and feast like a cohesive wolf pack, raising prices in unison. These need to be broken up into smaller pieces themselves to reduce the bonds of Cronyism. Big Union power is also oppressive and Parasitical. A Union should have to compete along with Big Business and Big Government by dissecting their monopolies so no Union can be bigger than the company it is involved in. Many other businesses look like they are competing but only fractionally because of Socialist grants, subsidized interest rates, special legislation, tax loopholes, and favorable regulation. We need more competition from Healthcare, Lawyers, Schools, Public Utilities, Non-Profits, and so many other areas, where our Government has got things screwed up. If we break up these groups and make them compete against each other, we will have much lower costs and better service as we free up a lot of capital to create further jobs and wealth. Below are some general observations on Competition.

Corporate Takeovers are rarely ever good for our economy even if there is no reduction in Competition. With 160,000,000 new high pay jobs, our employees need not fear takeovers, where jobs are eliminated to improve efficiencies. However, when there are only 5 or 10 producers in any market we have a problem and Parasitic or Predatory behavior is probably already occurring. We need more like 100s of competitors in most industries at a minimum. Uncle Jim regrets we haven't broken up the Big 3 and their unions. We must act quickly or I see this industry going the way of the textile, shoe, electronics and so many other industries now extinct in the U.S.

All individuals must compete responsibly and this includes speculators and those who over-borrow. Bankruptcy Laws should be tightened so people can't run from their problems so easily. When any Bankruptcy occurs it adds to our overall inflation, higher interest rates, and Parasitalism.

A big danger of a Capitalist system is in its maturity. In this stage of the cycle, wealth becomes too centralized, competition wanes and decay sets in. The Liberals and Collectivists have been able to keep their game going a while longer by pushing the Global Trade with foreign competition. This will eventually decay but the Government can stay big and bloated a while longer and avoid fixing its messes. But when the next depression strikes like now, the bigger they are, the harder they fall! Splitting up Monopolies and bloated concentrations of wealth must be done for a Limited Government to maintain dominance over Predatory Corporations and Robber Barons. Government's solution up till now has been to grow bigger itself, becoming more Socialistic. The problem with the bloat is the incredible amount of Parasitalism that is spawned in this environment. We are definitely out of whack with Nature. The Parasitalism will continue to grow until we fix the Predators who fight and stifle Competition more than they try to improve their products, service, market share and cost. Don't listen to their phony excuses about needing Economy of scale to compete in the Global Economy, they don't need 1/5th as much. You may not yet see the future with the untold and unknown riches and jobs, but it's out there, and so much more.

To keep a Government small and free from a multitude of Parasites, a Government must keep the wealth and power in the private sector in a decentralized manor, spread amongst many participants and protect its wealth from foreign Parasites. Or as we have seen, we get an explosion of Unions, Lawyers, Welfare recipients, Government Bureaucracy, regulation, criminals, Robber Barons, speculators, unemployment, huge taxes and other Parasites. Look I'm not saying we can eliminate all Parasites, they serve a function in Nature. Look at them more so as an indicator of an environment which is out of alignment and perverse to Humanity by having a large segment of our population not producing but feasting on the fruits of others, with little if any benefit in return. Parasitalism is not a form of Capitalism with Competition, it's an arrogant disease manifested from an ignorance and weakness in its Hosts. Yes, it's you the enabler.

The competitive Advantage of the U.S. is awesome. The Ports, Agricultural Lands, Climate, Raw Materials, Energy Resources, Fresh Water, Fewer Borders to Protect, Excellent Fishing Waters and large size all are Competition Enhancers. Let others collect Gold, Silver, Art and all that glitters. You can't eat these and they are nothing compared to a productive society. The question is, that with all of our advantages, how did our politicians get us 10 Trillion in Debt? I think we need our Government to compete and pay off their debts. Just imagine how much further we could have moved this country ahead if we would have avoided the pitfalls of Socialism and its sidekick Parasitalism.

A Socialist Collectivist thinking society with its Centralized Planning will eventually be tested by a disaster in which the People in Power are unprepared or unwilling to make the appropriate adjustment like a free Market economy would. There will be much pain and suffering because of the Socialist paralysis. Valuable time will be squandered as the people agonize for the Bureaucracy to funnel down a plan. Don't forget with one voice in the market; creativity, mobility, advancement and liquidity are sacrificed and snuffed out. As an example, imagine the stock market with only one buyer or for that matter, one seller? In a Socialist system where the Government owns the tools, resources and decides what the pay will be, the people are Parasitized and you can bet the exploited won't respect the Government or its tools. Theft, waste, riots and a lack of industriousness by the labor force will certainly result in shortages, with many opting for welfare. And why? Nobody has a stake or owns anything, so who cares? No pride of ownership here.

A Socialist system is virtually guaranteed to abuse its power over the citizens because it has a monopoly on power. Many checks and balances have probably already been swiped and snatched from our people, leaving People in Power to pilfer and oppress at will. And you want to let them take away your gun rights? Or further control Health Care? Or build more unneeded HUD housing? You gave them the right to collect the Income Tax and look where that got you. Limit Socialist Government or it will limit you. *(dis)Liberal* Government is not your friend, so keep an eye on it. Government isn't going to willingly supply surplus jobs because if it does, it can't Parasitize your wage and keep you running for your life on the treadmill to feed its growing Parasites.

Here is an insidious Parasitication by our non-competing Socialist Government. Government passed a law making it illegal to publicly disclose certain Bureaucrats' salaries. Now you not only won't know what they do all day, you won't know how much you are paying them. You don't even know how much they are sucking out your fruits. This is sinister. You own the country and expect people to go in Government to serve, not sponge on your salary. How many businesses do you know that give their employees blank checks and don't know how much it costs until the inevitable bankruptcy? This is our Lefty Government in action! The Bureaucrats love it. You won't see your **Salary 4 Times Higher** when we don't have competition in Government and they can pull the wool over your eyes. The Socialists aren't competing *for you* and your family. They are only Parasitically competing *for your salary*. It's time to end the secrecy in this and so many more areas of Government and let the sunshine in.

9.) *Balanced Trade*—Having a Balance of Trade Deficit over time can become Parasitical. A 600 Billion Trade deficit, assuming each 50,000.00 in trade equals one Primary Job, would be a Primary job loss of 12 Million. If we multiply this by the lost support and secondary jobs this is 48,000,000 jobs we are giving away hoping our job shortage helps our businesses in the Global Economy. But after the higher taxes and crime we will have, I'll take the 48 Million jobs for our people any day of the week!

If anyone doesn't think we can have balanced trade starting today, then they don't understand that our Government has set the environment with man-made rules to allow the foreign nations a favorable Parasitic advantage. We can even the playing field any time we want. Below are some strategies Foreign Countries use which we could also use, such as: Buy National Campaigns, Most Disfavored Nation Status

(MDN), Domestic Content rules, Tariffs, Quotas, Currency Lock, Labor and Product Dumping Laws, Pollution tax on imports, Profit Transfer taxes, Custom Stalls and Regulations, Sanctions, Currency Manipulations, Infant Industry excuses, Embargos, the fear of a recession, Partnership agreements for access, etc. We could use these but if we use the AMERIPLAN and boom our economy we will want somebody to provide products in these lower pay industries at a cheap price. But a moral and respectable Government should stop abusing its citizens by balancing imports and exports to reduce the Parasitosis and increase our jobs. This Free Trade mantra by the People in Power is insane.

10.) *Lower Interest Rates*—A strong economy has a strong business base in the Primary Industries. These businesses and their employees need Secondary Industries and employees to provide support services. In turn, the Secondary Industries and employees need products produced from the Primary Industries, hence the cycle is complete and all lives are enriched. We need to focus on creating an environment which channels investment into Primary Industries which will automatically create a strong market for important service jobs. When I hear the Politicians proudly announce we are turning into a service-based economy in the U.S., it gives me an ulcer. Service Industries are less desirable than Primary Industries because of their temporary benefit and total dependence from the products, profits and wages of Primary businesses. In other words, if you have few Primary businesses and we are all running around trying to service each other, we won't get very much for our services. The following examples show how low interest rates boost investment in Primary Industries so we dramatically increase our paychecks and create surplus jobs.

A construction company building Dams is a Primary business. It might take 10 years to complete the project before generating revenues. An environment of high interest rates makes a "Capital Intensive" project inordinately expensive because finance costs may push the completed cost of the project to double what it may cost in a lower interest rate environment. If money costs 8% a year to rent, as compared to 2% over 10 years the project cost will be (8%-2%)x1/2x10 years =30% higher for nothing. This does not consider compounding of interest, and the fact these costs can't be recouped till out years, wage inflation or material increases. With costs indeterminable they can't be stabilized. This is a risky and expensive venture. However, if interest rates and inflation are kept low for a long period of time, the environment is ripe to make long-term investment decisions of a primary nature which generally are the most profitable.

A fast-food company baking Pizzas is a Secondary service business. It might take only 3 months to start up before generating revenues. An environment of high interest rates has little effect on this project because less capital is required in a "Labor Intensive" business and finance costs do not overly distort the completed cost of the business which is only 3 months of interest. Low interest rates are of little value to service industries. After only 3 months, all of the future interest and labor costs are expensed against current earnings instead of being capitalized and depreciated over 30 years starting 10 years in the future. In a Parasitic environment with high interest rates, confiscatory taxes, cheap labor and high inflation, these service businesses thrive in the instability. In a stable environment of low interest rates, insignificant tax rates, well paid labor and low inflation, these businesses are strained from increasing competition and customer price awareness. The question is, do we want our children to twirl pizzas, flip burgers, etc., in Service jobs at $8.00 an hour, or build Dams, construct bridges, etc., in Primary jobs at $60 an hour? There will always be these low pay service jobs, and more people are forced to work in them in a Parasitic environment. Let's get rid of our Socialism and create a surplus of high pay Primary jobs that enhance our peoples' lives so we may reach our American Dream. Does everyone see why it's imperative to have low long-term interest rates? Are you with me?

All of the previous actions in this Chapter plug leaks in our economy, contribute to reducing interest rates, costs, making us more competitive and provide an environment for massive high pay job growth. But the most effective and powerful action we can take is to defeat Socialism with Asset Sales and eliminating Fiat, Income and Consumption Taxes. We can take back our Wealth and Power, returning to you the Fruits of Labor, improving Capitalism and Freedom from Parasitalism. Here you go Patriots, if you want to help Flint, Detroit, the Rust Belt and our entire country without welfare.

We can have the last laugh. While the Politicians In Power are wasting our time and money buying votes to get elected, with the AMERIPLAN we can solve their 10 Trillion Problems!

8

160,000,000 NEW HIGH PAY AMERICAN JOBS!

"Let us return True Capitalism, encouraging Hope, Faith and Compassion in our People, and as a stone is cast in the sea, let the ripples of the American Dream grow and send hope to every Patriot!"

The following are Macro actions we can use to improve our environment. These encourage the creation of millions of jobs and opportunities allowing us to reach our Dreams and help defeat the Parasitic Socialism in this country before it's too late to stop this train wreck. Keep in mind, Economics is more Art than Science. Do not get hung up on the numbers, just think about the possibilities. I could be off a few million jobs or billion dollars, but so what! We can always create more jobs! Real jobs!

Improve GATT Negotiations and this Parasitalism—With a 600 Billion a year Trade Deficit, we are donating our industries. It is said each Billion in Foreign Trade is equal to 20,000 Primary Jobs; 20,000 x 600 Billion equals 12 million Primary Jobs we can bring back home. Multiply this by the "4X Job Factor" we get . . . *48,000,000* new jobs. In my opinion, I would classify our Trade Deficit as a form of Foreign Aid Welfare. Welfare is addicting, the longer we wait to stop, the worse the withdrawal for the foreigners and the worse the permanent critical harm for us (we may never recover).

Energy Independence—If we spend a net 120 Billion a year buying oil from dictators, the OPEC Monopoly, and others, this is (120 Billion x 20,000 x 4) 9,600,000 jobs alone we can create if we plug this simple leak and become Energy Independent. This is our country. We can change our environment any minute. Too bad if the foreign Parasites don't like it. Just vote out our World Order Socialists People in Power.

Workfare not Welfare—There are millions of people in this country and worldwide getting Welfare from the American taxpayers to the tune of over 1 Trillion a year! 1,000 Billions x 20,000 p/billion equals 20,000,000 jobs. I know it's cruel, but let's use our tax money and have our reserve welfare recipient Labor Army work for their sustenance in an "Infrastructure Flex Plan." We need a productive environment, which will generate more jobs instead of eating up jobs and wealth with Welfare. We can't afford giving away a bunch of freebies (it's not really free, you pay for it one way or another). Let's have the Welfare recipients work in Desert Reforestation, Road, Bridge, Port, Airport, School and Mass Transit Construction, Timber Plantings, Clean Streets, Hazardous Waste and Landfill Clean-up, Recycle Trash, Riverbank Restoration, Building Dams, Drinking Water and Sewage treatment plants, Demolish Slums, Picking Fruits & Vegetables or whatever, assist in hospitals, schools, mental institutions, etc. They need to relearn work skills and at the same time we get something for our tax dollars instead of "Dead Weight" Parasitalism. With 20,000,000 Primary jobs multiplied by the "4X Job Factor" we get . . . *80,000,000* new jobs.

Debt Transfers (Asset Sales)—By growing the "American Pie" with Asset Sales creates jobs in Timber, Mining, Farming, Ranching, Oil & Gas, Manufacturing, Construction, Real Estate, Computers, etc. I figure each Basic (Primary) job needs about 250,000 in capital to generate a wage of $50,000 a year. By selling 6 Trillion in Government assets to pay off some of the National Debt, we create 24,000,000 new high pay primary jobs. If these assets are used effectively in the private sector and not wasted on Welfare, Government bureaucracy, taxes or bought up by bloated Multinational Corps., non-profits and others who leave the assets idle and unutilized like our Socialists and Parasites in Washington, then these jobs will be leveraged by the "4X Job Theory" to create 96,000,000 new jobs.

Asset Sales from Monopolies—If we keep an environment of zero inflation and encourage competition, bloated Monopolies and non-profits will have to compete or sell off assets to survive which will free up more wealth to create jobs. With all the big companies we have in the U.S., I will make a really low guess and say we can free up 4 Trillion dollars in capital, which is 4,000,000,000,000 ÷ 250,000.00 = 16,000,000 x 4 is 64,000,000 new jobs.[17]

---

[17] With each $250,000.00 in capital it is possible to create 1 primary job which could pay 50,000.00 toward wages (maybe more).

Further Government Asset Sales[18]—This action totally demoralizes the Socialist crowd and their degenerate philosophy. Let's sell an additional 2 Trillion a year in Government Assets over the next 10 years. 2 Trillion X 10 years = 20 Trillion÷250,000.00 p/job = 80,000,000 jobs x 4 (Job Factor) = 320,000,000 new jobs. Want one? Or would you like another dish of Socialist stifle?

We can **CREATE OVER 500,000,000** new jobs if we want; the price is the elimination of most Socialism, Parasitic taxes and Welfare spending. Unfortunately, do not count on any help from the People in Power with their Parasites. They will fight you every step of the way to steal your way of life. This is a game for them, but this is your life and your children's future.

Just imagine if we mastered the 10 areas of the "*4X Job Theory*" and actually put them into practice in this country. The job factor of 4 times each Primary Job could possibly be 20 or higher, which means we could create Billions of jobs in our country today! Yes, and the world.

Stop being a small thinker, we are only limited by our arrogant Powerful in Government and by our ignorance, so think big. It's all possible with the AMERIPLAN.

If you understand the job creation techniques in the "*4X Job Theory*", you are equipped to run a first class economy. Some in our country can't imagine how a Capitalist market will create the high pay jobs we desire. The Trade Imbalance of 600 Billion, or whatever the amount, is an obvious place to gain 48,000,000 new jobs but there are other job leaks our World Order Government has refused to compete for and has conceded to Foreign Nations, or just sold us out to the highest foreign bidder.

One area is the loss of Fishing Jobs. We should have a 300-mile buffer from our shores before international waters begin. Too many countries are abusing our fisheries with mile long dragnets and gill nets, leaving the water dead and harvesting all our stock and anything else that gets in the way. This is our resource that we are allowing foreigners to rape and

---

[18] I do not know exactly the value of our assets owned by Government. They have over a Billion acres, a multitude of buildings, trillions of dollars in Alaskan and offshore oil leases. We can offer technology, royalties, mineral rights, buildings, etc., for sale. We can dramatically increase the book value of these with Asset Enhancements to generate more fuel to stoke the job market!

plunder. I think we could help a lot of our fisherman by protecting their livelihoods, which is part of our heritage and bounty. By the way, stop the foreigners from dumping their raw sewage, toxic and nuclear wastes in our oceans and seas. They need to go back home and fix their own mess and catch their own fish in their own backyard. Otherwise they can buy our fish from our businesses, I think we could gain 40,000 Primary Jobs times the 4X Factor = 160,000 new jobs.

Another area our Politicians give away our jobs is in shipping. Some countries refuse our trade unless they can ship our products to their ports and they ship all the goods to our ports with their boats. We lose these Merchant Marine Jobs and we lose the Manufacturing jobs in shipbuilding. I think we could gain another 100,000 jobs in this area times the 4X Factor = 400,000 new jobs. Hey? Want one? If we can't get fair trade, then just forget these parasites and their free trade rip-offs. We are the U.S. of A. We don't need them. We produce everything we need. Our only obstacle is the Socialist mentality in Washington, D.C. full of trepidation.

Another area is in bidding on Government contracts. Government money comes from our working men and women, union or otherwise, who deserve the right to supply our needs, not foreign interest, unless they possess a technology we don't have. In this case the Foreign Company must team up with a legitimate local contractor and share all the technology as a term of participating in the contract. The Foreign Nations make our businesses open factories in their homelands if we wish to trade with them. Often we must find a Foreign National to joint venture with, in a customary 50/50 split on profits. We, unfortunately, have to consider the same to plug this wealth leak. This might add 100,000 jobs times the 4X Job Factor = 400,000 more jobs. It's our tax money people! Remember, it's *OUR* money! I never said these idiots could give away my hard earned money. Did you? This behavior is criminal Parasitalism. It seems like our People in Power care more about the foreigners than our very own people. *Where* are those PIPS? *Who* are these PIPS? *What* are these PIPS?

Another Global Trade concession we make is by stationing 300,000 troops overseas, which stimulates growth and development for foreign economies. If we spend 30,000 per soldier for base construction, maintenance and the miscellaneous spending off-base for foreign goods to support each soldier then this costs us 9 Billion a year. We can easily bring 200,000 troops home to plug this 6 Billion leak a year to create an additional (6 Billion ÷ 50,000) 120,000 Primary Jobs X (4X Factor) = 480,000 new jobs. This will certainly cause our Construction industry to boom. As a side benefit, we could use our troops to catch all the dope smugglers, criminals and illegal aliens sneaking over our borders for free! We are paying our soldiers anyway, so let's get a windfall benefit of dramatically less crime and have them do spot check-ups on all the Parasites getting Welfare to see if it is legitimate or another scam.

When you hear the government mouth pieces (manikins) spouting about how irresponsible people were borrowing 100% on their mortgages this is B.S. Listen up. The only decent tax deduction you have to avoid the insane tax Parasitalism of your wages has been the interest deduction on your mortgage. Plus homes were rising at 10% a year. The assumption was the Government would inflate and cheapen the dollar and even if the baby boomers sold some homes they still have to live somewhere. Your investment in your home was a great and prudent strategy. But no, your filthy greedy Socialists and Parasites tightened the money spigot and threw your jobs away with asinine free trade rip-offs. So, they sold you out by giving your job to the foreigners, which was how you were paying for your home (you weren't overleveraged). They sucked the life out of the stock market which was your reserves to carry you through the recession (you are using the little you got left in your I.R.A. but you didn't know and they certainly didn't, that this depression may last over 10 years). The next time the Parasites try to blame you for their crooked extraction sucking out your savings, job, and home, tell them you quit. No more surpluses for them to suck out of you. You don't care if they are the greatest teacher, public utility provider, trial attorney, G-man, F-man, politician, non-profit or professional healthcare outfit. You know some are getting a cushy ride from the fruits of your labor. The laws are artificially tweaked in their favor in violation of the free market where they got a windfall of ill-gotten gains. They don't compete in the market place except sucking for the fruits of your labors. They're just like crackheads—very good at talking, finagling and working their mitts into your wallet. And so would you if your very life depended on it. But it is horrifically wrong. By the way, why do you think the foreigners put their car industries in the south? Was it because they could procure and pillage more public influence and legislation to their advantage (shrinking the American Pie) with a few small states that have big power from their senators? Naaaaah, just coincidence. Let them contribute over 60 Trillion to our economy like the Big 3 instead of Parasitically sucking out the life's blood of our economy, leaving us with the short end of the stick, again, and again and again.[19] Are you learning how, just as a farmer, we control our garden environment and determine our destiny by what we do and just as importantly by what we allow others to do to us? Right now, our (de)Nationalist world Socialists are asleep at the post while it's a foreign free for all feast with rape, pillage, and plundering where they devour and lay economic waste. We sacrificed, slaved away, invented industries and had it all. Now when we finally give away all our industry, foreigners will cry "ok, we free trade now, America you keep free trade." Right! Okee Doekee! See you in the Homeless Shelter for soup and bread. Sorry, we have a shortage of American Pie.

We could sell off the over 1 Billion acres of our land the Socialists have locked up in Government. Let's say we got $4,000/acre on average. With this 4 Trillion we could buy 20 nuclear power plants each year for the next 20 years at 5 Billion a piece. We could build 50 dams a year (with fish ladders if you like) for 20 years at 1 Billion a piece. We could subsidize the building of 1 Million windmills a year at $10,000 a piece for the next 20 years. We could spend an extra 20 Billion a year to develop Star Wars Defense in Dayton, Ohio over the next 20 years. We could spend 5 Billion a year for a new AIDS, and other diseases, research facility in Ann Arbor, Michigan each year for the next 20 years. We could fund a new NASA project at 5 Billion a year for 20 years in Florida to subsidize science research in finding technologies to reduce Air, Land, and Sea pollution. We can take 5 Billion a year for 20 years to subsidize the clean up in our cities, encouraging businesses to locate in cities to reduce the habitat destruction of our farmlands and "Brown Out." We can have all these without any taxes and they get our country Billions a year extra in energy savings without any additional pollution! But all this wealth and jobs come at a price; the price is we must reduce Socialism by returning our wealth to our people! Freedom, self-sufficiency, personal responsibility and wealth all go hand in hand. Your choice Patriot. Let's start doing great things again in this country!

---

[19] The 60 Trillion like many other numbers, quantities and dollar amounts I refer to were heard on the radio, TV, or anonymous internet sources which I am unable to prove or quote the sources. However, they seem accurate and realistic to me.

The Environmentalists will love Habitat Reconstruction. This is done by a 1,000,000 or more welfare recipients or criminals in jail, they might as well be doing something instead of just taking up space, sucking up tax dollars. We could have them start at the perimeter of our deserts, planting hardy trees, working their way into the middle. When the habitat is stabilized with more vegetation, a moderate temperature with tree roots to hold water and prevent erosion, we can go back in with more preferred tree species and vegetation. Now we have created wealth and useable land that was uninhabited, only by snakes and cactus before. This is called a Reforestation project. This was done during the Great Depression. Another area we could create millions of jobs in is recycling. This reduces strip mining and pollution to refine raw materials. The Environmentalists who want Non-Profits and Big Socialist Government to buy up all our buildings, homes, and lands to stifle growth should bow their heads in shame. If they really cared about the environment and our people, they would insist on Government Asset Sales with a portion of the proceeds to go toward fixing our environment and create millions of jobs at the same time. Now, you know, most of our Environmentalists are really nothing but Socialist Parasites. Watch out when they cry over the environment and Global Warming, as they destroy jobs and encourage Government takings. It doesn't have to be this way.

We can transfer more technology to our private sector. This will increase efficiencies, save energy, reduce pollution and free-up more wealth to create more jobs. If we still need more jobs we can hire more accountants to catch the foreign businesses and tax cheats manipulating our tax code with profit transfers and we can hire more customs officers to catch smugglers. Or, let's teach everyone to be self-sufficient and operate his or her own business. Anyway, you get the idea, happy job creating!

WARNING: A crackhead and Socialists are very good at sucking money out of our productive. When you have a $400.00 a day addiction, you will do almost anything fighting tooth and claw to survive. When you beat the Socialist Crackheads in the arena of ideas they resort to labels. You are called names like Racist, Fascist, Communist, Stupid, Greedy, Mean Spirited and lacking compassion for these victims. Don't let their crack speak demoralize you. Hang in there. The Laws of Nature are on your side. And remember, talk and ideas from the PIPS are not enough. You must use your *Silver Bullets* to survive until they fix their mess. Don't produce a surplus they can siphon and steal from you. Grow your own American Pie. Invest in your self-sufficiency, abundance, create your own job if necessary and let the moochers feast on each other's spoils as their American Pie shrinks; not yours! Bon appetite.

POP QUIZ TIME: Circle the best choice.

1. How many jobs are created for each 1 billion in exports?

   A. 2 B. 20 C. 200 D. 20,000 E. 80,000

2. How many jobs are lost for each billion in a trade deficit?

   A. 2 B. 20 C. 200 D. 20,000 E. 80,000

3. With a 600 Billion Trade Deficit, how many jobs are lost?

   A. 1,200 B. 12,000 C. 120,000 D. 12,000,000
   E. 48,000,000

4. If welfare is increased, crime will *increase / decrease* and jobs *increase / decrease*?
   Circle your 2 answers.

5. If jobs are increased Poverty and Crime will A. increase B. decrease?

6. If jobs are increased most likely the 10 Trillion Debt A. increases B. decreases?

7. If taxes are increased on businesses, who pays the tax?

   A. Businesses B. Illegal Immigrants C. Government
   D. Rich People E. You

8. If the Socialists in Government borrow money for more spending, what is this called?

   A. Parasitalism
   B. Cannibalism where we eat our children

C. A Predatory rape, pillage and plunder
D. All of the above

9. If all taxes are eliminated with asset sales for 60 years, how much will your pay go up?
A. 4% B. 40% C. 400%!

Answers: 1.-E, 2.-E, 3.-E, 4. Crime-increase / Jobs-decrease, 5.-B, 6.-B, 7.-YOU! 8.-D, 9.-C

9

75% REDUCTION IN CRIME

According to the E.&S.P.T.I. Theory, we all should want to see our neighbors become financially secure and stay strong, reaching their American Dreams and having the best life possible. With a life worth living, few want to be involved in crime with the risks of losing it all. We all benefit by making our own American Dream easier to obtain with responsible secure and independent people around us. A Capitalist country is like a bundle of sticks, the stronger the individual people (sticks), the stronger the country (bundle). Socialism is like one giant log, but soon the log is infested with Parasitic termites and the core rots. Then the log breaks in half from its own weight. With time marching on, we can't afford another 30 years of sacrifice and punishment as we waste our lives before we fix our Socialist mess. This chapter as well as the whole book, is about the big picture. Hopefully, the ideas in the AMERIPLAN accelerate our understanding and desire to change our environment to one of Hope, Safety and Opportunity, instead of Fear, Crime and Parasitalism. In a limited Republic, we as individuals should have the right to live our lives in a responsible manner as we see fit, provided we don't infringe on the freedoms of others. Here Government does have a legitimate purpose and responsibility to protect our people and provide a secure environment. The solutions in this chapter avoid Government Parasitic repercussions. With a little common sense, anyone can come up with a lot of great ideas and even make the following better. **Help your freedom man Uncle Jim by emailing me your great ideas.**

1. *Create 160 million surplus jobs* to grow the "*American Pie*" and reduce the "*Crowding Out Theory*" problems. This will cure a large portion of our crime, including jealousy and hate crimes, all according to the "*E.&S.P.T.I. Theory*". Now we can utilize our resources on the remaining but much fewer and smaller problems. Job creation is the critical saving grace of Capitalism and crime reduction. If you want your Government to keep selling you and your jobs out in rip-off trade deals

causing shortages you will have more crime from this and get more Socialism. Got it? You'll get it.

2. *Reduce Government crime* by shrinking all Government Bureaucracies and taxes with fewer Bureaucrats for the citizens to keep their eye on. This places more responsibility on the elected officials and less passing the buck, blaming subordinates. Crimes reduce with smaller Government because there is a smaller Parasitic environment in which dishonorable people can hide and suck on our fruits. Government is a Monopoly and everyone knows a monopoly charges the most, giving the least in return. A bloated Government is weak; it crowds out jobs and is ineffectual in fixing problems. For example, welfare breeds crime where many people get something for nothing but taking up space, sucking up air and strolling to the mailbox for money. There is no appreciation or respect, they don't get this money from real people that demand accountability. If any idiot tells you that welfare doesn't add to our crime rates, get away from this Parasite. Use your head and think about it. Just ask your local police about the Government Housing Tax Credit housing scam. These fesspools waste 3/4ths of our police resources. You pay and subsidize their costs, Toastmaster Nincompoop.

3. *Reduce Parental Deprivation* of our children. Supervised children commit fewer crimes. We need an environment that invests in our children by changing our two-parent income system to where one spouse can afford to stay home if they want to and raise their children. We can do this by properly paying our working adults 4 times higher where they can afford this option or at least have leisure time to spend with them. Get away from these sick socialist dogs as you waste your life working to pay their taxes for their purposeless jobs at long hours away from your children. We need more high pay jobs and lower taxes to invest in our families, not more Welfare.

4. *Extend children's school hours* to match 8:00 to 4:30 parent work schedules. This reduces unsupervised time. Our unionized teachers get the big bucks. They need to work longer like the rest of us. Where is your cushy union job with

no competition? If they want those short work schedules you should have it first. If you don't produce something we don't have anything to pay them, or need them.

5. *Extend school year to 12 months*. This reduces unsupervised time of children and especially reduces summer crime. Parents work 12 months a year. Teachers and their unionized monopoly get long summer vacations, but don't deserve any better than you. They certainly aren't any smarter because if they did the AMERIPLAN, their pay could also go up 4 times.
6. All *violent crimes tried as an adult*. No two-tier justice. We need more movement to strengthen penalties on all crimes committed by juveniles. We don't want children to think they can get away with murder and other crimes anymore!
7. *Impose 9:00 P.M. curfews* on all minors on school nights and weekends unless accompanied by an adult. Minors don't have full rights of adults. Minors have no business being out on the streets this late, unless you want them exposed to sex, alcohol, drugs, guns, disease and crime. Good luck, kiddies.
8. Because parents spend long hours at their jobs away from their children, the schools have the obligation to help *teach right and wrong behaviors in school*. If teachers want the big bucks, our parents must keep working long hours to pay their salaries unless we do the AMERIPLAN! With big salaries comes bigger responsibility. The *(dis)Liberals* will fight prayer in school, but they better come up with more than a one-time lesson on the Golden Rule. Children are impressionable and if they make it to adulthood without delinquent behavior, it is highly unlikely they will take up criminal ways. If children avoid trouble when young, their good habits are well imbedded and they will likely avoid drug addictions and other pitfalls as adults.
9. *Stricter student policy*. Any student caught bringing guns or other weapons to school, caught in serious crimes of stealing, violence or causing a major disruption should be expelled for a length of time commensurate with the infraction and put in a working juvenile jail or home. Administrators need to exercise this tool much more to remove the rotten apples that are spoiling the whole bunch. A year in a work camp may help.

10. *More police visibility* on the streets instead of in the offices pushing papers. Police officers can do their paperwork on a P.C. in their vehicles at strategic locations. Especially near schools and high trouble areas.
11. *Gun Control*—I believe gun ownership is a right. However, to me, once a person is convicted of a dangerous crime, that criminal has sacrificed certain rights. This criminal may need the freedom and right to bear arms taken away forever.
12. *Use at least 2 ex-policemen and the victim or a family member on parole boards*. Who better to judge a criminal than someone who catches them in action all day? For example, we don't need some psychiatrist who has lived in an ivory tower and never witnessed violent life and death situations to be judging early parole on a smooth talking murderer. To take it further, early parole should be eliminated; instead, let's have late parole for the disobedient criminals. When a sick society releases criminals because they cry they don't have enough money, this Socialist Parasitalism will implode destroying innocent lives. This is another good reason for self-sufficient prisons. By the way, if the money runs short turn off the air conditioning and free legal paid by taxpayers. And turn the heat down to 60º, the criminals can put on a sweatshirt. Same goes for the Bureaucrats in Gov't offices.
13. *Require strict sentencing and interpretation of our laws* by the Judicial Branch. Most judges keep their politics out of decisions, but in today's era, more and more are becoming *(dis)Liberal* activists. These few and rare judges should be voted out whenever possible. This will shape up the rest of them quickly. Appointed judges are more difficult to remove and often the most activist. Some forget they did not gather support from the people in an election. There should be nothing uncomfortable in challenging the activist judges by eliminating lifetime appointments. They also need term limits. This cleansing will greatly enhance the system by taking the politics out of law where the rules matter again. Through all of this, we will have more clarity, the people will know where they stand and all the citizens will know right from wrong and can follow the rules. Plus, with turnover the laws will have to

be clearer and concise as appointed career judges won't have 24 years to figure all the loopholes and tricky laws out (*K.I.S.S Formula*), or play politics. "Ignorance" is a valid excuse for the Law, unless you have a Law degree. In other words, the legal system is broke according to the *Complication Theory*.

14. Besides the confusion of laws from Judicial Activists, we have problems with Lawyers and Lobbyists who write our laws. They understand the laws because they wrote them and this is all they do. You have a job producing something real you can use and see. You don't have all day to read the 500 page laws and learn the loopholes they dreamed up while you were working to pay taxes. Our laws need to use the *K.I.S.S Formula* (keep it simple, stupid) so we only have essential laws and we can know and live within the boundaries, or crime and Parasitalism will prevail. The Lefty Judges tell you ignorance is no excuse for the Law, but just possibly Attorney arrogance in writing the Law is the reason for some of our crime. And how do you like their laws that you need a law degree to be a judge? Give us a break! They ought to be ashamed! If everyone can't understand the law, we don't need that law. Nothing here but their job protection techniques. The whole problem is quite simple to solve. Just scrap out silly Federal laws, and simplify, where all of them fit on 100 pages. Or we don't need them. Look at our Legislature as a mirror of our entire country, which is a reflection of us. If we want complicated laws, then vote in Lawyers. If we want Monopolies, vote in Billionaires and their Politicians, if we want more Socialism, Crime and Parasites, don't vote at all. However, if we want more jobs, opportunity and freedom to reach our dreams, vote in more Patriots for short terms in office; not a tenure to decimate our jobs, pensions, and families with their Parasitic Socialism.

15. *Reduce Drug Abuse*—We need to change the environment by reducing the supply by bringing 200,000 troops home to protect our borders and beef up customs inspections. This will eliminate quite a bit of the drugs without an increase in taxes. Our schools have made some small progress reducing the demand with education to our children, but mountains more must be done. Increasing the penalties for using drugs,

bounties and whistle blower payments for the arrest and conviction of dealers and putting the criminals in tax-free self-sufficient prisons is a most efficient and fair policy.

16. Alcohol Abuse, Tobacco Abuse, Painkiller Prescription Meds, Gambling Addiction, Pornography, Prostitution, etc. These are non-productive activities, which are easily controlled if we really want to fix these. Because our parents both work full-time jobs to pay taxes, our schools need to do more by educating our children, hence reducing the future demand for these vices. Government can stop the assault of these vices on our people by *increasing the sin taxes* on Alcohol, Tobacco, Drugs, Pornography, Escort Services, Gambling, etc. Leftys love taxes but should the Government own Gambling operations like the state Lotteries, give tax-free status for Indian Reservation casinos where Government gets a cut, or Government protecting Tobacco companies from lawsuits for a cut. Let us instead eliminate taxes on the productive and only have sales taxes on these vices. For too long, we have allowed these parasitic industries to grow as we punish our productive people in a twisted environment. The taxpayers are Parasited and indirectly are picking up the bill for irresponsible consequences in the form of health care, police, and other social costs. It is Parasitic when a poor working adult playing by the rules is gouged with taxes on their fruits of labor from the ramifications of these vices. Where is the social justice? If a government truly needs revenue, then let it Parasite on its Parasites, not on the productive and the families of our productive citizens trying to eke out a living. "The power to tax is the power to destroy."[20]

17. If this country wants abortion on demand, then we may need capital punishment. A fetus is defenseless and has committed no crime, but gets death. A dangerous criminal has wreaked havoc on our society and surely deserves death more than a fetus. *Capital Punishment* serves two purposes. To reduce repeat crimes from repeat offenders and end the Parasitic burden on taxpayers. As a bonus, it surely will cause some to

---

[20] Quote by Judge Learned Hand.

think about their actions and maybe reconsider! If you don't want Capital Punishment, that's fine, but don't be rooting for Abortion Rights. Don't expect the American taxpayer to pick up the Parasitic tab on either, unless we have profit making prisons for murderers and tube tying and vasectomies for abortionees who crave for welfare cash and goodies.

18. *Reduce Teen Pregnancy* and VD Health Costs—Sex education on abstinence till marriage should be in the forefront of our school sex education. Single sex schools will reduce the fraternization at school where maybe the grades and achievement of students will improve without the distractions. There is plenty of time for dating after High School. If adolescents must be adults to drink beer, shouldn't they be an adult to be procreating? Only after these two steps do we need contraceptive education.

19. *Illegal Alien Deportation* with Amnesty—To help solve the *Crowding Out Theory* in a non-Parasitical action, we need to expel foreigners who are illegally sneaking into this country committing crimes with no regard for our laws. Before expatriation, we should have the criminals pay the State for the crime in a working jail for 1 year. Not only will this action eliminate the job deflation, overcrowding and Parasitic tax abuse, the rest of the illegal aliens and foreign criminal visitors will get the message quick and leave seeing we are serious about illegal immigration, crime, and their drug trade, etc. Crime will plummet in areas where the transients used to hide out. Giving our citizens 2000.00 a head bounty for turning the criminals in will help fix this mess in a hurry. Tell me if you think ending illegal immigration will greatly reduce poverty and crime, and provide more job openings for our own people? Email me. Ok, this problem totally solved in 5 minutes! Next problem please!

20. *Reduce Irresponsible Pregnancies*—The highest % of future criminals are born to unwed mothers, teenagers, and Welfare queens. The Lefty Government policies are the enabler, allowing these violations of *Breeding Rights*. These offspring have the greatest chance of being dysfunctional. Welfare loss will get the message across within 9 months and you can bet on it. If a human being wants Welfare, they must immediately

have an abortion and a vasectomy or have their tubes tied. This will end the Welfare Parasitic Cuckoo Bird crime cycle. The Welfarian may pay to have the operation reversed when they get off welfare and pay the state back all the money they got for free with interest, including food stamps, free medical, free legal, free electric, free rent, etc.! But no procreating until they pay back all the free assistance. Fare enough?

21. *Reduce Welfare Enabling Crime*—When Welfare is given, the recipients don't have to be responsible for themselves or to others because the Government guarantees them sustenance. These recipients can commit petty crimes, treat their neighbors disrespectfully, and avoid helping their families and friends because Big Brother Government will give them more money without consequences where they can get more drug action to supplement their welfare, hurt people, and steal at will! Thanks Socialist *(dis)Liberals*! Another good deed blowing up in our face! You are lousy stewards of our Tax Dollars. So much for your compassion. Of course, there are a few needy people we need to give a little of our precious hard-earned cash and Welfare tax dollars, but let's create 160 million high pay jobs and we won't have all this Welfare Parasitalism from our Socialists, where we work ourselves to the bone for a bunch of dead beats and criminals. I did a study and series of interviews and discovered 9 out of 10 on welfare can work when they need to. In fact they don't even need or deserve welfare. Just create 160 million new high pay jobs *(dis)Liberals*.

22. *Military Interventions*—Do you really want to solve the illegal drug problem? Since our Police can't control the foreign drug cartels that are chopping the heads off of people and destroying us . . . . we may have to call in our military to remove their kingpins and help the Banana Republics. The Mexican people will be glad to see us! Let's fix this in a week. Next problem please.

The more of the above ideas we use, the less crime we will have. Maybe you have some good ideas, let me know. Yes, I know I'm not perfect but let's do something, besides wasting our cash and lives put in danger as we hypocritically pretend we love them and everybody loves us.

By the way good Patriot, I want you to know I know you are a WINNER! We can fix our mess together. Thank you so much for who you are!

And hey deadbeats, jealous and criminals, I have compassion for you! This is why I'm telling the world how to create 160,000,000 new American jobs! I don't want you to have to look too hard.

I don't know why someone in Washington couldn't figure this out. Maybe when we do the 70% Solution and fix the Socialism with our economy growing at 10% yearly GDP rates with no debts and no inflation, I can go back to my livelihood as a homebuilder. Or do you want me to dedicate my last remaining years to building an American Windmill Dynasty of Energy Independence? Picture the landscape as far as the eye can see and in every backyard or roof where every homeowner has a beautiful windmill. Why, we all can be Windmill Sheiks of energy independence. And Oh No! We will have millions more new jobs! This will be a piece of cake compared to solving and developing the 70% Solution to our Socialist Mess! Email me and let me know. *unclejimameriplan@yahoo.com* or check out the website at *www.UncleJimAmeriplan.com*

10

PAYING OFF THE 10 TRILLION DEBT IN 4 YEARS

This Chapter shows one way with huge tax cuts to balance our National budget instantly and begin paying off the 10 Trillion debt as our people are rewarded in a prosperous and compassionate environment based on incentive without the Parasitalism. ***All are winners*** in these strategies, even the Parasites who will gravitate to the new high pay jobs, which are created with the AMERIPLAN. There are many more solutions to solve our problems and I welcome any you have. I am very proud of the AMERIPLAN and how this book captures the big picture defining and providing the understanding to our one major problem. Problems like racism, jealousy, crime, high taxes, huge debts, unemployment, the 10 Trillion debt, pollution, etc., are all merely drops in the bucket of Parasitalism. Our Parasitalism is a result from the Environment of Socialism, which allows this phenomenon to exist and spread like a cancer, decaying every institution, nook and cranny of our civilization. Our Government Bureaucrats and supposedly wise men in this country, blame it on you and your lack of altruism, decline in morality and lost respect, even as they suck you dry. How arrogant and foolish these people really are who can't even identify the crux of this matter!

By the way, I have identified over 20 macro solutions to solve most of our countries problems today. I share 2 in the last chapter. See if any government geniuses in this country can figure out 10 macro solutions and use the K.I.S.S. Formula. By the way, every one of these solutions and more are mentioned in this book. Big Socialist Government truly is the problem and this is why it should shrink to a quarter of its size; to wring out the Parasitalism. This is the only way if you ever want a better country. Alright, let's stop the blood sucking on The Fruits of Your Labors. The following are areas where we can dramatically raise your pay and reduce the Parasitalism. I have included dollar amounts we may benefit. You may benefit more or less, but everyone benefits. Do not get hung up on the estimated amounts or calculations, this chapter was designed to make you think of the possibilities.

1) Interest Savings on the National Debt—There is no excuse for the U.S. Government borrowing over 10 Trillion dollars. This increases our taxes about 253,000,000,000.00 a year just to pay interest welfare with no benefit whatsoever. How would you like a yearly tax cut of (253 Billion ÷ 100 million full-time workers) ***2530.00?***[21] We can end this debt bondage simply with asset sales. Let's stop punishing our people with gimmicks like inflation, taxes, borrowing and spending in the wrong areas as we try and fail to pay off the National Debt and advance our society.

2) You will get much more than lower taxes by paying off the National Debt. You will get hidden savings especially if you have a home mortgage, business debt, are paying dues in a club which has debt, have a car loan, credit cards, lease payments, and taxes to any municipality, utility, state or local government which issued Bonds or borrowed money. Let's say you owe a share directly and indirectly of 200,000.00 at an average interest rate of 8%. With a flood of new capital, interest rates could easily drop to 3%, assuming Lefty Government doesn't increase the inflation rate with Fiat, raise taxes, start reborrowing, or spending Welfare. It's really not hard to lower interest rates even more if you stop listening to all those Bankers and Parasites pretending to be economists. This works out to 200,000 x 5% interest savings a year equals ***10,000.00*** a family. This would be a nice raise by doing nothing more, just working smarter, not harder.

3) The savings go even further as everything we buy will cost less because a large part of the cost of production is paid to rent capital. By the way, monopolies love regulation and high costs for capital preventing new competition in the market. Suppose 50% of an average companies capital is rented for the production of goods and services, with a 5% interest savings x 50% borrowed capital X 30,000 as an average family spending for food, utilities, gas, clothes, etc., this would save ***750.00*** each. (This is greatly simplified by not calculating business mark-up for profits or the interest on hypothecated capital,

---

[21] 2008 National Budget

etc.). Paying off the National Debt could save an average family approximately 13,280.00 a year. How's this for a yearly tax cut? Do your math, what do you come up with?

The only way I see we can pay off this 10 Trillion atrocity without destroying our people is to reduce the Socialism in this country by reducing Government bloat and sell off, for starters, 10 Trillion in Government assets to retire the debt and stimulate the economy. Some think we have 60 Trillion of our assets held by Government, some think closer to 100 Trillion, regardless, these resources will be worth several times more if Government learns how to increase the values with *asset enhancements*. Throw those Karl Marx, Keynes and Hitler books in the trash. These Socialist systems always bloat out with the excess baggage of Locusts, Parasites and Predators. I sense a growing fanaticism in Government to dominate all facets of our lives along Statest extremes. But these collectivist idiotologies have to face reality by understanding a Federal Government can only do a few things well, such as National Defense, print money, Civil Protection and Enforcement of simple Laws. Governments always fail when they over reach their purpose like trying to be the world's policeman, and in the process destroy our freedom, trust and cooperation. Wouldn't you think the Socialists would have figured out their philosophy was doomed after Russia's implosion and further after they needed to prop *(dis)*Liberalism up and buy off our voters with the first Trillion they borrowed? They knew it and didn't care about you, but were too dishonest to stop the next 9 Trillion waste and 40 Trillion more they promised on our behalf. Our money—not theirs!

4) Workfare Not Welfare—You know it's cruel to allow people to starve if they truly can't work, but when we create 160,000,000 new job opportunities, there will be no excuse for our Socialists to spend 300 ± Billion for business and bureaucracy welfare, food stamps, AFDC and other Parasitic wealth distributions. There are some legitimate needy who have no friends, have become alienated from our wealthy charities whom won't help, and are unable to find a job to maintain their sustenance. We could allow our State Government to efficiently spend a few precious tax dollars on this Welfare, but it's time to

stop failing at helping so few, while we succeed in hurting so many. Socialist Federal Government is a failure in this area. It can never help more than it hurts with all its Parasitic baggage, plus it is an enabler creating more of the problem it pretends to solve. With 100,000,000 full-time workers, each will get a tax cut of ***3,000.00***. The Socialist have some pretty slick techniques to separate you from your wallet such as their Parasitical plea for compassion with higher taxes to spend on the children. But it's a sinful trick with their job shortage, high taxes on parents, and working long hours away from our children. $3,000.00 for each family is a heck of a compassionate act to help our children and putting our money where our Socialist mouth is.

5) HUD, Education, Transportation, Physical, Human and Community Wasteful Spending Reduction—We need to cut this spending where our people can make these same investments at 30¢ on the dollar if these investments are even needed and I said needed, not wanted by Parasites. Federal Government has a poor track record with too many failures such as causing unemployment, bankrupting farmers, mass transit boondoggles, Parasitic waste of education funds on administration instead of children, job training for jobs that don't exist, community development pork barrel, Socialist regulations which are ineffective, all cost a fortune and are unnecessarily intrusive. Often grants for twisted environmental programs and studies are awarded for political purposes to enhance and lay the groundwork for Socialist Government takings of private lands, tools of production and other resources, and to enhance the collectivist power over individual rights. I suggest we reduce this category of Parasitic spending by 100 Billion. You won't miss it. Really? Yes, Really! We can leave 20 Billion a year in this spending all earmarked for space research. Reducing this spending will net you ***1000.00*** a year. So far in this chapter you can increase your pay 17,280.00 a year by doing nothing. I know some of you are crying you don't even make this much a year at your job. Don't worry you soon will when we end the oppression of Socialism. You are really paying much more than 17,280.00. Many taxes are hidden and don't show

up on a paystub, but they still reduce you over-all pay and Fruits of Labor. Hang with me and ahead I will give you an economics lesson that will change your life for the better, forever.

6) Reduce Parasitic Social Security and Medicare Expenses—It is often human nature to be weak, lazy, make ones' life as comfortable as possible. The problem with Social Security and Medicare is costs are much more than they paid in. Since the people have no responsibility for the costs, Parasitalism has set in with a strangle hold on this industry where costs are 4 times higher than a free market would cost. You know this to be true. You are actually paying these bills yourself. And don't be happy when the Socialists say with socialized medicine, costs will come down 10%. Tell them to totally get out of the way so costs come down 75%! The Leftys in charge of the system have not properly invested the Trust Funds and have tragically spent the money on themselves and Illfare programs buying votes to keep themselves in power. When the baby boomers begin to retire and the music stops, those still remaining in the hollowed out workforce will have to work even harder to pay these Parasitic bills before they get any fruits from their own labors. Some say your children will pay an 83% tax rate. (The chapter on Freedom will show you how to avoid this abuse). The old are sick and dying. You need to keep the promises made by our Socialists by sacrificing your wage and work another 1000 hours a year at your job to properly support them. Show some compassion. So what if some of the poor and some elderly never paid much into Social (in)Security or Medicare and were burn outs, but all your life your fruits of labor have been taken away for the infirm and welfare Parasites. When it's your turn, you realize the Ponzi Scam collapses or it gets so watered down you get 1/10th the benefits the old get today. Quit crying and understand the longer we wait to cut off these Illfare beasts, the more abuse we inflict on our young. Our Politicians insulted us and promised our old a Parasitic non-solution where the children become the sacrificial lamb. The Socialists kept power for a time with this deceit but the money is gone and the jig is up. The lesson you need to learn and the moral of the story: **"When you leave Socialists and**

their Parasites in charge of your money they will consume it and leave you the waste."

Below are some solutions, which keep our promises, but stops the Parasitic abuse. The longer we wait to fix the mess, the more drastic the measures which shall be instituted. Don't forget the payroll tax rate is not 6% plus 1.5% Medicare, but is 15% of your wage. If your employer didn't have to pay half, your employer would pay you this much more! This is 75.00 more a thousand! Or about 3,750.00 for free to you a year! Do you get it that there is and always was only 1 tax: it's a tax on you and your labors.

A) Immediately end all benefits for anyone with a net worth over 2 million dollars or having an income from all sources a year over 100,000.00, (especially when we eliminate taxes). These individuals can support themselves and obtain their own insurance, or self-insure. The limited funds in Social (in)Security and Medicare must go to the destitute in their Golden Years. The rich already received their Social Security checks through the propping up of our economy as the Leftys spent all the surplus in the S.S. and Medicare Trust Funds. There has been a great wealth transfer from the middle class to the wealthy through the payroll taxes. The wealthy only pay S.S. Tax on 65,000, now 105,000 in wages but pay nothing much above this and don't pay these taxes on rents, capital gains, dividends, interest, royalties, etc. Do not be jealous of the rich; just realize the Socialists confiscated the middleclass wealth, granting loopholes and low taxes to buy off the super rich by dramatically freeing them to grow their nest eggs while the Parasites ate yours. In this environment only the Socialists, Parasites, and Super Wealthy benefited. Now it's your turn for a better life, as Government has to face the crimes from another era. This means restitution by Government starting with a dramatic shrink in the size of ***ALL*** Government levels, including its tax rates, power, people and it must sell back ***ALL*** our assets and resources it has hoarded from its very own citizens. Don't worry, there will be 160,000,000 private sector jobs for the ex-government bureaucrats.

B) The abolishment of the Social Security and Medicare plans—These two noble but foolish Socialist systems prove my point, that Socialism always fails sooner or later from the excess Parasite baggage. You can't ignorantly expect these wolves in sheep's clothes who forced you to allow them to hoard your life savings, to treat you with respect, trust, and fidelity. Nope, the Parasites will arrogantly and selfishly consume your fruits. Only you can be responsible for you. Wake up. Do you think the Socialists live to serve you and really give a darn? Their words say yes, but you better watch their actions. If you were in charge and were trusted to guard our citizens Social Security Funds, you wouldn't have spent this money, would you? Is there no honor among thieves or morality in Government? Are you beginning to see the wicked Parasitalism that is dominating our life and culture? Even one penny improperly spent by a Government regime is a crime against humanity. The Socialists have proven they can't be trusted and this is why these programs must die. Oh sure, they will find a handful of destitute lost souls and victims who don't have healthcare or retirement savings because of no fault of their own. The Socials will try to find ways to make you feel sorry as they pick your pocket. Let the bloated State, local Governments, Unions, and Fat Non-Profits paying out ginormous salaries to their employees do something to serve and help our people, instead of so much for themselves as they don't pay income taxes, sales taxes, or property taxes but sponge off ours hand in hand with the illegal immigrants, foreign free trade countries, and the People in Power. Again so you know I'm not overly cruel to them; their pay will also go up 4 times!

C) Offer buy-out plans, ending the tax oppression of the S.S. and Medicare to everyone over 50. We have plenty of Government assets we can sell to accomplish this noble deed. The people can still stay in the system as we keep our promises, but at least we are offering a win-win Capitalist solution to end the Parasitosis. Asinine describes the idea of forcing people to pay into this blood sucking Ponzi Scam, but this is Parasitic Socialism for you. Also, we better not let them take out any more earnings for retirement from any Government worker with their track record. The Government foot soldiers don't know it yet, but the PIPS ate their Federal pension too. Oops they aren't supposed to know this. Oh sure they'll get it up the kazoo, a watered down trickle down pittance. By the way, if we don't do the solutions in the AMERIPLAN, count on a decade or two depression starting now. Hey, only 17 more years to go!

D) All wage earners under 50 will have the option to forfeit all monies paid in these deceitful systems and totally opt out. These workers will provide their own retirement and insurance plans in a non-Parasitical environment where they are totally responsible for their success. Many wage earners will have 10 times the amount of savings at retirement over which the Socialist Insecurity system would trickle in each month for the rest of their life. If these workers wish to stay in the system, all promises to them must be kept, but no new workers with a collectivist bent will want to be stupid and *donate*, I mean *invest* their life's savings in the Social Security *scam*, I mean *system*, they may continue *wasting*, I mean *contributing* their money. In 50 years, or whenever they retire, the Government Bureaucrats will pay these now retired citizens whatever money the Parasites in Government haven't siphoned off (I mean invested, invested, invested) of these retirement funds, if there are any funds left and if the wage earner hasn't smartened up sufficiently to get out of this rip-off (I mean noble plan to save the elderly). In 80 years or so, we will finally be saying good riddance to this Parasitic human tragedy. Is it any wonder the young have lost respect for the retired? Is it any wonder church and family are less important to our people with all our Welfare safety nets where the unproductive can abuse the productive without consequences? For a long time these Ponzi gambits like the 10 Trillion borrowing, creating Fiat funny money, raising taxes, Social Security, Welfare and Medicare appeared to be great noble deeds. Unfortunately, the horrible truth became that Social Security and other Social policies were a hoax and gimmicks concocted to fool the middleclass in a false sense of security that capital ownership was not important or honorable, while the Social Government could scoop up our assets and resources on the cheap at bargain basement prices! The rich like this because it created scarcity and inflated the value of their holdings. Now the Parasites pickings are slim from the middleclass hosts but it wet their growing appetites. The Parasites to survive must now feast on themselves. Not many suckers left.

The Socialists next target is the rich. I think you will soon see the rich crawling out of their castles to battle Socialism. It won't be an easy fight because the Socialist mentality is entrenched in practically every institution in our country, plus we are 10 Trillion in debt. This battle will cost the super rich plenty, but they can spare the money and it is better than losing everything to the Socialists. It will be a circus observing the Parasites at war with the Billionaire Robber Baron Predators, sitting on the sidelines observing these two powerful classes scavenging on each other. The bloodier and more crippled these groups become, the less suffering for the productive class playing by the rules. Their struggle is intensified with the silver bullets you will want to use to stay out of the fray. Let's go back to these Ponzi schemes.

In Uncle Jim's opinion, the total savings on this Parasitalism is 750 Billion a year.[22] Divide this by 100,000,000 full-time employees and the additional income per average worker is ***7,500.00***. Or would you still like the 12.4% Social Security tax and 2.9% Medicare tax as the Parasites eat these spoils and when you retire there is nothing left? You Chicken Littles keep donating your $10,000.00 but not us!

7) End Medicaid by creating 160,000,000 new high pay jobs everywhere. With health care costs reduced ¾ we can save 201 Billion a year or ***2010.00*** per worker. If you got to have some of this, do it only on the State level as the Federal Government is failing here.

8) Savings By Ending The Inflation Tax—With a 50,000 salary paid over a year and assuming we have a 5% inflation rate on the things we buy, (not the Government quoted rate), these savings are (50,000 x .5 x .05) ***1250.00*** a year. What do you think the Leftys in Washington are spending all this money on? It doesn't show up in the budget, you know? We don't need any inflation and with the AMERIPLAN we won't have any, even when your **Pay Quadruples**. We already played the inflation tax game, been there, done that, the last 80 some years since we started the New Deal, which wasn't such a Great Deal and this Parasitic Deal will soon be the Dead Deal. Our people are figuring out this Socialist philosophy with its evil Parasitalism, is what is decaying and rotting our country into a piece of rancid meat. Only a vulture could love this Socialism. To think it was once noble and compassionate.

9) Improved Competition—So far, by cutting out the Parasitic taxing and spending, we have cut over a Trillion off the National Budget. With this savings we can afford to eliminate business taxes. Forget about trying to make businesses pay

---

22 A 66,666.00 salary a year multiplied by 15% in these taxes is $10,000.00. If ¾ of our people opt out, we save 750,000,000,000.00 a year. If we end the Medicare and Medicaid subsidies along with a few other simple environmental changes, health costs will drop precipitously as competition returns.

their fair share in taxes because they totally pass all the cost back to you or they soon go out of business. If you want a tax on the super wealthy and the monopoly businesses, make them do the one thing they hate and fear to do, which is Competition and lots of it! Big businesses can easily reduce their costs on average over 10% (maybe over 50%) with better service and value by increasing Competition. Lest you forget, no matter what the tax is, it is still and always will be a tax on you (the consumer) and the fruits of your labors. With 50,000 a year in average family spending, this is a savings at the very least of ***5,000.00*** a year. Ok, if you really want to destroy the rich then charge them luxury and net worth taxes. But remember, it is still a tax on you with higher product costs and shortages, so you lose again!

10) 160 Million High Pay Jobs—I haven't put a dollar value on the wage inflation which will occur or the added value of a higher paying job but this is **BIG** and substantial and may **Triple a Wage** earner's pay all by itself! Oh what the heck, figure ***20,000.00*** a worker. With surplus jobs, each worker's pay goes further from reduced crime costs for prisons, welfare, security costs, police enforcement, drug rehabilitation, judicial spending, insurance premiums, etc. This is according to the E.&S.P.T.I.T. Plus, with a labor shortage, our businesses will pay for employee training and education to help their workers reach the highest productivity and pay so these companies can make bigger profits. Oh, my, do I mean **FREE EDUCATION** as you get paid, instead of paying someone where you sit in class and don't make a cent? Do you realize when I (Uncle Jim) went to Central Michigan University, a great education, but the cost for tuition today is 18 times higher? Unfortunately pay rates for students only went up 2¾ times what I earned. I never could have afforded it today. Boy, don't you just love our Parasites?

11) Make all Federal prisons, asylums, halfway houses, etc. self-sufficient without cruelty. I don't think requiring work out of criminals is cruel. Work is rewarding and gives purpose to one's life. It is Parasitic to punish American taxpayers, playing by the rules with supporting the criminal through tax extraction. If criminals are able-bodied but refuse to work, they can stay in

their 4'x8' block walled cell in solitary confinement. No A/C, TVs, radios, legal aid, medical or dental. Us knuckle heads better help our people playing by the rules with medical, dental, food, clothing and shelter before we waste another penny, not one more penny on our affected Predators. We can reduce Federal Government spending 10 Billion a year to save each family ***100.00***. It's not much, but it will feed a family for a couple days. We can also do this at the State level; save big bucks!

12) Vice Tax—Instead of taxing our productive and their families, playing by the rules, let us put a tax on the Parasites. Some of the idle and destructive pursuits and products where surplus income is begging to be taken are Gambling, Alcohol, Cigarettes, Sport Events, Bulk and Junk Mail Rates, Prostitution Escort Services, Pain Killer Drugs, Massage Parlors, Nude Dancing Establishments, Pornography (including print, TV, on the Internet, phone sex, sex toys), etc. Sin taxes kill two birds with one stone. These vices are discouraged and at the same time Government gets money to pay the bills for the social problems caused from these vices. It is time this society quits penalizing the productive and their families by making the hedonists and other Parasites pay for all the social costs they are causing. Let's start small and tax these vices 30 Billion more a year and give each family a ***300.00*** tax break with less social problems.

13) Healthcare Competition—To stop ripping off our people we need to Unsocialize healthcare by eliminating Medicare and Medicaid, which will encourage our people to be price and value conscious. If necessary this could be attempted at a State level but never Nationally. Federal Government can't micromanage without eventually failing us. It wastes 70% Parasitizing its people often in bankruptcy. Any major operations will be helped by our tax-free charities. That's why they don't pay taxes, remember? Costs can drop well over 50% with much better service. Lefty Government is an enabler, permitting monopoly costs by limiting competition and insulting us with crude regulation tinkering, which is keeping healthcare unaffordable to a large segment of our productive. When is the last time you saw Doctors and Hospitals advertise their rates, give references, testimonials from satisfied patients and a list of their successful treatments and deaths

that occurred in their hospitals? You need information like this so you can judge value. It's your money they are trying to eat up with tooth and claw. Buy yourself some home medical books and get proper nutrition. You can eliminate 80% of the hospital visits, colds and operations. Don't expect the hospitals to tell you this one. It's all about money, not competition to be the best. With lower healthcare costs from lawsuits and malpractice suits with **At Risk Rules** and less visits, your family can most likely save well over ***4,000.00*** a year. Remember that healthcare is an earned privilege, not a birthright, but it shouldn't cost an arm and a leg. If your employer pays your healthcare, it isn't free. You still pay for it one way or another with your pittance salary shrunk. You want a new law I'll give you a law that by itself will reduce health care costs over 20% alone. ALL HEALTH CARE SERVICES OFFERED MUST HAVE MANDITORY POSTING OF TREATMENTS, DRUGS, SERVICES AND ALL OTHER POSIBLE COSTS IN TWO INCH LETTERING IN THEIR LOBBY OR ALL SERVICES ARE FREE!

14) Reduce Unnecessary Regulation—Use the K.I.S.S. Formula (keep it simple stupid). I heard the Heritage Foundation did a study showing each family would save over ***3500.00*** a year by eliminating unneeded regulation. Figure it out yourself and you might save 5 or 10 thousand. A Consumption Tax or better no income tax or sales taxes would save a lot of us over 100 hours a year, which we could use spending time with our families or becoming more productive at work. Imagine how much further we could move our country forward without this Parasitalism. Are you beginning to understand all these costs are because of Government and its ineptness at solving anything? But gee they sure eat up a lot of your cash while you run longer on their treadmill!

15) Reduce State and Local Taxes—Eliminating Federal tax deductions on these siphons will force the Parasitosis out of the fruits of your labors by bringing reality back where a dollar spent is a full dollar somebody earned from their labors and not a tax deduction. Note that we won't need tax loopholes and deductions by eliminating all income taxes. Higher earnings for our people with 160,000,000 surplus high pay jobs will

end the Parasitalism, so our good citizens will have the leisure time to fix all the waste. We will be able to reduce our property taxes, sales taxes, State income taxes, etc., to less than half we are paying now. Save ***4,000.00*** or more a year.

The following are the hidden costs each American producer pays to prop up the Global Economy. Not only are we spending Welfare in our country, we spend worldwide Welfare and give away our businesses to artificially stimulate foreign economies as we injure and Parasitize our children. I guess our sissys in Washington fear the foreigner threats to bomb us so we buy them off. How pathetic with our unemployment rates. Listen up, Patriot . . . . "Live Free or Die!"[23]

16) Trade Deficit Elimination—A Trade Deficit is like a hole in a damn or an oil pipeline leak that is losing precious resources and in need of repair. A trade deficit results in idle decaying factories and unemployed workers in the Host country. With a job shortage this artificial stress dislocation decimates the Host country's tax base and capital stock but causes up to a 10X boom in the surplus mercantile nation's economic growth. If trade is not balanced within say a year, the trade deficit is not making us more competitive but may be said to be Parasitical because the Host country permanently loses wealth and jobs (causing increased social problems) not only in these primary jobs but there is a multiplicative effect resulting in a magnified loss in secondary jobs. The country with the trade surplus gains more jobs, wealth, and a positive transfer of industry and a boom results from this favorable condition, which with lopsided trade is a Parasitical win-lose situation. It is nice to do a favor for the foreign nations but let's not destroy major parts of our economy and millions of patriots in the process any more. $600,000,000,000.00 is too much foreign welfare in trade deficits. According to the 4X Job Theory, if $50,000.00 equals one primary job, balanced trade would add us 12,000,000 new primary jobs plus 36,000,000 secondary jobs. Let us stop punishing our 100 million workers by taxing

[23] A popular freedom lover's slogan where if you aren't free, you might as well be dead.

them ***6,000.00*** a year for global trade as we are preventing ***48 million*** of our people from having a high pay job and we stunt our economic growth to falsely reward other nations. And why do we do it? So the foreigners won't become Communist, go to war against us, won't bad mouth our Politicians in Washington, or is it the Parasitic deal making with future promises of lobby jobs, wealth, power, and influence at the expense of our very own patriots! Yes, and according to the E.&S.P.T.I. Theory we have mushrooming crime and other social problems from this foolishness.

With *competition enhancers* we can keep Government, big business and Unions in line as we dramatically grow our economy at 10% a year and treat our people with respect in an environment of opportunity and incentive. We can't keep waiting on this free trade stuff when no one else will do it until we got nothing left. Forget about deals where they will do free trade with us in 10 or 20 years as we let them Parasitize us now, by then a lot of us will be grown up from a pittance poor childhood, decrepit and old or just plain dead with unfulfilled hopes and aspirations. You know the Global Economy will shut down as soon as it's the foreigner's time to stop their quotas, tariffs, custom stalls and ridiculous regulations. When the riots and financial crashes start in these countries, watch the trade walls go back up and our PIPS in Washington will hand you the empty bag again. If People in Power want free trade, that is fine, but we need a clearinghouse mechanism where our imports and exports balance out each year or we are Parasitizing the American people with serious injury. A 600 Billion trade deficit is an arrogant Global Economy tax with each family's share *6,000.00* a year. If we have a 600 Billion surplus, you would each get a 6,000.00 a year global economy profit. Fat chance, along with the additional 48,000,000 extra high pay jobs! Unless you use the Silver Bullets, but keep reading.

17) Grant Territories and Possessions Statehood or Free them—The possessions are getting a Parasitic free ride by not paying taxes for the costs of military protection and other Federal Government costs. They get grants and other spending deals. Regulations in our country have encouraged our businesses to set up shop there because of the artificially created advantages.

These costs are difficult to tally. I will make a wild guess and say this is costing us at least a 20 Billion tax indirectly each year to prop up their uncompetitive economies. Ending this leak should save your family ***2 C-notes*** a year plus add 400,000 direct and 1,200,000 indirect jobs.

18) End Profit Transfers—Multinational and Foreign Businesses are avoiding their share of taxes by claiming all the profit in foreign tax havens. Since they do not pay taxes here but sell here at a tax-free advantage against our own home based companies, we lose production jobs and we pay their share of taxes in a doubly Parasitical situation. This is one of the ways the Parasites fool you into believing they are more competitive and work harder. They are not, they just have an artificial advantage by us paying their tax to prop up their Global economy not yours. This leak of profit transfers once patched could net us 40 Billion. This will give us 800,000 new primary jobs and 2.4 Million new secondary jobs and raise your pay or lower your taxes ***400.00*** from the costs of Global Trade. Ok, too difficult? Then institute a 10% tariff on every product entering this country and eliminate all sales and income taxes. Instead of the tax cheats and the foreigner rip offs let them pay their fair share of taxes. They use our ports, customs inspectors, roads, railways, airports, police protection, fire departments, government services, etc. all for free. You think they are competitive? Get me out of here. And you know what? This is our country. Since big businesses shipped our jobs out of our country not giving a darn about our people, let them pay for the privilege of coming back. We don't have to throw away our jobs just because the People in Power want to. It's our country, not the Parasites! Vote non-incumbent to fix this garbage in a hurry. These Bureaucrats are destroying our ability to compete as they critically injured our industries.

19) End Foreign Aid—Foreign aid is a tool, along with the other Global Economy taxes, to buy favors with the Foreign Nations. Debt forgiveness, low interest loans, grants, trade deals through G.A.T.T. etc., all fit in this Welfare category. No matter the spin on these giveaways, they are still a Parasitic rapeage on our productive citizens. Direct Foreign Aid by itself is not overly large but taken as a whole with the Global Economy taxes it is

a large bitter pill for the American people to swallow. Cutting 10 Billion a year out of our Federal Budget will be easy. Our World Order People in Power say this shouldn't be cut because it is such a small amount. However, since this is such a small amount as they say, they shouldn't miss it when we cut it out of the budget. Put another ***100.00*** back in your pocket or get one of the new 800,000 jobs as we plug this bleeding. If any Parasitic people in this country want Foreign Aid, then they can pull out their own checkbook but no more Parasitalism on our people through tax extraction without representation.

20) Bring Home 300,000 Troops Stationed in Foreign Bases—This will keep our tax dollars working to support and build our economy instead of them leaked overseas to prop up the Global Economy. Because it's our money! This is a Foreign Aid Parasitalism where we suck on our productives' fruits limiting their potential while we prop up so called strategic areas around the world. When we close bases, they often are in our homeland, which absolutely devastates local economies. Before we punish our own people, we might want to close all the foreign bases. Our PIPS say Global Trade reduces wars between Nations. Since they believe this, they won't mind bringing home 300,000 troops because we don't need them over there, now that we have the Global Economy. Here's another guess . . . if we spend 30,000 per soldier stationed in foreign bases per year for salary, equipment, and base construction this is 9,000,000,000.00. Put another ***90 buckaroos*** in your pocket plus how much would you like one of the newly created jobs from this cash flow? How many Construction jobs would you like? 180,000 x 4=?

21) Don't worry about nothing for the troops to do. They can protect our borders and catch all the illegal aliens and drug smugglers for starters, as crime plummets and we save 200 billion from the *illegal* drug trade! Talk about one heck of a Global Economy Tax! Save ***2,000*** a family and let's use the savings and create 4 Million Primary Jobs and 12 Million Secondary Jobs. Don't you want a decent honest job for your sons and daughters or are you good with them getting hooked on dope? How about tweaking their brain cells, becoming a dull witted moron committing crimes from theft, drug dealing

to murder. You can manage their life till the day they die. **LIFE REALLY SUCKS UNDER SOCIALISM.** Pssst . . . We could use the troops to do pop inspections and catch all the waste, fraud and abuse from the Welfare cheats. 9 out of 10 can work but won't as long as they can be lazy and beat the system. Don't be gullible and fooled by the crackhead lies and behavior. They have you buffaloed. But you'll get it when you finally go broke. Wake up, Patriots!

22) Patent Protection and End Technology Giveaways—Our Government has a legitimate responsibility to protect our technology, which was created from magnificent sacrifices by our people. Our productive must not be Parasitized in this area, but allowed to recoup their R & D (research and development) costs along with a large profit for the risks they took. Politicians shouldn't have the right to give or trade it away in its Global Economy Deals either. Who can know how many jobs and wealth are lost in this field where Socials dropped the ball. I'll estimate this is costing us 50 Billion a year, which is another ***500.00*** a family to prop up the world economy. Our Politicians went and gave it away for pay-offs. But friends, how will we ever reap the rewards and satisfaction and desire for capitalism if the Socialists and Parasites rape pillage and sell us and our sacrifices out for their false glory and hollow praise from the foreigners? Put another way, we have to eliminate all these Socialist Parasitic rip-offs, coming at us from every direction, if we want to save this country. The foreigners told me our Politicians are gullible, full of themselves and a joke. But they won't say it to their faces; they only laugh and snicker in private at our people in power.

The cost of the Global Economy to all American families is 600 Billion Trade Deficit, plus 20 Billion cost of running possessions, plus 40 Billion tax advantage for foreign operations through profit transfers, plus 10 Billion foreign aid spending, plus 9 Billion cost of troops overseas, plus 200 Billion illegal drug trade, plus 50 Billion loss in technology equals 929 Billion. This works out to a cost of 9,290.00 per year, per family to support the Global Economy the way it is currently set up (no wonder we got a 10 Trillion debt). Our Government thinks it will get paid back this time. I hope we are getting these imports really cheap to pay for the 9,290.00 per family tax and don't forget all the social problems and crime we suffer when we lose 18,580,000 primary jobs and 55,740,000 secondary jobs. I say, did you or one of your kids need a $50,000.00 a year job? Now you know why the foreigners love our career politicians! Wouldn't you for 929 Billion a year and 74,320,000 high pay jobs? Since the foreigners pay their workers about 1/4th of what we pay ours, we are actually creating 300,000,000 jobs from our 929 Billion stimulus. Unfortunately, when the baby boomers retire and the music stops, the foreigners won't like us so much when these jobs start to disappear. We will be sacrificing a lot more as the cries for bailouts intensify all over the world. I anticipate this and suggest we keep a strong Economy and Military, so we won't be intimidated when the desperation explodes from a trade dry up. You better become self-sufficient starting now Patriot. Ok, don't believe this? Then eliminate illegal immigration which deflates wages and watch your pay go up in the stratosphere. You don't need to be a genius just really loopy believing the Socialists, Insiders and the Parasites. Stop listening to these Crackheads.

The following chart "A" shows how much each family can gain per year. Some will do better; some will do worse, but put in your own estimates. The second chart "B" shows most of the taxes we pay. You might be paying up to 75% of your earnings in Parasitic taxes with little left to survive on. If you are making 40,000.00 gross pay multiply it by 4 times and you should really get 160,000 a year. With all the crazy taxes our people are paying in our Socialist environment, it is easy to see why our citizens don't respect our politicians, one another or have compassion. But still, let's fix our Government and help each other multiply our income with the two big factors; wage inflation from surplus jobs and the step up to higher value jobs by our people based on incentive. The sky is the limit on how high your pay could go up with these two factors! I think you can reach your American Dream and invest in our Human Capital with a **Quadruple in Your Pay** (better in your pocket than in theirs). You deserve it and now you know how. But if the Socialists keep standing in the way of Government reform, you will succeed with the 6 Silver Bullets despite them.

And don't let them tell you we can't do all of this or better. Wake up! You've been listening to those smiling, conniving, bungling, lying bureaucrats for years and what's it got you? The 1st time they say we can't fix a problem and it will take years and these ideas won't work, you better remember on the next Election Day to vote non-incumbents only. I am positive any problem we have can be fixed immediately. Hold their feet to the fire and it will get done and even quicker. Remember—it's your country!

CHART A

Cost Category	Individual Workers Share
Interest on National Debt	2,530
Paying-off 10 Trillion Debt (interest savings per year)	10,000
Product Interest Cost Savings from debt pay-off	750
Workfare not Welfare	3,000
Physical, Human, Community Development, HUD, Education, Transportation	1,000
Social Security and Medicare Resolution	7,500
Medicaid Savings	2,010
Ending Inflation Tax	1,250
Enhancing Competition	5,000
160,000,000 Surplus high pay jobs	20,000
Self-Sufficient Prisons	100
Initiate Vice Tax	300
Healthcare Competition	4,000
Reduce Unnecessary Regulation	3,500
State and Local Tax Parasitalism reductions	4,000
Global Trade Tax[24]	6,000
Statehood Tax or Freedom[24]	200
Profit Transfer Tax[24]	400
Reduce Foreign Aid[24]	100
Bring the troops home[24]	90
End the drug trade[24]	2,000
Technology Protection[24]	500
End Illegal Immigration wage deflation	??????
Yearly Gains Per Person	***$74,230.00***
Yearly Gains Per U.S. Economy	**$ 7,423,000,000,000.00**[25]

---

24 The job costs of Global Trade - $9,290.00 per American worker X 100,000,000 American workers = $929,000,000,000 X 20,000 jobs per billion = 18,580,000 jobs X 4 (add secondary jobs) = 74,320,000 lost high pay American jobs in all the mad rush to free trade rip-offs! Now do you think we can create over 160,000,000 jobs with the Ameriplan, Patriot?

25 And they say we aren't competing? Give me a break! How about 7,423,000,000,000.00 a year! Now you know why our country is dying and rotting at the core according to the *Super Power Exhaustion Theory* and the *Shell Theory*. How would you like another 74,000.00 a year added to your salary? Do you think you could stay off the dope, raise your children properly, pay your own health care and be a good American citizen? Your good Buddy Uncle Jim thinks you could! Now do you think we can pay off the 10 Trillion in 4 years, Patriot?

CHART B

The following chart shows a list of taxes and an estimate of rates you may be paying. Put in your taxes to see if your rate is even higher.

Example	Your Costs
Social Security Tax	12.4%
Medicare Tax	2.9%
Federal Tax	16%
State Tax	5%
Local Tax	1%
Sales Tax	6%
Gas Tax	.5%
Utility Taxes	.5%
Property Tax	6%
Interest Expense Tax	6%
Pass Through Business Taxes	6%
Retirement Tax	2%
Inflation Tax	3%
Capital Gains Tax	3%
Dividends Tax	.5%
Gift Taxes	1%
Estate Taxes	1%
Import Taxes	1%
Excise Taxes	1%
License Fees	?
Govt. Penalties & Interest	4%
Franchise Fees	?
Transfer Taxes	?
Other Taxes	?
Unemployment Taxes	?
Sin Taxes	?
FCC Fees	?
Regulatory Taxes	?
Postage Fees	?
	75%±

If you are paying this much in taxes, by eliminating taxes and doing nothing different, your pay goes up 4 times!! Then imagine how much further your pay will go up with regulation reduction, lower Health Care costs, lower insurance rates, lower education costs, higher competition, fair trade, wage inflation (instead of product inflation), surplus high value jobs, ending illegal immigration, reducing Illfare etc. **Your Pay Will Surely Quadruple!!** Guaranteed with your Silver Bullets or your money back! But wait! Do you think I mean to tell you if nobody else has to pay taxes, theoretically, your money could go 4 times further because if no one else paid taxes they could afford to sell you their products for ¼ of the cost? This is a multiplier of 16 times your current pay rate! The sky's the limit. Can we just settle for **4 times your pay** for now?

Federal Government Budget after eliminating Parasitalism

Expenses:	
National Defense, Veterans, Foreign Affairs	737,000,000,000.00
Science	200,000,000,000.00
Law Enforcement, General Government, Education, Health, Welfare, Transportation and other Pork	150,000,000,000.00
Total Spending	***$1087,000,000,000.00***
Revenues:	
Miscellaneous User Fees	57,000,000,000.00
Vice Taxes (to reduce Parasitalism)	30,000,000,000.00
Gov't. Asset Sales for 60 yrs. to Reduce Socialism	1,000,000,000,000.00
Total Revenues	***$1087,000,000,000.00***[26]

26 You see how simple this is people? All we need to do is use the KISS Formula and reduce the Parasitic Socialism. If you want more Government spending then raise the tariff 10% across the board and get an extra 200 Billion for free. It's our money and our country you know. The foreigners can set their own rules. We don't have to put up with their foreign Parasitalism.

By sacrificing the Socialism in this country we can stop our unnecessary punishment and gain 160 Million new jobs, 75% less crime, pay-off the National Debt in 4 years, vastly improve our National Security, and **Quadruple Your Pay**. The only price is to reduce Socialist spending and sell Government assets back to ourselves. It's truly your choice. Or let them keep buying you off with their meager welfare spoils.

Picture our productive as a herd of Antelope. This is how the Socialists see you, (the Host, food and beast of burden). Next picture the Socialists as a hungry pack of Jackals. The Jackals are dependent for survival on eating the Antelope. Jackals don't survive independently on their own productivity but live a specialized predatory existence in a pack and hunt out weaknesses in a herd, singling out the young and defenseless productive for their next meal. Our Socialists parallel this. The Socialists clique or pack survives by feasting off your labors in a dependence on your productivity. With the Social Security Ponzi scam, they even take the bread out of our children's mouths as they spew out how they want to help our children. Socialism will continue tearing us up unless we escape their clutches and strengthen ourselves with the Silver Bullets. What really counts though, is how much you have left each year after all your expenses for food, clothing, shelter, transportation, medical, services, other costs of keeping a job, utilities, taxes, etc. If you make $50,000 a year and only can save $2,000 a year after expenses you aren't much of a fan of Capitalism. But by **Multiplying Your Pay 4 Times** with an extra $154,000 you can thrive in Capitalism as you invest in your self-sufficiency, our children, provide for your retirement and have no desire for Welfare and Socialism!

Oh, this isn't good enough tax? Then tax the Big Charities and other non-profits sucking up your resources as they pay their hot shots at the top 500,000.00 salaries but don't pay sales tax, income tax, or property taxes. Add another 200 Billion a year in revenues. This is another 2000 a year apiece you are donating to them and you probably didn't even know it. I want you to give to who you want with your hard earned dollars. I don't like you forced to contribute to the Fat Cats, making deals behind your back. What's that? You mean to tell me you donated another 50.00 this year? You mean to tell me you did a food drive for them on 2 days? Boy, I sure bet you wish you got the fat cats 500,000.000 salary. Hey? Is this really a charity? They got plenty of money, why do you have to cover their share of property taxes, sales taxes and income taxes? Why can't you get their deal and keep your money? You earned yours; they got it for free. Be quiet! Get back on your treadmill! So they say, but not so fast, your good Buddy Uncle Jim has 6 Silver Bullets and a 70% solution to even the playing field. Remember don't hate the Parasites—they are arrogant and don't see the critical harm they caused.

11

VASTLY IMPROVE NATIONAL SECURITY

We are blessed being citizens of this country, but that doesn't mean we have to be satisfied. Many have heard it said that the U.S. has the worst Government in the world, except for all the others. Assuming we still have a great country, we need to fix our problems on our own, instead of hoping the foreign nations can solve something or even help us. Thank the European Liberals earlier this century for convincing us of the virtues of the Income Tax (Not). Many countries in the world are envious, jealous and want to see the U.S. fall. These countries want our wealth, prestige and respect. Some will do anything outside of war to get a piece out of us. They won't go to war as long as we have the best military. They may be jealous, but they are not stupid.

The magnificent sacrifices by our forefathers and families today are what makes this country great. Once we do a little more work to create *160,000,000 new jobs*, *reduce crime 75%*, and *pay off the 10 Trillion debt*, we will have gone a long way toward improving our *National Security*. You can't be a military super power without being an Economic super power, which is why we need to create many more new jobs, industries and produce surpluses. Also, you can't have a Military super power if a large amount of resources must be devoted to paying off debts and controlling the crime and civil unrest of a war at home. And let us not forget a country is strong when it has strong individuals. Not strong when a Government is bloated and can topple from the weight of its lazy Parasites when the Welfare bribes run out.

Besides improving our environment with *160 Million new jobs*, *75% less crime* and *paying off the 10 Trillion Debt*, if we do the following our *National Security* is virtually secured.

1. *Increase Star Wars and other Defense Technology Spending*—(For further info see the 160 Million jobs chapter). This can be easily done by diverting a small amount of defense spending. Our Military budget need not be cut just because the Politicians spend our money on pork and Bankrupt the country. Let's stay strong with high tech investment spending

so we are not technologically passed by other countries and put in a dangerous position of weakness. Once we fix our economy with the AMERIPLAN we can easily afford the 1st class defense spending we need.

2. *Continue Normal Funding of the C.I.A. and F.B.I.*—Whether a domestic terrorists, corrupt politicians, international terrorists, Communist Regimes, aggressive dictators, or Parasital behaviors from any group, country, or individual with their evil plots must be thwarted. This Funding is the price we pay (a Parasiticide) to keep these Parasites and Predators in check.
3. *Self-Sufficiency*—Just like an individual, a country should strive to have the ability to supply all its needs. A self-sufficient country is strong, can stand on its own, and is free from Parasitic foreign influence and domination in its decision making. Therefore it is prudent for the U.S. citizens to demand its Government *pay off the 10 Trillion Debt*, stop the decimation of its manufacturing base and begin rebuilding it, staying the leader in technological innovation, continue surplus food production and become totally energy independent. How do you like it when OPEC arbitrarily raises and lowers oil supplies ultimately causing the stock markets to go up and down? If you were in on these secrete meetings you could make a fortune with this inside information just like them and their buddies. No wonder you go broke in the stock market! Get out of this Parasitically rigged scam. Watch out for these scalpers and shavers. Start your own company and be self-sufficient.

The AMERIPLAN solves our self-sufficiency problems so we don't have to fiddle around with the Saddam Hussiens of the world, trying to trade for their oil or some other product which we are critically dependent on. The U.S. is at risk of oil shocks. The OPEC monopoly or a couple of the members could violate the free market of oil by lowering production to achieve windfall profits. A well-timed price increase could throw our economy in turmoil and affect the outcome of our elections. This is a Parasital abuse that the AMERIPLAN stops.

Having said all this, a country with its act together, having at least 1.2 high pay jobs per worker, a trade surplus and with no debts, is in a position to influence world developments because it can take the moral high ground without succumbing to Parasital pressure. This country should Fair Trade to stimulate the economies of friendly nations and take a well-deserved role of leadership. But before we prance all over the planet telling everyone else how to live we need to pay off our debts and create more jobs. Are you listening Elite and Wealthy?

Fair Trade-Yes. Free Trade-No. Free Trade never works in the long run between dissimilar countries. The host country is in the best position to benefit and profit from Free Trade. The less developed and poorer countries are at most risk. The host country develops trade treaties which usually are slanted in favor of the poor countries in the short run with a gradual opening up of markets with lower tariffs and less restrictions in the future. At first the Host citizens take a big hit in their lower skilled industries and with intense negative pressures must work twice as hard in these jobs, advance to a higher pay job or create a new niche to compete in the onslaught. During the dislocation period of the Host country, there will be numerous social problems. To reduce the pain of this evolutionary process, the U.S. has initiated welfare programs. As time progresses and the poor countries must open their markets, the host country now has the advantage assuming they still have a healthy economy and haven't sacrificed too much of their human capital and industry. When the times get tough for the poor countries from the Free Trade dislocations, riots and other social upheaval often occur. This is a good excuse for these counties to back out of their promises. So much for Free Trade as the U.S. is left with the short end of the stick.

The original argument for Free Trade is to increase competition, with the AMERIPLAN, we have "*Competition Enhancers*" which satisfy the competition argument. Now we can leave the foreign nations alone to develop at their own pace and we can develop at an accelerated pace without punishing our people.

4. *Government Ethics Reform*—Believe it or not, I think there are a lot of people going into Government to cash in or they become tainted while in Public Service and are out to advance their own careers, gain prestige, profit financially and use

power for their personal agendas. Really? These actions are Parasitic diseases of Socialism which must be stopped if the Government is to survive and improve its citizens' lives. The American people lose confidence and trust in their Government when they see all the perks, pensions, big salaries, lobbyist paid martini lunches, easy working conditions, free vacations, etc. paid by the special interests. There are other hidden Parasitic payoffs taking place after the Bureaucrats leave public service. Some are in the form of transactions with low interest financing, receiving Government grants, under market asset purchases for the bureaucrats or over market asset sales by these bureaucrats which are bought up by Parasites. More direct and obvious payoffs are offers of high pay jobs after the devious bureaucrat leaves public disservice. These jobs could be $300,000.00 a year Lobbyist positions, a $20,000.00 an hour speaking engagement, a position on the board of directors of a Parasitic company, jobs for the bureaucrats friends or relatives, a partnership offering, stock options, book deal, endowments, or whatever.

With so many of our Bureaucrats up for sale, is a most compelling reason for balancing the budget, abolish the Income Tax, require term limits, ending inflation, reducing taxes, drastically shrinking the size of all Government levels and *multiplying your pay 4 times!* The bigger Government gets the more Socialistic it is and the more space in the environment in which Parasites can hide in its web crowding you out. Socialism is not a Limited Republic with maximum freedom and opportunity but is the domination by a clique over the many. I suggest the following if we want to cure our political Parasitosis. Let's pass laws on all these Parasites like they have done to you and your family the last 60 years.

A. Any U.S. Elected official Government Bureaucrat or family member shall not receive any type of consideration from a foreign Government, foreign business, or any unapproved individual or source. This consideration includes any American company or its subsidiaries who are receiving Government contracts, or special gifts, tax breaks, money, property, jobs, legislation, etc. These Bureaucrats must not become Lobbyists or have any business dealings with these entities, either during Government service or the immediate 10 years after. This applies to "ALL" Bureaucrats at any levels of Government. All current and ex-Government Bureaucrats and their family will have a yearly questionnaire to complete and return to the I.R.S. during service and for a continuous 10 year period after Government service. The questionnaire will cover the applicants net worth, incomes and expenses, finances, jobs, contractual undertakings and all other areas where Parasital consideration may have occurred. This form will be submitted with the Bureaucrats income tax forms for public and I.R.S. review and prosecution if necessary. At the bottom of the form, the Bureaucrat will sign a sworn statement under the oath from a notary that he or she committed no Parasital act. Each of the 50 states will stipulate an appropriate jail and restitution penalty for the violators. There will be trials by an impartial 12 member jury with only independents and an 8 to 4 majority will determine their fate.

This questionnaire will be made public. A public servant works for us and can't be allowed to keep financial secrets or they don't belong in Government service. Isn't this fun! Let's pass laws on all these Socialists cramming laws down your throat and give them a taste of their own medicine. Or just have massive spending reductions with Asset Sales to reduce the Government crime and bloat and all the Parasites hiding in their Socialist web. Your choice.

B. All foreign lobbying must be done through the State Department with no political contributions from any source. All Government elected officials will have to keep a public list of all calls answered from any lobbyist or any chance meeting in the hall, letter, text message or email received. If they don't answer truthfully, they are sent to a hearing with the ethics committee and suspended till the investigation is complete with appropriate penalties! We can start by enforcing all the laws we already have on the books. Any past politician who peddles his services out as a lobbyist to represent foreign interests contacting any Politician or Bureaucrat is no friend of our people. These Lobbyists efforts may only be directed to the State Department and no further! These Parasites need to be arrested on site and put on trial for their treason against our people. This is an example of a modern day Benedict Arnold. These Lobbyists' efforts may only be directed to the State Department and no further! Once the 10 Trillion and 40 Trillion other Parasitic promises are paid off, we can relax the standards as obviously we have gotten most of the crooks out of our Government.

C. Campaign Finance Reform is crucial to reducing the Parasitalism and the disasters our country faces with the 10 Trillion debt, 40 Trillion other promises and the coming retirement of the baby boomers. I suggest we reduce the buying of influence to get your money. They are Parasitizing money from your family with twisted laws which they then use to grab more of your money to buy more influence and further Parasitize your salary and so on. P.A.C.s, Unions, Corporations, Special Interests, Foreigners, Foreign Countries, Bureaucrats, and Lobbyist groups don't vote so they must be forbidden from making any contributions, Soft money or even buying lunch should be eliminated. When we catch the Politicians cheating we throw them in jail for 5 years. Candidates may only take money from voters in their district. The question is do we want strong Political Parties and Socialism or strong people and freedom.

D. It won't be easy to catch the Parasites in our environment of bloated Socialism. If we return to a Limited Republic and shrink the Government, most of these Parasites will just move on and be forced to go to work like the rest of us instead of Parasitizing on your family. Tell them to get real, and get a real job.

"PREVENT GOVERNMENT BRIBERIES and hence THE PARASITAL PAYOFF SUBSIDIES"

5. *End Foreign Parasitalism*—Our Government is an enabler allowing the Parasitalist environment that we are struggling to survive in. We can stop foreign Parasitalism easily as long as we keep our sovereignty. Here are a few areas where abuses occur from time to time by our Bureaucrats:

- Selling or Leasing military bases and other lands to Foreign Governments.
- Tax breaks and loop holes to the foreigners. Allowing them to buy our companies and other wealth for pennies on the dollar.
- Profit Transfers by foreign businesses and Government owned industries.
- Favorable legislation to special interest groups selling out our jobs and wealth.
- Trade agreements with huge trade imbalances. (GATT)
- Incompetence and lack of protecting our technologies from foreign theft.
- Low interest loans, grants, Treaties and Pledges, debt forgiveness, other welfare, etc. to foreign Governments, groups and individuals paid for by American Taxes (IMF, World Bank, etc.).
- Nuclear or other defense technology given or sold to risky countries.
- Currency bailouts and manipulations.
- Use of Military, including spending at overseas bases to prop up foreign economies in foreign countries.
- Environmental Zealotry at the expense of the U.S. economy. (Global Warming)

When the Socialists give away our resources and industry, our people are denied Capitalism, "*Crowded Out*", stressed, and subject to further Parasital Attacks in a downward spiral. This is when people cry Racism, jealism, give up or become paranoid. You don't become stronger by going on a crash diet; only get diseases and a heart attack. Nor does a country become stronger by denying and starving the citizens from the fruits of their labors. These fruits are the magnificent sacrifices our people make to improve our society. When people are not properly rewarded they will cease to produce wealth. All will be poorer.

It is a sad excuse to give away our technology and wealth to entice a country to do what it should do anyway. For example, our People in Power give the foreign Governments our Nuclear and other technology, trade subsidies and welfare so 1) they won't sell bombs to unstable countries and 2) they won't invade their neighbors to plunder and pillage wealth and resources. I ask you this . . . What will the foreigners do when our baby boomers retire and we stop buying all the foreign toys and trinkets? They will do exactly what they want with our advanced technology, the bombs they sell or use will be a lot more deadly. And you know one day some nations will need to raise some cash to keep their system going, especially in the face of riots from their oppressed citizens when Global Trade dries up. We will truly have created our own monster. They will do bad things, be ready.

Let us start investing in our own people, grow our economy at 10% a year, advance our technologies and stop regressing to the status of a petty 2nd world nation.

6. *Annex the Provinces of Canada* when they become ready. The only true deterrent to nuclear or biological war is size and strength. Our goal should be to become so big and strong that any country attempting the use of weapons of mass destruction would also be committing their own suicide. An aggressor would have to jeopardize the whole world by bombing our country because to kill enough of us would include such an enormous portion of the world's landmass.

We have a similar culture with Canada. We have the same language, close histories and values. Canada is the best friend of the U.S. It's a perfect marriage. Canada has the natural resources and we have the agriculture and industry. Together as one, our Nation can battle the assault of global Socialism. In a Socialist world, you can't go it alone and protect your freedom. If divided, the Parasites of the world will chew you up. But together, we don't have to keep looking behind our backs in fear.

Don't count on the New World Order Socialists to save the freedoms of men. The Socialists as always will cut a Parasitic share out of your hide. And if you don't cough up, they will socially unite, like a swarm of angry bees and sting you. Plus, why should the U.S. succumb to the unholy alliance of the U.N. when we want our sovereignty to call our own shots and live our way of life, liberty and the pursuit of happiness. We are not the World Oppressors like the Dictator, Communist and Fascist countries. We shouldn't be oppressed into their Altruistic sacrifice for the world Socialist Parasitic culture. Our country is more advanced because we have more individual freedom with a system based on incentive and opportunity. The entrenched Socialist systems have oppressed their people in a negative environment which is smothering their economies. Don't let the World Order Socialists blame us, the U.S., on their failures and don't let them play Parasitalism on you or our country. And get the rest of the NeoLiberals and Socialists out of our Government.

7. *Reduce Pollution*—To protect our health and long-term survival, we should eliminate most of our pollution. If you believe in Capitalism like me, with some positive incentive, we can easily fix most of this. I don't believe in ruining our citizens' lives by sacrificing their jobs and businesses, taking their lands, or causing hardships with high taxes and regulation. Sure, changes must be made with concrete evidence beyond question when a real disaster exists. But the changes must be done in a Non-Parasitical exchange by willing participants who are treated fairly with honesty and respect. Below are solutions we can do now to improve our environment in a win-win solution, instead of the typical Socialist solutions where both sides lose, but not as much as they could have and/or both sides win a little, but not as much as they should have. Don't fall for the disingenuous arguments of the Environmental Zealots. They are nothing but Parasites with an immature philosophical outlook who are scared of living life. They will sell your freedom in a second, to feel the false security in a Government womb! If these hypocrites

really cared, they would stop polluting themselves and have spent their time and energy creating pollution free energy sources and systems. But being the Parasites they are . . . . they don't want to work—just cut a slice out of your labors for themselves without so much as a thank you.

A. *Recycling Project*—We have hundreds of thousands of hardcore unemployed and millions on the welfare system. These people need to end the Parasitic lifestyle and learn some work habits, so they can become productive citizens. Have them recycle trash to receive their welfare checks. Have a couple million people recycling trash instead of sitting at home in front of the miserable Boob Tube, waiting for their paltry check (really our check) in the mail. Think of the possibilities! Energy consumption would be reduced. This would mean less smog, less Greenhouse effect of CO_2 and Global Warming fears, less Acid rain polluting lakes and lower health costs. With recycling, we need less strip mines, less timber clear cutting, less landfills and less primitive factories spewing dangerous chemicals out the smokestacks polluting the air, tainting our water supply and killing our ponds and lakes leaving nothing living but pond scum.

Where are the environmental zealots on this one if they really wanted to clean up pollution? I'll tell you, they are propping up the Socialists, trying to get our Government to take away your lands. The zealots are worried about the pittance pollution you may cause on your land, burning some leaves, never mind that leaves have been burning for millions of years in the cycle of nature. But where are the zealots when their Socialists in our Government collect the big fat permit fees, allowing big companies to burn tons of poisonous chemicals out their smokestacks in the middle of the night into our Air supply and expensive ineffective public sewage monopolies over-taxing the users polluting our rivers? Every time we get a rain, they can open the sewage gates without treating the sewage. How sad! I ask every Zealot Environmentalist, who do you think is really killing you? The Socialists and/or your stupidity? Read on!

B. *Reforestation Project*—Could we take a couple more million unemployed and have them plant trees to receive big fat welfare checks to end the Parasitalism, With a healthy paycheck, I'll bet not many will risk selling drugs for extra cash.

For starters, we can plant a 100-foot tree line on each side of all rivers, ponds and lakes. We can start on Government property and try to purchase restriction rights with landholders. This action will prevent soil erosion, reduce farm chemical run-off in our rivers and shade the water supply to allow for cooler purer water.

Secondly, we can take the unemployed and our criminals to our drier regions and at the outside perimeter of our deserts begin massive reforestation projects. This will reduce the CO_2 Greenhouse effect, improve the air we breathe, possibly reduce erratic temperature fluctuations, reduce desert erosion, enhance the beauty, and increase the habitable lands in our country.

C. *Infrastructure Improvements*—Our sewer systems in many areas of the country need to be improved or rebuilt. In times of heavy rains, raw sewage is allowed to flow into the rivers. Many systems are old and don't purify the water sufficiently before it is released back into the rivers. Our storm sewers need more retention basins and erosion barriers to prevent silts from entering our river systems. Also, we need people to pump out both the Sanitary and Storm catch basins on a more regular basis, along with riverbank improvement to reduce erosion.

We can take a few million of our welfare and put them to work with dignity repairing and building sewage treatment facilities and maintaining our Storm and Sanitary sewers, instead of living as a couch potato, parasiting on the productive.

D. *Landfill Restrictions on Materials*—Besides the recycling of materials, there is no sense in hauling grass clippings, leaves, branches or scrap wood to landfills. These products make a good mulch or can be run through a wood chipper by the unemployed for our people to use as a thatch around trees and shrubs. Leaf burning is prudent, along with harvesting our mature old growth timber (except for a few scattered sections of Sequoias). Or should we continue dumping our trash in landfills and letting our forests go up in smoke, just like many environmentalists are doing to this country?

E. *Nuclear and Toxic Waste*—Let's stop burning chemicals into the atmosphere or creating dumps which later cost us billions to clean up. Instead, let's bury these materials in the North Pole, well below the permafrost or work a deal with a country in Africa to bury our waste there in exchange for free food. But let's not bury these wastes in our own lands where our children live. We can't afford this stuff leaking in our water supplies. I don't like hearing rumors of foreign countries dumping nuclear waste in barrels off the Californian coast. They can dump their waste in the North Pole too, or in an African desert and feed millions of people!

F. *Household Technology*—Use of the internet should be further encouraged where more letters and documents are transmitted without using paper products, gas guzzling delivery trucks and wasted time buying and licking stamps. Paying bills, doing research, writing, advertising, shipping, etc. can all be done without consuming paper or the time, transportation and energy costs to obtain it and think of the trees you will save. Faxes are a big help reducing delivery costs. Thermostats with temperature timers should be encouraged to reduce energy consumption. I suggest if these have Mercury, we pay a $50.00 deposit to ensure few end up in our water supply. Fireplaces that actually help heat a home instead of just for show should be encouraged.

G. *Food Pollution*—Foreign producers of our food supply don't have restrictions on the toxic chemicals they use to produce the food. Many can make you sick or worse. In today's era of Global Socialism you don't know where the food is coming from or what is in it. Think about growing your own to be really safe. Save on your wallet, reduce worldwide pollution, get some exercise and improve your health.

H. *Industrial and Household Cleaners*—We should only be using products that are biodegradable. With the AMERIPLAN, let's sell a Trillion dollars of our assets the Socialists locked up under Government control and pay our companies to permanently convert their productions to Earth Friendly systems and products. This will rot the Socialists socks, but we can afford to shrink Socialism by giving our people and companies incentive to do the right thing. Are you with me Environmentalists? This is the Socialist price to pay for their failure to clean the environment for us!

We can further reduce bottle pollution with 25¢ deposits per every piece of plastic, tin or glass man-made containers. In the meantime get our criminals and welfare recipients to clean up these messes and continue discouraging those recklessly disposing of trash and find incentives for our businesses to use biodegradable packaging and bottles.

I. Reduce smokestack burning of toxic chemicals and contaminants released in our air and ending up in our lungs and our waters—See "A" and "E".

J. *Alternate clean renewable energy sources*—With the AMERIPLAN I show how we can create millions of jobs in nuclear energy and many more in building Dams and Windmills. With these who needs oil? Acid Rain? Pond Scum? Oil Spills? Smog? And who wants energy independence? Who wants the high health costs? Let me know if we should open a windmill company, and will you help by investing and agreeing to purchase a windmill? Email me. And tell your friends.

K. *Ozone Damage*—CFCs are ruining our Ozone layer, so let's reduce the usage. See technique "H". With the millions of jobs created in the AMERIPLAN, I'm sure a few scientists can solve the problem with Freon and its effects on our Ozone Layer. Or possibly a brand new technology could soon be developed. But for now, plant trees you can hide under to prevent heat exhaustion and catching cancer, wear American sunglasses, keep a gas mask handy, stay out of the sun between 11:00 a.m. and 2:00 p.m. and don't build your home on the beach or below potential mud slides.

L. *Self—Sufficiency can be pollution free*—The following are healthy, profitable activities you can do with your family and get exercise all at once. Plant a garden, grow an orchard, Hunt and Fish for food, help heat your home with a Wood Burning Stove, grow your own Christmas trees and landscape your yard for summer shade and a wind break in winter. While you're harvesting in your self-sufficiency without adding to mankind's pollution, you might live in the country, drill your own well for your drinking water rich in vital minerals and install a septic drain field to prevent pollution runoff in our rivers.

M. *World Population*—The 2nd and 3rd World countries are increasing their populations at alarming rates. Their food production and infrastructure can't support or keep up with the explosion. Their water is full of sewage, their people are malnourished and their polluted, crowded conditions are a spawning ground of mutating diseases. Forget about giving them Welfare, all the food in the world won't solve the disorders. There is nothing wrong with helping them in the area of birth control and self-sufficiency, as long as it isn't done Parasitically with our tax dollars to pay for it. Accepting their procreation spillovers won't help because this worsens our country by placing a "*Crowding Out*" Parasitalism on our own people. Eliminating Welfare Parasitalism will also help reduce *Breeding Rights* violations in advanced countries, but Nations far out of tune with their environments must structure their Governments much closer with the Laws of Nature or Nature will solve their dilemma in a very uncivilized manor. I see a massive plague, bigger wars, more dislocations, riots, starvation and early death if they continue violating a Capitalist system of unlimited opportunity with self-sufficiency and personal responsibility.

N. *Is CO_2 Greenhouse effect and Global Warming a Hoax?*—CO_2 is converted by Flora (Trees and Plants) into the Oxygen we breathe and the Carbon is stored in the Flora itself. Flora also absorbs many other airborne particles which improves our air. Nature has a way of balancing things, I suspect with an environment of increased CO_2 our Flora can actually thrive over the Earth and take advantage of the conditions with expanded growth. If we want to increase the habitat for Fauna (animals, including man), we need more Flora to keep balance in Nature, whatever that balance may be if we have even reached it yet. It is prudent for countries to protect the integrity of their rain forests by selective cutting and ending the slash and burn methods which turn the environment into a dust bowl unfit for human habitation after a few years of ranching on the poor soils. We need to encourage these countries to smarten up, but not pay them off in a Parasitic fashion. Don't get suckered into paying them money to save their forests because they are causing too much pollution. They have to sacrifice for their own benefit. If they want a country, they better start helping to save it themselves, instead of putting a guilt trip on you so you loosen up on your wallet, even as they burn down their forests faster than ever. And don't fall for those jealousies about how you must shut down factories and sacrifice jobs for the 3rd world as they accelerate their populations.

In the developed Nations, Desert Reforestation expands our habitat, looks beautiful and gives our Welfare people a chance to learn some good work habits to prepare them to reenter the workforce. And to hedge our bet, reforestation will reduce CO_2 Greenhouse effect if it is eventually found to be a danger. But at this time it seems to me the Global Warming from the Greenhouse effect of CO_2 is not a concern to worry over. As nature seeks a balance from temperature increases, we will experience more evaporation from our oceans and lakes. This will cool the earth along with the resulting clouds and rain, which repeat the cycle. The warmer the temperature of the air, the more humidity it can hold, hence more clouds and eventual rains on the plains and deserts which will now be more hospitable for Flora growth. With more Flora to change the CO_2 into Oxygen and Carbon stored in the trees, the Global Warming moderates back into balance. Possibly this whole concocted scheme of Global Warming was developed by the disingenuous Socialists as a tool to advance their agenda of Government ownership of the land and other tools of production so they can dominate you by taking away your self-sufficiency. Do the Socialists respect your property rights and freedom or, are they taxing away your land as they run you on their eternal treadmill for their glory and your money? You be the Judge. This is the argument based on the Laws of Nature. Feel free to copy this Global argument and give it to the Socialist Demagogues. Another thing . . . . if these hypocrites and World Order Socialists were really serious they would practice what they preach by staying off private jets. In every Government building they would set the heat at 65°, and the air conditioner at 78° in summer; after hours and on weekends have the heat at 55° and turn the air conditioning off. Those imbeciles in Government and on welfare are the ones that need laws passed on them. They obviously can't run the country.

I suggest to the Socialists and their Parasitic Putricites to quit taking away our citizens land but instead take their 40 million plus dependants they spawned with our taxes for welfare and get them planting trees, recycling trash and cleaning up their sewer systems before the next rain washes their pollution over our lands and into our rivers. The bad news—we have a filthy mess. The good news—we can use about 20 million American jobs in this area alone.

8. *Lords of Democracy*—In the future I see Socialism withering as the information age can fully expose the dealings of Governments and their Bureaucrats. U.S. citizens will demand more direct control over policy and will have the information to make informed decisions. (The Internet is the Genie the Socialists ineptly let slip out of the bottle).

Before each vote, time will be divided equally to each side of an issue up for vote by the people. Now the elected politicians' only purpose will be to bring legislation to the American people to vote on through the internet. (Politicians will have only trivial power but will be kept for custom and ceremony). The citizens ballots will be tabulated instantly and the money then appropriated accordingly if even at all. Most will see the Parasitic scams and Government will become smaller, leaner and more trustworthy as the people won't allow the wasted spending anymore.

No longer will the special interests, Plutocrats, Politicians, Putricites, Parasites, and other People in Power be able to dominate the American Citizens with shady, behind the scenes, backroom maneuvers and deal making.

With this great dispersal of power to every corner of the country, it would be meaningless for a crazy dictator to drop a nuke on our capitol with the hope of turning our country into full-blown anarchy. There will be no physical location of our Government. Sure, we will still need a military and local police, fire departments and town halls, but the White House and the House on the Hill will be just another memorial and tourist attraction.

This great wave of decentralized power is the great fear of Dictators, Robber Barons, Multi Nationals, World Order Socialists, Parasites, Big Unions, Fascists, and Communists. Carl Marx and the Elite of today's World Order will be proven wrong in their theories on the direction of Government to eventually reach a One World Socialist state where the Government owns everything! Freedom, Opportunity, Individual Responsibility and Capitalism will thrive in our future. If you doubt the failures of Socialism . . . . Look how these philosophies collapsed and how they violate the Laws of Human Nature. Ideology based on the domination of the masses (hosts) by the few (Parasites) is the great evil of mankind. Socialism always ends up in this camp to its eventual destruction sooner or later. Stick with your good patriot and partner Uncle Jim. We got some really great stuff to talk about coming up.

12

FREEDOM

"If citizens are weak and dependent, they cannot appreciate the benefits of Freedom and Capitalism. Since our Socials are making our people weak and dependant with high taxes, borrowing, inflation, excessive regulation and control, rampant crime, Special Interest Factions, Welfare, illegal immigration, and all the other Parasitosis, is it really any wonder why our people, to their ultimate doom, fall into the evil clutches of Socialism with its two evil brothers: Fascism and Communism?" And now the third—Parasitalism.

Don't get sucked in from all the Parasites by default. You don't have to play their game of Parasitalism having yourself and family taxed, oppressed with regulation, sued, independence and jobs destroyed, scalped with debt foreclosure or let them steal your savings with Fiat Inflation. Save and make an extra 50,000 to 60,000. Do as much as possible for yourself eliminating all foolish spending where possible. If you don't spend they can't suck your fruits. Invest in yourself and family, always striving for freedom through self-sufficiency with the best quality of life. It may never be your destination but your goal is to be a Sovereign (an Island unto yourself).

One day when Socialism has totally squandered enough wealth and our heritage, just maybe when nobody is stupid enough to be Parasited, the PIPS will look out their ivory towers and see the people will no longer follow their insanity. With a little luck, we can all then work together to realign our limited Government with the Principles of the Founding Fathers and our outstanding families who fought, sacrificed and gave their lives to make this country great for us. It's ours to save or lose (and work smarter, not harder for nothing).

When our Socialists tell our productive you aren't competing and you are the greedy selfish and uncompassionate one, stick up for yourself. You have been competing your butt off during the Cold War and then after. In the meantime, the Socialists and Parasites have bloated out protecting and expanding their interests and wealth at your expense; not by productive effort, but by increasing regulation, taxes, interest rates, inflation and by restricting you (their competition and meal ticket). Also, they increased their wages with Government help as these Parasites ate yours. Let's reduce interest rates to 2% and eliminate all taxes on private production and stop the Socialists from running our businesses. They get free postage and shipping and don't pay any sales taxes, property taxes, or income taxes and these parasites take your tax money to buy property, collecting rentals, royalties and run businesses. When these idiots lose more money they just tax you more! They never make a profit in the long run. This is why your salary is ¼ of what it should be. They are just running you on the treadmill till you exhaust. This is why capitalism doesn't work. They took away all the incentives and opportunities—they queered it! These corrections to lessen the Parasitosis will set the productive at only a 2% disadvantage, against the Socials which will almost even the playing field. The rich don't care if you also join them by accumulating your own capital with sweat and hustle from your Productivity. You are frustrated because the Socialists gouged you with Social Security taxes preventing your growth and ability to accumulate capital and then they Parasitically spent it, but you don't want to hurt the rich like you are hurt, using net worth taxes. You only want a fair shot at keeping your productive earnings. No more inflation eating your savings or regulation preventing you from operating your own business. It's wrong. They are sucking you in to their Socialist mentality abomination. Wake up and stop blaming the rich. It's the Socialism, stupid!

Patriot, the joke is on you. Go ahead and let them have it . . . "Socialists and Parasites, I quit. The Cold War is over. I'm not feeding you any longer, only my family. No more. I'm working for myself now. It's your turn for 25 years. You, your cliques, and the rest of the Parasites build the cars and cut your fingers or get your hands smashed. You grow the country's food and breathe in pesticides and shovel manure. You mold the steel as you get burned from the heat and spillage. You build the homes; get the slivers, crushed toes, and broken bones. You drive the trucks and fly the airplanes in dangerous weather. You drill the gas and oil but try not to fall off the derricks or get blown up. You saw the timber but don't cut off your arms as you're looking out for Spotted Owls. You dig the coal and get black lung. You collect the rents from your tenants and since we can't afford any more taxes, I guess they live for free. We can't pay it anymore. You fight the wars as we dump Agent Orange on your head and inject you with plutonium, without your knowledge. You unload all those boats stuffed with foreign imports we already produce. You arrest your drug dealers and illegal alien criminals you let flood in here along with your repeat offenders given early prison paroles and try not to get shot. You provide your Parasites Welfare out of your paycheck, not mine. You send your kids (if you even wanted any) to the drug rampant, undisciplined and uncompeting public schools and while you are at it, have them have another abortion. You live next door and rehabilitate the drug addicts, criminals, illegal immigrants, gangs, dropouts, prostitutes, homeless, etc. But you aren't getting away with more rampant unchecked illegal immigration to take our place and continue the wage deflation and Parasitosis. You do the work and Parasitize yourself."

"I quit Social PIP, I'm jumping off the treadmill, the game is over. I wasn't so smart, I took you at your word when you said you would fix all my problems with Socialism, Taxes and Welfare. You said you would be compassionate if I gave up all the fruits of my labors. But after decades and all my money, nothing got solved. I finally figured out after 20 years, it isn't about solving problems, being compassionate, ending racism or jealicism, solving crime, or creating jobs, it's only about getting my money! I won't forget what you did the rest of my life. So, get out there and compete yourself, since it's so easy and your job is, oh, so difficult and you are so smart. You can have all of our paychecks. You already get most of it. The only thing you have to do is a little work (about 10 hours a day, and get your spouse out there, Good Luck). It's easy right? And after you do this easy work you have time leftover. You can figure out your taxes and mail over 75% of your wage back to your Parasites. Then you can figure out all the regulations you passed and how to follow them (should take 8 hours of study a day for 60 years—do in your spare time, your brain won't be numb from your full-time job. Then you can pay your 18% credit card bills, your under water home loan and interest charges, which prop up the non-productive. Then get sued for the legislation you just passed. Then argue with the local drug dealer, who hooked your children on dope, you have the spare time. Then call the early paroled alcoholic next door who lost his job from the Global Economy. He owes you 15000.00 for totaling out your car. Duck! Bullets are flying through your windows. Oh well, guess the crack dealer hit the wrong house again. Come out of the ivory tower, Socials, time for you to compete. I quit. I'm taking my life back."

We have Parasites in every nook and cranny of our Socialist country. Become a sturdy oak above the Parasites grasp and let them feast on each other in a competitive cannibalism. If you do not become self-sufficient, you are a slave pushed and pulled by whipsawing policies. When you invest your little nest eggs do you really understand what happened when you made a small profit or suffered a loss? It was good or bad luck, right? Wrong! Somebody always knows and they are the ones pulling the strings using Government policy to change the environment. You can't compete with these people and rarely will your luck hold out so you are a winner in the long run, unless you have vast resources to understand the policies. Your best bet is self-sufficiency. Start with some self-discipline and throw that TV in the garbage, it is costing you a fortune! The media is run, owned and fed information by the PIPS rich elite and special interests. Slaves, with their free speech you are being managed like a herd of cattle.

Your body, mind, time, energy, and capital must be closely guarded if you desire to be a free man. Without super caution you are subject to the whims of the Parasites. So, when you ask, "America what went wrong?" look at yourself and then in your own wallet.[27] To follow are pure and divine ideas to clean off the Parasites. They won't make you a billionaire, but you get the fruits of your labors and the life you morally earned and deserve based on your efforts, which is **4 Times More** than now for most of us including most of the Parasites. Follow these and you will thrive in an environment of Freedom and Capitalism. This is the promise of the AMERIPLAN!

1. ***Vote In All Elections***—Vote non-incumbent in most circumstances.

People should go into Government to honorably serve short terms then go back home to work. We don't need career politicians—every one of us must understand every law or government is dysfunctional. Vote non-incumbent in most all cases. Work smarter, not harder. Don't listen to the rubble about how the Lobbyists will have more power over newly elected officials. The fact is, the Lobbyists have no power as the officials aren't bought off or owe political favors. Lobbyist Parasites always heavily contribute to the incumbent career politicians and work on them over the years. Eventually, the Parasites breakdown the incumbent's defenses. Over time, your politician gives up the fight for our interests, throws his hands up in the air and cashes in, making deals, taking the path of least resistance, selling you down the river. You've seen it

[27] From the book, "America What Went Wrong."

too much before, so stop it. Voting non-incumbent destroys Parasitalism and is your most important tool! Get your bigger deserved slice and end the Parasital attacks with this Silver Bullet. When you are enjoying 10% growth rates, 75% less crime, surplus jobs, the 10 Trillion debt being paid off and your **Pay Quadrupled**—STOP VOTING NON-INCUMBENT! In the meantime, make our Government compete for your vote by continuously churning the pot with new officials from a fresh untainted perspective, and watch the Lobbyists scramble for a new food source. Don't become a radical or dangerous extremist; you can easily change things within the system! In other words to change the system you must change them. Their performance is terrible. They don't write the laws—the Parasites do. Your politicians don't even read the laws they pass! This is sick.

Stop listening to the PIPS when they say your vote doesn't count. 75% or more of the people in our country don't or can't vote, such as the old or minors. Your vote is a *multiplier vote* worth 4 people. Depending on whom you vote for, it is a vote for 1 and a lost vote for the other. This is a *swing vote* and a value of 2 (this is assuming you always vote, can vote for only one candidate, and there are only 2 candidates in the race). Most elections are decided by a margin of 4% which means 48% for one side and 48% for the other side (these people are the sheep) with only 4% (the independent thinkers) of the vote making the difference. By voting non-incumbent, your vote is leveraged to 48% ÷ 4% which is a value of 12. By voting non-incumbent your vote is equivalent to 96 people (4x2x12) in this country. If you get 100 people to vote for real change, you have a voting block of 9600 people! Now you know why the People in Power spend billions in Pork Barrel (to buy votes) and why the Politicians spend millions of contributions in the media (to brainwash) to capture your vote. After they have your vote, you are a meaningless number, Socialist sucker.

Because we can't trust what they say, we can't let them get away with computerized balloting. We need to have every ballot hand counted by 3rd party officials. They will tell us how much time, efficiency and all the money we will save. Yeah, right. Are you going to trust them with your ballot, like we trusted them with our money? Look at the 10 Trillion debt and a Ponzi scam called Social Security.

How do you like the Politicians who say they are retiring but don't really want to retire, but they know in their hearts they will get clobbered in the next election? They retire instead of getting trounced. These PIPS don't want the citizenry to learn that ordinary people can make a difference with their vote.

Always vote your conscience. The politicians already know what you want and where you stand. Politicians have to lead the entire country and will have to pay attention to what you want if they know you vote. Certainly when you vote in the future for neo-politicians who have no excess political baggage, they will want to take your views into consideration if they wish to be rewarded with re-election. If you don't vote your conscience by voting for the best statesman, you are giving a mandate you don't want that will probably hurt you and at best you are truly throwing away your vote! And when these political mannequins tell you not to vote for somebody because you are throwing your vote away . . . you are only throwing it away if you vote for them. Stop being their sheep and don't waste your time working like a fool on their campaigns for free. If you are going to keep working against your better interests, and throw away your future, then at least get $20.00 an hour 'til they sell you out, which they always do—you'll see.

2. ***Vote Down All Tax Increases***—shrink the blob. The more money sucked out for taxes, the more Government Parasites find a need in the near future. The more they take the more power over your life and the longer hours you have to work to pay the taxes. The Socials can get by on ¼ the tax revenue they currently rake in. Your family suffers from this neglect. The dollar in gas you save by not driving to the polls is costing you 50,000 a year off your salary—pennywise and pound-foolish! Don't stop here start a petition to shrink spending in your state by reducing Income and Property Taxes 50% across the board for starters. You will save a fortune and get better service without layers of bureaucracy. Let me know how to do it and maybe I can help us succeed. Email me. We could be the 1st state and many of the jobs, businesses and wealth will be yours as everybody who will take personal responsibility, wants freedom and is productive will move here.

3. ***Vote with Your Money***—Buy American from your friends and neighbors. This helps them and keeps the money in your community and is a job creator for our people making you richer, according to the *American Pie Theory*. Don't waste your money with Free Trade scammers. Boycotts are useful to show disapproval of inappropriate behavior by multinational businesses, foreigners, Parasitic behavior by some movie stars, entertainers, foreign lobbyists, sports figures, and any offensive cliques. Try not to get sucked in and buy from companies that spend too much on advertising; they usually sell fad impulse and temporary products at inflated prices that break. It would be nice if we could boycott the parts of Government we don't like. We can't, so strive to change the Government laws and shrink the size of obese Government. The less you buy the less Government has power over you.

   Exchange favors with your friends when possible, the politicians do. However, if you join a barter club, you must pay the tax. A way to vote with your wallet if you disapprove is by not buying any Government obligations, such as treasury bills. If nobody loans the Government money, it can't borrow any money except from itself and this can't last long or efficiently. Let the Chinese loan our taxaholic welching Socials their money.

4. ***Buy A Gun For Defense From Crime***—The Socialist won't save or protect you. Don't keep it in a closet or in a drawer. Children have a way of finding things. Cut a hole in the bedroom closet and place the gun in it. Then drywall back over the hole and paint the area. If an emergency ever occurs, you can easily kick in the drywall with your foot and obtain the gun. Don't forget where you hid it.

   Socials in Government think you don't need guns anymore because it will be safer for you (really them) and they will protect you in your hour of need. But if you have been around a while, you realize there are a lot of bad people in Government who you may need to protect yourself from. Percentage wise, there are probably more crooks in Government and out on early paroles than in the general public. You cannot possibly know all the motivations of these dangerous people, but with every citizen having guns it is a check on a potentially power hungry Government clique or individual trying to ram things down your throat or annihilate anyone in their path. You don't think our Government will hurt you and you believe all that bunk about compassion? Do you still believe in the tooth fairy? Who spent the Social Security trust funds, put us 10 Trillion in debt and all the other promises? What do we have to show for it? What will the Socials do now that Government is out of money? Will our Power Mongers be meaner or kinder when they can't get any more of your money? As proof of the need for citizen gun ownership, throughout history, citizens who are armed and can defend themselves are very rarely attacked by their Government. Even the most extreme and radical zealous Government would commit suicide by directly attacking these subjects it wishes to dominate. Just in case Government and others get cocky during their 10 trillion austerity you get some insurance and pray you never need it.

5. ***Form Your Own P.A.C.***—With all of your friends, pool a small amount of resources and fight like heck to get in line ahead of all the other lobbyists. Don't bring cash, time for that later. Just start bending the Politicians' ears, write lots of letters and monopolize their time with your issues so they can't pass any more destructive legislation from all the Parasites. And don't worry about being polite and courteous to the Lobbyists. Cut in front, shout them down, and get aggressive. Just like they aggressively are picking your pocket to the bone and robbing your children to the tune of 10 Trillion. You are there for moral, honest reasons. They are like the thieving crackhead in the middle of the night. Our Government is for sale, so buy your slice of pie before the Parasites eat all of yours. Buy a cheap computer to track the untrustable politician's side deals for their benefit and email them your complaints. It's too bad Government is in our pocket so much we can't concentrate on our businesses like we should. But since the *(dis)Liberals* love to calculate and split up the electorate to win office, since they want Faction, give them more faction than they ever dreamed,

where they drown in it. One cynic told me a P.A.C. stands for Policing Awful Congressmen. I hope not!

6. ***Raise Your Own Family***, not the Parasites—It's nice to give some of your bounty and hard earned cash to charity. But when you figure the thousands of billions we are spending in Government welfare, it is obvious you and your spouse are raising a lot of Parasites and some deadbeats as you work long hours at your job to give your money to Government. You are on the treadmill as your family is neglected and you are unable to give them the love and attention they need. You are the Host in the "*Cuckoo Bird Phenomenon*". There are about 8 billion people in this world. They have enough children already without forcing you to support them. If you want a family, you deserve one. Don't you let the Socialists control your "*Breeding Rights*" as they flood this country with umpteen millions of illegal immigrants and sell out your jobs overseas to "*Crowd Out*" a good life for you and your family. Make sure you do everything legal to avoid paying any taxes and paying Government anything. Don't throw up yet, you have almost completed your education. Hang in there.

7. ***Protect Your Fruits of Labor From Multi Nationals and Lefty Fiat Inflation***—The best way is by investing your earnings in the knowledge and skills of yourself and family. Secondly, invest in products and resources that build your self-sufficiency such as mini-farm, garden, repair and replacement supplies and a small business. Don't count on a job, you want to get rid of it before it kills you or you get fired with no capital reserves. Whenever reasonable, resist buying products from Multi Nationals and other big businesses, when comparable products can be purchased locally. And better yet, don't buy that new foreign junk. Go to your neighbors' garage sales. I challenge you to avoid buying anything new until we vote all the New World Order Trade ripping off Socialists out of Government power. You want wealthy local merchants who will have more money to buy your products and invest in your neighborhoods. If you buy from distant big companies, in one respect, they are your Parasitic competition. They rarely ever give back to your community, maybe once in a blue moon for

show. On balance they suck out more capital to invest in their countries and big cities than they invest back in your local economy. Once the big competitors have put your neighbors out of business, watch the prices skyrocket locally and your local community suffer and decay into fesspools like many small towns all across America. The Socialists environment of excessive regulation, high interest rates, tax loopholes, orchestrated booms and busts, etc., have all worked in favor of large businesses which can use economy of scale by hiring experts to manage the Social assaults. The bigger the business, the bigger it gets, not by competing and producing on a level playing field but from successfully managing these extracurricular impediments from a Parasitic Government. With economy of scale advantages the big companies can buy out the small competitors on the cheap or just put them out of business with price dumping in specific target markets. This is not competition, only a Parasitic plague of Socialism which has swept over this country. Now you know how so many of our industrious small businessmen met with ruin. It is our environment of Socialism, which is the reason we have illegitimate capital distribution and few competitors from small businesses. Also resist investing in big bloated company stocks. These are fairly priced, may drop 90% in value when the baby boomers retire and when big stocks become overvalued, their money men water down the stock earnings as they quickly raise their own salaries and act to buy up competitors with stock buyouts, diluting your shares instead of competing with the best products at the best prices (the "Brown Trout Phenomenon"). Another rip off.

In the past, one of the most abused tools of the Socials is Fiat. This is creating money supply for the Government to spend without having honestly taxed it. This is the John Maynard Keynes evil sneak of your money when you trust your Socialist Government and turn your back. Yes, Keynes philosophy is criminal and an abomination to nature, not to mention dishonest according to the *Loose Money Equals Loose Morality Principle* Theory". Possibly if enough care, I will share this in detail. Further, this Economics Monetary Solution is not a solution but a problem transference causing social upheaval which boomerangs in a circle to more economic problems! There you go all you economists, this is the textbook spark to intellectually wet your appetites! There's more of course but they can complete the puzzle. This is theft, but they passed a law making it legal, even if dishonest and sneaky. Dollars are the chips used in the Government's card game. Government is the dealer increasing or decreasing the supply of chips which determines the value of the things you buy and the value of those businesses. Increasing the money supply inflates stock and real estate values, rewards the rich, punishes savers, increases inflation and increases consumer prices causing labor to run longer and faster on the treadmill just to stay even and afford the price increases. Decreasing the money supply deflates stock and real estate values, rewards savers, reduces inflation and increases bankruptcies causing labor to run faster on the treadmill at their jobs to keep from being fired. With these policies and money games, production will continually be whipsawed and Parasitized as long as there is dependence on a job working for a wage in an environment of scarce capital (Socialism). Unfortunately, the increases and decreases in Fiat do not always have an immediate cause and result relationship. Fiat effects may go on for years without a reaction in the economy. Only experts have the experience and time to hunt out true values in our markets. To amass a large fortune, you better be the lucky one out of a thousand speculators or have the resources to hire expensive professional economists. What a waste of our productive energy having everybody running around to figure out what scam they will pull next. If you aren't rich to begin with, forget it (unless you have friends on the Federal Reserve Board). With unstable money, the strong get stronger and the weak get weaker, or the rich get richer and the poor get poorer. Eventually, there are only a few strong left and a multitude of weak, which means no more stabilizing middleclass. It is one thing to get strong and wealthy from productivity; it's another thing to get strong and wealthy in a Socialist Parasitic environment of excessive regulation, tax extractions on productivity, wage deflation from illegal immigration, warped trade policies, capital scarcity, asset confiscations, speculation and insider information, and the stop and go pump priming with Fiat money. What do you want? Honesty or dishonesty? Incentive or theft? Now you know why some say that "work just doesn't pay any more".

A good defense against Fiat money maneuvers might be to leverage your productive assets in your small business and mini-farm by borrowing approximately 40% of the value (no higher). Don't be discouraged when you don't show much profit. You aren't supposed to. You don't want to pay too much in income taxes. Just hang in there keeping the business going and when the PIPS run the money spigot, you make all your profit through inflation as it deflates the value of your debts and your assets increase in value. When the PIPS deflate the economy your cash flow normally doesn't go down too much because interest rates start declining after a short lag time and you can reduce your interest rate costs by refinancing. While interest rates are low and the economy has already bottomed out and becoming stronger, maybe rates have even started to trend upward, raise your prices. Look to accumulate more productive assets to get your debt ratio back to about 70%. Now you are a Capitalist just like the multinationals and big businesses. Instead of making profits and surpluses, you make money borrowing to buy assets, timing your purchases, avoiding taxes, pay off your debts with cheaper dollars in the future and speculate which asset class the Socialists will pick on the least in the near future. 70% may not be the ideal leveraged ration, but it is very safe after a long recession or depression and capital preservation must be your top priority. You aren't working your whole life to lose it all in a recession back to the hoarding Socialist. Now remember we are in a once in a 100 year recession. When we come out, you will be able to recoup some of the losses the Socialists scalped out of you with their intentionally orchestrated depression. The whole thing is sick, isn't it?

Fiat stimulus is a tinkering of our economy, which is a favorite of monopolies, Socialist Governments, speculators and billionaires. They make their money with inflation, tax loopholes and borrowing, not work and the sweat off their brow in productive activities. You can do the same and make more than they do percentage wise if you stay disciplined. Look at your small business as a pine tree and the increases and decreases of fiat stimulus as changing seasons.

When the Leftys prime the economy with increasing Fiat, is the time to expand your holdings and grow your business with borrowing like the billionaires. Make your small business like a pine tree in Spring, which has prepared and stands ready for the massive increase and growth in its branches. As soon as the threat of a freeze has passed, its buds expand rapidly because the next Winter comes quickly and the growth must slow before Fall and harden-off. The new growth must become firm and strong to withstand the cold winter winds, ice and snow. If the tree has tried to grow too quickly and is still expanding in the fall at a dangerous pace without building reserve strength into the new branches, the branches will snap from snow accumulation and the winds. This will have been a wasted year with effort and energy put out with no growth and possibly a loss of prior year's growth if branches from previous years break off.

In your business, borrow when the Fiat is increased (Spring), immediately expanding your business in the improving economy (Summer). Then when or before the Government Fiat is cut back (Fall) causing the economic growth to slow, make sure you have sold and eliminated the inefficiencies and dead weight out of your business. Do not borrow more at this time, try to sell some assets and raise cash because a recession (Winter) is on the horizon and if you over leverage with reckless growth in your business at this time, watch as you give it all back (snapped branches) in a possible bankruptcy (dead tree) during the coming recession (Winter). Of course, if your business is growing even in a recession, reducing you debt ratio well below 40%, you can afford to further expand your business and acquire more debt with caution until things turn up, then, BET THE FARM! Just like the Billionaire Speculators.

Pay attention to the demographics because the rules will change and serious deflation will hurt borrowers and businesses when enough baby boomers have retired. Consumer and equity markets will deflate with retiree asset sales and less demand for goods, especially from our foreign suppliers. Foreign economies will deflate from job loss. The foreigners will now have less money to buy our exports as they try and sell more here at even cheaper prices. Investors in equities will be hurt at this stage and workers may see their job disappear or their boss cutting their pay scale. To stem this disorder, I would like to see our Federal Government accumulate a 10 Trillion surplus in the next 10 years where it can supply capital from a position of strength instead of in weakness trying and failing to meet the 40 trillion in obligations, even with their extreme taxes to wring the money out of the collapsing economy and our families. I'm not buying the argument some economist say the 10 Trillion debt is good for us, do you?

You will know our Government is failing and a depression is going to happen when they pull out all the stops and start to re-borrow, run the Fiat printing presses, consume and nationalize more capital and raise taxes to meet their monstrous obligations from the heavy burdens of Social Security, Medicare, 10 Trillion debt and unfunded Government employee pensions as the labor force shrinks. This is when our Socialist style Government will be challenged and meet its match. We shall see how they handle their crisis, or more likely try to make it your crisis! (Hopefully they will have the foresight to use the "70% Solution"); doubtful.

WARNING: We need action now if we want to stem the coming 10 year plus depression I see on the horizon. Government needs to be a net seller of assets while it can sell them for a good price. The price gets cheaper each year! When the boomers retire, in desperation PIPS will flood the market with asset sales. Unfortunately, there won't be much demand for equities and our Government will still owe its 40 Trillion in debts. At this point, our Government will be the cause of the problem. We need Government to be part of the solution. We need it much smaller but want it much healthier, which means less Socialistic without all the Parasite Baggage.

QUESTION: Why does the Government continually run us through all this stress with their punishing taxes, fiat inflation, shrinking our environment by sucking up our capital and choking us with destructive regulation?

A. For the glory of Government. The Leftys think if they keep you weak under the imposed stress without capital, self-sufficiency and freedom, you will have to compete and work harder to produce more fruits for the Government agenda and to feed the clinging Parasites. The Socialists must take your capital and lands keeping you in a subservient relationship of dependency on the Government for their hoodwink to work. The proponents of a one world Government must weaken you to the point of despair where you willingly *sacrifice your sovereignty* to the World Order Socialists.

B. With their inflicted pressure, it is hypothesized the American people will *create new technologies* to advance world civilization. Actually, people clam up over time, become fearful of the Parasites and avoid risks. Imagine the gains we could have achieved within a positive environment over the last 40 years!

C. With the extraction of the Fruits of your Labors, you will avoid having a large family (their "*Zero Population Growth*" agenda), or maybe no offspring at all. This only works if you are smart enough to be responsible. This policy doesn't work on the dysfunctional who recklessly breed with the propping up from Welfare. With free subsistence they live day-to-day and don't have to be responsible to their communities for their actions but further increase your problems. (I think you see that our Socialist Welfare system is enabling a large part of the crime we are experiencing today. Welfare may prevent a few riots in the short run and create more addicts, drunks, HIV infected, criminals and malnourished dysfunctional, (but this is no way to run a first class country).

D. Because Lefty inflation and high taxes keep you busy at your job with your nose to grind stone, you won't have time to figure out what they are doing or fix the messes. This is the "*CONTAINMENT THEORY*" Socials use for crowd control and to give themselves a free reign at running their parasitic agendas, which are diametrically opposite to your interests.

E. With an environment of conflicting and expansive regulation, you will break some law no matter what action you take (even if you don't act) or you may be so lost, the fear of some infraction or violation you may have committed will be sufficient for you to want to keep your mouth shut. Again, this is their "*Containment Theory*" used on you. Ignorance is no excuse for the law they tell you. Unfortunately, when the baby boomers retire, markets deflate, and if the Socials raise taxes to 83%, people will speak up in ugly protests, crime and riots, regardless of the consequences. We need the "*K.I.S.S. Formula*" to uncomplicate things so we can solve our problems before it is too late and tragedy results.

8. ***The 6 Secret and Simple Habits***—Before you can deal with all the Parasites and Predators, you must get strong both physically and mentally. Look at your body as a machine, which needs regular maintenance to prevent a costly breakdown. In good health, you will have a higher resistance to the Parasitosis and can prosper and win in an environment of Freedom and Capitalism. Remember that a Parasite is always seeking out a weakness it can exploit. Shake the Parasites off your back, force this disease into remission and make the Parasites hunt onward for a defenseless Host. Every hour of your life, take a few seconds to review and act on the following critical areas. If you do, you are *ahead* of 99% of the people in this world. First the PARASITAL DEFENSE . . . .

WAKE UP,
THINK FAST,
GET HEALTHY, AND SELF-SUFFICIENT
EVERY PARASITE IS WATCHING!

AIR—Get your head out of the spent oxygen and smog, get a gulp of fresh air upwind or in the country. You may need to move out of the city so you can think straight, keep your health or get it back. Breathe deep to get plenty of oxygen into your lungs and have it flowing through those arteries and brain cells. Consciously take 10 consecutive slow deep breaths each hour you are awake, everyday, to keep your mind alert. Cells in your brain begin to die when deprived of oxygen. Your brain cell connections develop more efficiently with proper breathing. When you exercise, don't forget to take deep breaths to maximize muscle growth and reduce potential heart attacks. Don't wait for your body to send a message to your brain to breathe more, because your cells are facing a critical oxygen shortage. Pay attention to what's happening to your body.

Don't let your brain get hijacked from the second-hand smoke and inhaling illegal drugs. You don't need more health problems and a mixed up mind on dope or you truly will be nothing but Parasitic food in your sorry station of life as you are led around by the nose.

HYGIENE/HEALTH—Cleanliness is next to Godliness. Consciously strive to stay healthy, avoid germ exposure and risks of contracting diseases. Obviously, casual sex and sharing drug needles are no-no's, but drink from your own glass, keep a safe upwind distance from sick people, when possible, avoid large crowds and hospitals. Shower and wash your hair (at least once daily), wash hands regularly as needed, brush teeth after meals, wear clean and dry clothes, dress properly to match weather conditions, etc., to maintain good health and keep the Parasites at bay. At home or work, avoid taking risks where an accident could injure you physically or emotionally. If you do get hurt or sick, get it corrected right away. Most of this is plain obvious, the problem is, many don't consciously act on common sense and caution. You must take this *serious* . . . . as serious as cancer.

Watch and pay attention to your own health. Get a Medical-Health Encyclopedia which gives cures to most any injury or illness you may feel you have. Look up the problem on the internet and diagnose yourself. I would be careful of the Health industry. You can do just about as good fixing yourself. When you are sick and frightened not knowing what to do or if you might die, don't buy into their Parasitalism when they tell you how much you need them as they take advantage and pick your pocket for treatments which should cost less than ¼ what they stick you with. And how do you know? They prescribe dangerous pills, ignoring the value of nutrition and good eating habits, and don't forget these 6 powerful habits. They don't even post their prices and don't have any competition! This is not Capitalism; it's miserable and grossly unjust. And further, now you have to pay healthcare for the illegal immigrants who get it for free? Get back to your job and shut up you livestock, you are food for the Parasites.

A chronic health problem is when they give away your jobs in free trade rip-offs. This causes stress and Health issues leading to Heart Attacks and mental disorders. Get self-sufficient and work for yourself. Don't freak out, and don't let the Parasites suck you in their black hole of despair. You can outwit them just follow me your good neighbor Uncle Jim and learn what you're up against. Then it is child's play to cure the diseases they are festrating over our lands.

EXERCISE—First you need 20 minutes a day of solid physical exercise to get the heart pumping. The main reasons are to improve circulation, strengthen the heart muscle and lungs, strengthen the body to resist diseases and increase the ability of the mind to remain focused and alert. Always warm up with stretching or another low intensity exercise and after your workout use a cool down activity to slowly bring the heart rate back down. Do not over work any muscles during the workouts, but use many different muscles. Breaks in between sets are fine because all you are concerned with is getting a strong healthy heartbeat for 20 minutes. Also, spare your body some of the aches and pains by not working out within ½ hour of eating, working out within 1 hour of waking up in the morning or working out within 1 hour of going to sleep for the night. If at all possible, find medium intensity exercises or sports to do with your family and friends, so it is a fun social experience. A note of caution—don't overdo it. Workout in moderation and stop if any chest pains or other unnatural pains, don't blow a gasket.

Second, you'll need 20 minutes a day of intense mental exercise to build up your mental ability and strength. Your mind is like a muscle, use it or lose it. Pick a mental stimulus and push yourself to comprehend and react. The exercise could be flashcards, writing, math, singing, playing an instrument like the piano, technical reading, debate, memorization or whatever. Get your children or friends to exercise with you so they also sharpen their cognitive skills.

ATTITUDE—Before you can control your emotions and improve you outlook, you need to get a passing grade on the five physical areas (breathing, hygiene, exercise, diet, and sleep). These foundations are the most basic to life and one can't expect to act in a civilized manner when you body craves these from a deficit. Only when the basic needs are satisfied can you move forward with a better life. Don't do the minimum to get by, do the best you can in all these areas (it gets easier over time) or you are hurting your future and limiting your potential. If you are weak in anyone of these areas you are susceptible to a Parasital Attack.

Careful with that idiot boob-tube. TV is a brainwasher by the advertising Media, elite Government Socialists, News Stations with their *(dis)Liberals* etc. TV is the People in Power's greatest tool managing you and your children to be their Parasitic food. TV is nothing but a 24 hour a day Commercial subliminal message to control your mind. You may have to throw that Television in the garbage. Don't be a mind of mush and live a life of couch-potato desperation.

A positive attitude is great to open your mind to opportunities but you also must see the negatives and protect yourself from dangers if you want to survive and have a chance to succeed. Instead of getting sucked up with a bunch of motivational hype, with the inevitable emotional downs, decide what you want out of life and write down these goals. When you need motivation and discipline to reach your goals, visualize your goals.

To reach your goals you need to take all the little steps one after another and keep moving in the direction of your goal with discipline. If you religiously follow the 10 Words of Success, you will succeed to a level surprising yourself and leaving others mystified by your achievements. But your accomplishments are not mystic or supernatural, only the result of a few Simple Habits and discipline.

Say the following in your minds voice to yourself every 5 minutes, of every hour, of everyday, for the rest of your life, then act on it, if you DARE TO REACH YOUR AMERICAN DREAM . . .

"I DO THE MOST PRODUCTIVE ACTION POSSIBLE EVERY SINGLE MOMENT"[28]

DIET—Get the proper raw materials to fuel you machine (body). You are what you eat and an apple a day may keep the Doctor away. Take a daily multi-vitamin with a weekly mineral supplement of 70 or more minerals. Vary your foods with a large variety, while you cut down on greasy foods, bleached flour, pop and other junk food. Have a high protein intake in the morning, you need this for cell growth (especially in your head so you can think straight). You need at least 8 glasses of water a day to help wash all the chemicals out of your body from the food. Get plenty of fiber with some fat. Fat is necessary for your body, but not much more than 5 grams a meal should be your goal. Keep your weight down to prevent fatigue, avoid early diabetes and other diseases. See a Nutritionist at the Vitamin Store as they may likely have more helpful information for 20 Dollars of vitamins compared to a 200 dollar doctor bill with drugs causing side effects, and 2 hours wasted catching diseases waiting in a filthy hospital.

If you want to lose weight but love food, don't torture and worry yourself. Eat as much as you want, however, lay-off the fats and sugars. If you still have trouble cutting pounds, then before each meal (3) and snack (1 a day), drink two 12 oz. glasses of water and eat 5 carrots or celery sticks. If you do this small step and exercise 20 minutes a day, you will lose weight quick enough. If still not good enough, space your meals out to 6 a day of smaller portions and add a second 20 minute work out a day and don't eat anything 4 hours before you go to sleep and no booze. Just stick to it. You will look and feel great. Never go on a crash diet, they harm more than

---

28 A quote as best as I can remember from Tommy Hopkins; a great real estate salesman of our time.

they help. Get a book on nutrition and stay away from taking diet pills or fad diet plans. You have the time and discipline; you can succeed! (NO potato chips or Twinkies).

Back in the Dark Age, people were browsers going from tree to tree and insect to insect, eating small quantities all day long. The point is never go on eating binges or stuff yourself. If you like to eat a lot, eat a lot slowly and spaced out over the day. If you still can't lose weight lay off the breads.

It goes without saying to avoid excessive medications, illegal drugs and more than two alcohol drinks a day or your mind will be lost in the fog, you will shorten your life span and have a tough time coping in a Capitalist environment of Freedom and personal responsibility. Or go ahead doper zombie meathead—let the Socialists prod you in their milking stall.

SLEEP—If you take the first letter of each of the habits above, they spell "AHEAD". As important as these are, they are meaningless without this 6th Habit which starts with an "S" meaning sleep. It is simple, even though many abuse it. Get 7 or 8 hours of uninterrupted sleep each night at the same time. The quantity, quality and consistency have been proven to improve memory and sharpen other cognitive skills. Rest is essential for the body to repair itself and prevent the onslaught and infection of most germs and diseases. When you sleep, breathe a fresh air source, don't weaken and kill off brain cells by sucking stale air with the covers over your head. And resist drinking liquids within an hour of bedtime or the rest won't be high quality with the middle of the night trips to the bathroom. I know this is all very simple common sense such as limiting alcohol, caffeine and nicotine intake which all create sleep disorders, but a little review now and then of self examination never hurts because with a good mind and a healthy body you can keep the Parasites at bay.

Grade yourself daily on your progress with these simple but essential activities. Physical and mental health are first and most important factors to improve your quality of living. It's your life, stop complaining and take charge of your own mind and body for starters. Don't take these 6 habits lightly. I think you will find you aren't as tired, you have less pains and headaches, you will end depression as your spirit and enthusiasm soars and you will finally see the deceit, oppression, hypocrisy, and Parasitalism from Socialism. Also, don't be surprised if you find your work an enjoyment as you complete your assignments in a fraction of the time that previous tasks were seemingly impossible to comprehend, let alone solve. Take a moment each day writing down your progress and see the results. You owe it to yourself and your family. Tenaciously applying the combination of these habits is crucial to your freedom and reaching your American Dream. You can't have a happy life, become rich, own a successful business or manage a family until you can manage yourself first!

AIR—Consciously take 10 deep breaths every hour
HYGIENE—Review and make any adjustments each hour
EXERCISE—20 minutes each day, both physical and mental
ATTITUDE—Every 5 minutes ask yourself and do the 10 Words of Success
DIET—Take a daily multiple vitamin/mineral supplement and a minimum of 3 balanced daily meals
SLEEP—7 hours every night, at the same time, of uninterrupted sleep as a minimum

Some people are lucky, have good instincts and satisfy the needs of their mind and body without much thought. Don't count on luck. Freedom in a Capitalist environment works when you take responsibility for your own mind and body. Once you do this, your American Dream is right around the corner, no matter how many Parasites are slithering around and licking their chops for an easy Host.

When you are neglectful in any one or more of these Simple but Essential Habits, you magnify your potential to make mistakes using poor judgment and increase your risks of illness. You may not even realize it but you are subject to the Socialists and their Parasites in your pathetic state. To prevent mental illness and physical disease and a lethargic life, you must get a high grade in these 6 Simple Habits. You are best prepared to solve your problems by maintaining yourself in a disciplined, responsible grown up manner. This is how we keep Capitalism alive in the world, truly prosper and live for our own sake in Freedom. Don't count on Government or our Public Schools to teach you these divine Simple Habits. They gloss over them in a hit and miss fashion, ignoring the critical importance in combination they possess. Oh sure, you hear a fragmented sound byte here and there, but these Habits must be reinforced on a continuous daily basis. And keep your religion—you need balance and must realize that Government is a false idol you can't trust blindly.

When your mind and body are fixed you won't get suckered or have anything to do with Socialism. You will clearly see how Socialism continually destroys human spirituality, creates the very crime and unemployment it talks about but never solves, robs you of your Fruits of Labor and Freedom, how it confiscates our lands, resources and time with regulatory control, and how it Parasitically taxes for wealth redistribution as it sees fit (to themselves first of course). All this further crowds you in their rotten Skinners box, becoming stunted, lobotomized, and weaker as you cry for more Socialism. Socialism is never a cure but an expansion of the disease. Get away from this human suicide before this travesty kills you.

Karl Marx and the rest of the degenerate proponents of Socialism truly lack understanding of Human Nature and Universal Laws. The Socialist philosophy actually increases the human misery it desperately hopes to solve!

9. *One action which may improve your life in 30 ways,* ***"MOVE TO THE COUNTRY'!***

A. Less crime.
B. Less safety concerns.
C. Less security concerns and costs.
D. Less drugs, prostitution, gambling, alcohol, and other vices.
E. Less pedophiliacs, parolees, gangs, carjackers, pimps, prostitutes, drug dealers, scams and con men, sociopaths, violence mongers, homeless, transients, illegal aliens, addicts, perverts, fugitives, and all kinds of crazies.
F. Less diseases; too much human exposure increases potential of contracting a cold or disease.
G. Less traffic, lines, and other time delays.
H. Less noise pollution.

I. Less land pollution.
J. Less water pollution.
K. Less air pollution.
L. No impulse purchases when you have a good drive in to town.
M. People are much more friendly in the country.
N. Safety of food, especially if you grow it yourself or buy from your neighbor. With Global Trade, you don't know where the food has been. Before you dare eat any of this imported food, you better act like a rat and graze your sniffer over it first to see if it is foul. Then eat just a small sliver and wait 3 hours to see if you get sick. Don't be a guinea pig.
O. Self-sufficient living with excellent opportunities to keep more of the Fruits of Labor.
P. Utility cost savings on water, sewage disposal, garbage pick-up, and on heat bills if you have a source of firewood, a wood-burning stove, well and septic.
Q. Beautiful scenery. Enjoy the walks in serenity and see the stars at night.
R. Planting room for flowers or a garden.
S. Land to go hunting.
T. Good areas for fishing.
U. Less pestilence in the environment. Rats, flies and other pests such as stray dogs and cats are kept in check by nature, the same goes for the human pests, (Parasites and Predators).
V. Plenty of room for pets, for defense and advance warning of strangers.
W. Room for children to play and grow safely from traffic
X. Plenty of storage space.
Y. Space between you and your neighbors.
Z. Few pesky solicitors and cold call salesmen, wasting your time.
AA. Lower property taxes
BB. Landscaping options.

CC. Peace and tranquility without the potential of a terrorist using a weapon of mass destruction and you becoming a statistic.

DD. Plenty of activities to get exercise, such as gardening, orchard picking, fishing, hunting, rake leaves, wash car, shovel snow, cut lawn, chop firewood, etc.

EE. Less laws and more freedom. In the city, you have the Federal, State, City, and County bureaucrats throwing roadblocks in your path. Some things you will run into in the city are no fences, no barns, no sheds, no pools, no ponds, no burning of leaves or trash, no livestock, no antennas, no compost piles, no temporary rubbish piles, no inoperable vehicles, no parking in the street, no open garage doors, no pets, no dog runs, no home business activity, etc., etc., etc. The bureaucrats like giving tickets, penalties, compliance letters, licenses, and inspection fees, special assessments, tree removal permits, uncut lawn fines, sidewalk unshoveled citations, sign approvals, etc., so they can Parasitize more cash out of you and justify living off their wits instead of having a real job.

Competition in the city has become fierce with all the Parasites looking for an easy meal. But in the country, the Parasites must become self-sufficient or move on. Be careful of the Parasites and *(dis)Liberals;* let them take turns Parasiting on each other as they rot under their 10 Trillion debt. Hopefully you can live in the country or isolated for your own sake. Get away from the unnatural habitat and negative bombardments, get your head clear, and start thinking straight.

10. ***Self-Sufficiency*** *is the cure for the common Parasite.* If you have a couple million in the bank, you are free from the Parasites, but you can never be secure and self-sufficient if you depend on a job from someone living paycheck to paycheck. You could get fired and sued for discrimination, sexual harassment, jealousy, a mistake at work that ruins your career, even if it is not your fault. A bad economy caused from poor Government regulation could also do you in. Do not depend on others or Socialists as they have a habit of letting you down. So many struggles in life can be avoided with a little common sense. Below are actions you can easily take to increase your independence, spend quality time to raise and teach your children, save and earn an extra 60,000 or more a year by working smarter, not harder on the treadmill of taxation. These actions won't get you to a multimillionaire status, but with self-sufficiency you will have a higher quality of life and won't need all that money to pay taxes for survival. But once you are free of the Parasites you can try and go for it. You can speculate in stocks and real estate, but first get your self-sufficiency because demographics are against you and as the baby boomers retire, there will be less demand for housing (except nursing homes) and stocks will have their profits held in check with a smaller workforce demanding higher pay to pay their 83% tax rate for past Socialist Government debts and current expenses (Unless we demand the Ameriplan). This is your good buddy Uncle Jim checking in. How do you like the book now? Are any of you still mad because I criticized you? And are you OK with a 400% increase in your salary? Give a little and get a lot.

Start a mini-farm—If you don't live on one, you might buy one. Take out a mortgage if you need to and build a house on 10 acres. Only build the amount of house and land you will use productively, no more. This will be a great business producing a stable return, giving you self-sufficiency. You have just learned 30 reasons to live in the country. To follow are over 70,000 a year more worth of money making and savings ideas. All of the following could be done on a mini-farm but with a little creativity you can find methods to increase your *Self-Sufficiency* no matter where you live. Team up with your trusted family and friends. Don't count on Welfare; the easy pickings are gone and Socialism with its Parasitalism has broken the piggy bank. Don't waste your money on taxes for this diseased infested Socialist defilement of Life and Humanity, or are you a worker or soldier bee for the glory of the unproductive People in Power? A Beast of Burden?

a. *Grow a garden*—This food is much safer for you than the toxic laced stuff in the supermarket. Get your grocery receipts for a month and look how much you spend on food you could grow yourself, such as beans, peas, corn, tomatoes, cucumbers, radish, turnips, onions, squash, pumpkin, sunflower, strawberry, raspberry, grapes, potatoes, asparagus, rhubarb, peppers, cabbage, lettuce, broccoli, cauliflower, Brussels sprouts, carrots, eggplant, beets, watermelon, cantaloupe, horseradish, etc. You can eat these fresh, canned, dry, cold storage, juices, freeze, dehydrate or fry them. What you don't eat, you can sell by posting on the internet or sticking a sign in your front yard. You can add further value by processing these for your own consumption, making pickles, horseradish, potpies, salsa, ketchup, tomato paste, sauces, edible-pumpkin, sunflower and hot pepper seeds, popping corn, raisins, jams, cocktail sauce, instant potatoes, noodles, bread, spaghetti sauce, wine, beer, soups, stews, tomato juice, casseroles, stir fry's, chili, etc. You could grow pumpkins, gourds, squash, Indian, cherry and miniature corn to sell at Halloween or at least grow enough for yourself. You can also grow your own teas and tobacco. The list is endless. Grow your own birdseed and food for pets and wildlife. Grow spices such as garlic, oregano, sage, savory, rosemary, dill, bay, basil, thyme, parsley, etc. With a family of 6, you could easily save *5000.00* a year, or more. Remember, you pay approximately 50% of your wage in taxes, so by not spending this money or not having to earn it, you could save the equivalent of 10,000.00 a year or this is 4 months a year you don't have to brown nose up to a boss and waste all that money on transportation, lunches, car depreciation, clothes, and all the other costs you can't write off against your massive taxes. Plus you always have friends, relatives (you may even have your parents or friends in need live with you for a time) or especially your kids help you in these pleasant tasks so you teach them work skills and you share your time, experiences, and talk about things of interest to improve your lives. Don't do it alone, ever. This is quality time with your family! In all of these activities you don't have to worry about employees but always get company. If you don't have a family, you help your neighbor one day and the next day he or she helps you.

b. *Plant a small orchard*—Plant fruit and nut trees you like such as apple, pear, peach, cherry, plumb, crabapple, maple, mulberry, apricot, nectarine, lime, lemon, orange, grapefruit, cranberry, blueberry, blackberry, hickory, walnut, pecan, chestnut, butternut, beechnut, etc. Sell what you don't consume. You can even sell small trees, Christmas trees, and bushes. You can refine the fruits into jelly, syrup, cider, juice, vinegar, applesauce, wine, etc. You should be able to save and make *4000.00* a year real easy. Remember to have a loved one to help and spend quality time with, I don't want you lonely for the Parasitic Cities.

c. *Hunt* on your land for game—If you have time, plant some wildlife friendly trees and shrubs such as oak, birch, locust, willow, cedar, juniper, spruce, fir, pine, mountain ash, yews, arborvitae, etc. besides your regular orchard trees. These will attract deer, rabbit, squirrel, wild pig, woodchuck, goat, elk, pheasant, turkey, geese, grouse, dove, quail, woodcock, duck, etc. If you hunt for pigs or venison and bag 3 deer, that's 300lbs of meat times 4.00 a pound you save *1200* bucks before taxes plus this is much cleaner, healthier, and leaner with less fat than most meats in the grocery stores.

d. *Fish* in the nearest lake, river, or pond with your family—This is a great outing. With a family of 6 having fish twice a week each eating ½ lb. a meal is over 300 lbs. a year. At 5.00 a pound, you save *1500* a year before taxes. Some fish you could catch are bass, pike, walleye, rock bass, sunfish, bluegill, perch, pickerel, smallmouth, crappie, catfish, steelhead, salmon, smelt, whitefish, frogs, turtles, rainbows, browns, Lakers, and brook trout. These are the highest quality fish and when you know where they came from you won't have to worry about the toxic chemicals locked in tainted meat you are eating. For those who like fresh salmon they are a prize with each having about 10 lbs. of meat which at the store sells for 10.00 a lb. Catching one of these is like finding a 100.00 bill! Between fishing and hunting you can process your game into hamburger, steak, roasts, friars, barbeque, cold cuts, deep fried, smoked, beef jerky, stews, chilies, casseroles, etc.

e. *Burn & Bury* your trash saving over *200.00* a year in dumpster and garbage collection fees. You can even profit from charging others who live in the city. You could make several thousand easily.

f. *Chop your own firewood*—Get friends to help, of course. Save on the wood, heat your home and get exercise all at once putting at least *300.00* in your pocket a year. 2 cords of wood will cost you 150.00 alone. Chop more and sell it for a profit. Hey, use a wood-burning stove and save more on utility bills as you cook your food for free!

g. *Have* a German Sheppard for *a pet*—Feed it your table scraps. Dogs are a great security against the Parasites and will protect your property. Much cheaper and better than an alarm system. Save over *200.00* a year and sleep better. You could even raise dogs, watch your friends' dogs while they are on vacation or have a kennel. Have a cat or 2 for pets. They will keep the rodents in check.

h. *Grow flowers*—Liven up your home with beauty and fragrance. Give them to your loved ones, husband or wife. Make arrangements or decorative wreaths for friends, sell them either fresh or dried. Save or make over *100.00* a year. Save the seeds and plant them every year.

i. *Storage*—Save on storage fees or make a profit letting city friends store their campers or whatever on your spare land. Save or make over *200.00* a year.

j. Have your Banquets, Reunions, Birthday Parties, Weddings, etc. on your own property. Save over *300.00* a year on average. Each wedding hall rental might cost well over 2000.00 itself. By the way, have your friends over, forget wasting money at bars.

k. Wash your own car and shovel your own drive, don't hire a maid, do the housework and home repairs with your kids, cut your lawn, rake your own leaves, etc. for exercise and good health, you need it. Why waste 200.00 a year in a Health Club. Oh? How much are you wasting? Did you catch any staff or the flu touching the equipment or in the pool? Save money on medical bills and look more attractive. Keep much more than *500.00* a year in your pocket in this cleaner environment as you get your daily exercise instead of paying somebody else as your health goes to pot.

l. Learn how to cut hair it's easy—12 visits a year times 6 people at 10.00 each is *720.00* in savings. Have the hair stylist, as a treat, get his or hers done in exchange for doing another friends who also cuts hair. Cut other peoples hair for more money.

m. Public Utility Savings—With your own well and septic, you can save *200.00* a year or more depending on where you live. To increase your independence from monopoly utility companies, you could install windmill or solar systems for electricity and a satellite dish for cable channels or see the programs you need on the internet. Cancel your phone and just use a cell phone or us a Majic jack for your phone service off the internet. How about a clothesline in the summer to save the cost of a dryer?

n. Insurance cost reductions—In the country, insurance for car and house are generally less than the city, where carjacking and riots occur. Save *100.00* a year.

o. No association dues—Save 200.00 or more and all the regulation headaches.

p. Interest expense—Your lot in the suburb may cost you 100,000.00. Ten acres in the country might cost 60,000.00. This 40,000.00 in savings at 8% over 30 years saves you *3700.00* a year! Yes, you might have to commute to work. But no matter where you live get others to join you and split the cost and make your phone calls as you drive to and from work; cell phones are cheaper now.

q. Property tax savings—With a 40,000.00 savings on your lot and if the tax is 3%, you save *1200.00* a year! Note, you won't have as many public services, but you won't need them because there aren't as many criminals, Welfare people, psychos, or other Parasites feasting on and consuming your tax dollars with no useful return.

r. Rental income—By renting a spare bedroom or having your parents living with you, instead of in a nursing or retirement home, they might pay you what they are spending in rent. Possibly make 600.00 a month or *7200.00* a year.

s. Daycare—With your parents or friends living with you on your mini-farm, they can help watch your children while you go to work. Your parents will be much more loving and attentive in raising your children, than some daycare operation that is more concerned about paying its bills. Also with all the savings in this book, your spouse can stay home instead of working to pay taxes. Save over 7000.00 a year! Assuming you still like your parents and aren't hooked on welfare.

t. Dinners out—Instead of going out at a restaurant or carry-out, where strangers cook the meal and you don't know if they are sick or what they stick in it, take turns going to your friend's to dinner and then entertain them. This will be superior in both price and quality as you enjoy dinner and socialize with friends. If you eat out twice a week with 6 people and it costs 50.00 a dinner, you can easily save half of this and keep *2600.00* in your pocket each year.

u. Entertainment—Forget about spending a lot of money away from your family at expensive professional sporting events, movies, and casinos. These cost you 50.00 a piece by the time you calculate the admission fee, food, transportation, parking, exposure to diseases, your time, etc. If you have 3 of these events at your home or a friend's a year per family member that's 6x3x50=*900.00* savings a year before taxes! If you need to get out for entertainment then go to tax-deductible business seminars, where you can learn something. For the kids, go to a $3.00 afternoon movie or rent a video at the library.

v. Buy products in bulk quantities—save another *100.00*. You certainly have the extra room for storage on your mini-farm.

w. With all the money saved, one spouse can stay at home to raise the children instead of wasting money paying income, state, and other taxes, which are mostly Parasitized. You could get by with one car or at the very least you will pay less in gas, car maintenance, tolls, driving tickets, parking fees, insurance costs, lunches, business clothes, and wasted time. Save another *1000.00* a year. As you stop having the computer, TV, IPOD, cell phone, video games, and DVDs raise your children.

x. One great savings of living in the country is the end to materialism and foolish consumption. The advertising blitzes and impulse buying don't work as well if you have to drive 20 miles to get that nonsense. You will have plenty of time to think about what you really need. You just won't be brainwashed and you will be able to maturely think for yourself. Review your checkbook, credit cards, and receipts to see all the garbage you bought that already broke or you're tired of. My suggestion is to donate it for a tax right-off and don't buy anything else, unless you talked to your friends and family and have had a week to cool off and think about it. Save at least *1000.00*. Some of these savings could be by waiting for a garage sale, buy clothing and goods at the Salvation Army and Goodwill, buying presents at 50% discounts after Christmas, buying used books and magazines, or getting them at the Library, shopping at dollar stores. Or waste your money buying junk from foreigners that don't pay any taxes or listening to advertising on TV. Hollywood says TV doesn't affect you or your children. If this is true, why do advertisers waste billions in TV advertising every year? Throw out the boob tube and avoid this Parasitalism! Listen to the radio and read books or you will wake up in 20 years with nothing accomplished except being 20 years older, fat, sick and your vision shot from sitting by the TV and penniless.

y. Other big savings can happen with a little planning. Carpool with friends. Buy once to last a lifetime and profit from inflation instead of wasting time and money replacing cheap products. Pay off credit cards and car loans quickly. Reduce the debt on your home with these savings. Raise your insurance deductibles. Get a wood-burning stove for heating. Plant shade trees to keep your house cool in the summer and reduce electric bills, use a fan and maybe you won't need an air conditioner. Increase the R-value of your insulation. Communicate through the Internet. Use a clothesline to dry clothing. Go to church as an activity and learning environment for your children. Everybody hates junk mail. One old fella I heard got on thousands of mailing lists. Every day the Postman delivers a large sack of magazines and junk mail to this man's house. He gets enough junk to roll it into 3 logs a day, which he burns to heat his house! How would you like to have your firewood delivered to your door for free? You could save another 1000.00 by working smarter, not harder, every year, with a little creativity.

Your goal is to become, or at least have the potential of self-sufficiency as you spend quality time with your family and friends teaching them survival skills, good habits, about tax Parasitalism, welfare, big Unions, insiders and other lazy and unproductive scammers, and teaching responsibility. Don't expect your Government or schools to do any of this. Get your children helping you with all these money saving and profit making activities. Talk with them and teach them. Then make sure they study 2 hours every night. You keep your kids busy. They will have plenty of time to do what they want when they are adults, but not until.

Get yourself a daily planner to keep track of important dates, appointments, and errands. This will save you a lot of time and money. If you ever want to succeed in business or amount to anything, you need to take charge of your own life and get serious or the Parasites will be happy to control your life. Write down your goals and progress each day on the 6 Simple Habits to a better life. Keep track of what you spend your time doing and judge if this is what you want to do in life. And write down everything you spend your money on. In life it's not how much you make, but what you save.

Start a small business—You will get great right-offs on interest expenses, your home, vacations, travel expenses, car, utilities, gasoline, repairs, supplies, insurance, food, phone calls, etc. Visit your friends and sell them something so the visit is tax-free. Be prepared to buy something when they visit you. Get into a business with your family where you can use the products, get them for free, or at least at big discounts. Remember that you can right-off samples for demonstrations and use them for free for a while. It shouldn't be too difficult to earn *5000.00* a year in profit or savings in this part-time business in your home or apartment, at least you will save all the rent which may be 5 or 10,000.00 a year! Below are some more home savings and businesses you might like.

- build wood furniture, toys, bird feeders, picnic tables, cutting boards, napkin holders, fence building, etc.
- become a fishing or hunting guide or organize bird watching hikes
- sell garden seeds, flower seeds and produce grown in your garden

- build signs
- farming wheat, corn, potatoes, soybeans, hay, straw, etc.
- ranching raising pigs, goats, sheep, cows, emus, geese, horses, fish, etc.
- create paintings, birthday and holiday greeting cards
- make clothing, or sewing
- trap or raise furs, such as raccoon, rabbit, fox, muskrat, beaver, deer, mink, beekeeping, etc.
- start a home bakery, can fruits and vegetables
- have hayrides, concerts, bonfires, picnics, seminars, dinners, field trips, kite flying, insect collecting, knitting groups, tree color tours, barbecues, chili cookout contests, haunted house, horseback rides, amusement rides, canoeing, candle dipping, petting farm, paintball war games, cider mill, dances, gift sales, craft shows, dance lessons, etc.
- start a microbrewery
- do data processing and computer systems design, internet work, income tax returns, etc.
- skeet shooting, bow hunting club, outdoor game workshops, etc.
- Christmas tree sales, orchard and fruit tree sales
- bait shop, gun shop
- recycle materials
- sell garden equipment
- write for magazines or newspapers
- frame shop
- sell computers, teach usage or fix them, or work on them at home
- antique sales or have garage sales
- baseball cards
- sell jewelry
- repair shops for cars, appliances, lawn mowers, painting
- sod farm
- mail order business

- sell woodchips, firewood, lumber, mulch, burn pits, topsoil, etc.
- u-pick veggies and fruits
- lawn mowing service, housecleaning, furniture moving, landscaping, newspaper route, snow shoveling
- piano lessons, dance, coaching sports, etc.
- join a multilevel marketing company as an Independent Contractor
- car washing, home mechanic fixing, motorcycles, bikes or autos. You could also sell them.

Or any other service or trade you enjoy and can think of. Find a need and fill it! The list of business is unlimited when you can use your own labor.

Follow this chapter to defeat Parasitalism!

Below are savings you may obtain with Self-sufficiency and Freedom. Figure out how much you will save in your situation, it may even be more! Only by regaining your self-sufficiency can you beat the Socials and their Parasites. This is true to nature and irrefutable.

Grow a garden	5000
Plant an orchard	4000
Hunt game	1200
Fishing for food	1500
Burn and bury trash	200
Chop firewood	300
Security savings	200
Grow flowers	100
Storage	200
Home parties	300
Health savings	500
Cut hair	720
Utility savings	200
Insurance	100
Association dues savings	200
Interest expense	3200

Property tax	1200
Rental income	7200
Daycare	2000
Dinners out	2600
Entertainment	900
Bulk purchases	100
Transportation costs	1000
Impulse buying	1000
Miscellaneous savings	1000
Small business tax shelter	*5000*
Total Income & Savings before taxes	*39,920*

Total Income & Savings including tax savings if all taxes cost you 50% and are now eliminated by producing for your self-sufficiency!

79,840

You are not self-sufficient if you have leveraged wealth or depend on a job from someone else. You could get fired and sued for racial discrimination, sexual harassment, a mistake that ruins your career (even though it wasn't your fault), or, a bad economy caused by poor Government policy could get you laid-off, or bankrupt your nest egg. In the Great Depression, stocks lost 90% of their value. Don't quit your full-time job yet, but immediately get your self-sufficiency and home business going. Build up a couple years worth of reserves to pay your living expenses. Becoming self-sufficient in a Capitalist environment allows for the moral disbursement of wealth without exploitation and Parasitalism. Self-sufficiency strengthens people where they are capable of making good choices for themselves. And only after our people have self-sufficiency and the ability to provide for themselves with reserve assets are they in a position to help their family, friends, and country. Do you get it?? Change your lifestyle and watch the Free Loaders scurry off for a new food source. By you being strong and independent our nation becomes more strong and independent. Not stronger with a bunch of bloodthirsty vultures breathing down your neck.

11. The Socials, *(dis)*Liberals, Parasites, Non-Productive, People in Power, etc. have been getting real cute abusing their privileged position, picking your pocket, running you on their tread mill as they ruin your life for their benefit and glory. You own the country and better start taking control and limit the Socials before it's too late and they totally own you, lock, stock and barrel!

Do the following to defeat the Parasitation . . . Amend the Constitution with the Big 3:

1. **Balanced Budget Amendment**—
For Federal, State and Local governments with only 1 set of books and all spending on that 1 master budget—no more tricks!
2. **Term Limits**—
2 terms maximum in lifetime at any position Federal, State, or Local and a life appointment is good for 8 years.
3. **Abolish the Income Tax**—
We never needed it, it's all about controlling you.

If you believe in this and can help, email me and let me know what we can do.

12. ***If All Else Fails, Then Split***—After obtaining food and shelter, learning to flee and protect yourself from Predators and Parasites is the most basic and important instinct or lesson of nature and your life. This is called Survival and Self-Preservation.

People move for rational reasons and understand it is very expensive to uproot ones family and sell their home for pennies on the dollar. The cost is enormous but it's better than continuing to sacrifice their freedom, fruits of labor, and risk their lives and property fighting a growing environment of tax Parasitalism, jealousy, violence, drugs, lawlessness, crowding out and a lack of regard for life. To put it bluntly, if you are exposed to enough diarrhea, sooner or later you'll catch it.

If you are suffering in the city, maybe you should get to the country and start a mini-farm. If you can't get away from the Parasitosis in the country you have one last option . . . leave the nation and go to a better place where freedom is cherished in a limited Government and where ones pay is based on what one produces. People who live off their wits, avoid work but try to Parasitically suck out a share of your fruits, are dysfunctional and not much better than a pickpocket, only smarter. Get away from this insidious mistreatment now to multiply the quality of your life with freedom!

13

The AMERIPLAN

This chapter is an outline of the most important problems and solutions we face in this country today. Socialism is the all-encompassing problem, which always decays into an environment of Parasitalism. When people are Parasitized, they have their time, money, children eaten and their energy sapped. This is why you and the American people are unable to **reduce our crime 75%, create 160 million surplus** jobs, **pay off the 10 Trillion debt**, and vastly **improve our National Security** along with solving the rest of the Parasitic Socialism running rampant in this country. The Spin Doctors tell you how great we are doing, but compared to where we should be as a country, our economy is sick. We have been brainwashed for so long, many of us don't even believe it is possible we should have a better life.

Don't become frustrated with all the arrogance and ignorance around you. The lost sheep won't even wake up until a disaster shocks them. You have read about the "*not so tiny bubbles*" we are sitting on that can burst from a little pinprick. Some already have. Fortunately, you can think ahead but for most people as long as they are fed, can consume drugs and alcohol, and can sit in front of the boob tube 5 hours a day, everything is hunky-dory. But you want more Patriot. You want freedom and self-determination. You want to keep the Fruits of your Labors, live in peace without the Parasitalism, random crime and fear of Government tyranny. To have this, we need to solve our problems now with the energy and productivity of our baby boomers and stop squandering this precious resource before it's too late when they retire.

The most important thing you can do is to give your all and live a responsible life doing honest work producing something of real value, solving problems and making this place better for everybody. Don't count on anything from the Government and watch it like a hawk. Too many promises have already been broken in the past. People solve problems, not a bloated Socialist Bureaucracy full of Parasites sinking their teeth in your wallet. If you can understand this chapter (the AMERIPLAN), you are a Master Economist and a political genius (better than any politician) who can truly help our people reach their dreams. It all starts by solving your own problems on your own, eliminating the pressures of Socialism, so you can actually help others. Now for you, your *6 Silver Bullets* and the simple solutions to our country's 4 major problems . . . .

Your SILVER BULLETS

Why do the People in Power always need more of your money before they can solve anything? Use these to guarantee yourself a better life regardless of how the Socialists try to Parasite on you and put you on their treadmill. They don't need money to solve our problems and never did. They only want *your* money to solve *their* problems! They don't want to get a real job doing real work! Although, if they do the Ameriplan, they can easily make 4 times more themselves!

- Vote Non-Incumbent always and always vote (if your pay goes up 4 times, stop this immediately)!
- Vote no on all tax increases and vote yes on all tax decreases (they just squander and Parasitize 70% of your hard earned wages). If they come up with a tax and can prove it is revenue neutral . . . vote it down, they are probably lying.
- Diligently use the 6 SECRET AND SIMPLE HABITS. (You can out smart them)
- Be a free man or woman by becoming "SELF-SUFFICIENT". (You can't be Parasitized on anymore as you are a Sovereign).
- Buy American to help your family and friends or do without—shrink their Parasitic environment.
- Amend the Federal Constitution with 1. Balanced Budget, 2. Term Limits, 3. Eliminate the Federal Income Tax.
- If all fails, SPLIT! (Get away from these Parasitic Animals!)

160,000,000 New High Pay American Jobs!

So, you want 160,000,000 new American jobs and to **Quadruple Your Pay**??? The greatest reason for job growth is Incentive (potential profit). This is done by improving the odds in our business environment with less risk and more rewards. There is no limit to the number of jobs we can create. The only thing limiting us is Socialism itself. We set the environment and if we want to value our people, families and children.

Well, this is it Patriots, the 10 Commandments of Job Growth.

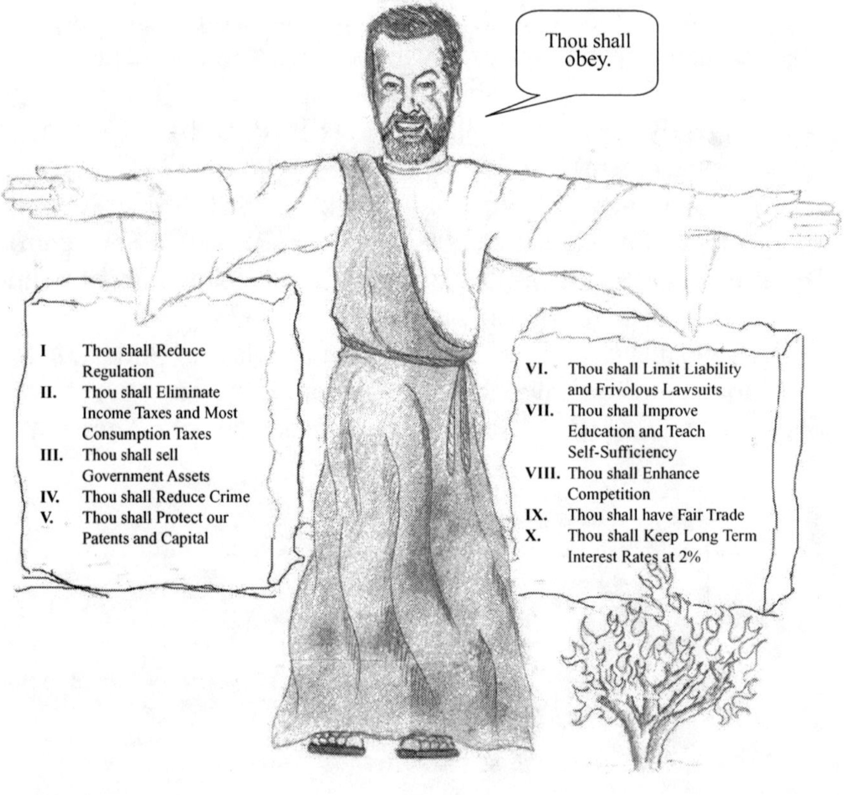
Thou shall obey.
I Thou shall Reduce Regulation
II. Thou shall Eliminate Income Taxes and Most Consumption Taxes
III. Thou shall sell Government Assets
IV. Thou shall Reduce Crime
V. Thou shall Protect our Patents and Capital
VI. Thou shall Limit Liability and Frivolous Lawsuits
VII. Thou shall Improve Education and Teach Self-Sufficiency
VIII. Thou shall Enhance Competition
IX. Thou shall have Fair Trade
X. Thou shall Keep Long Term Interest Rates at 2%

Pay off the 10,000,000,000,000.00 National Debt In 4 YEARS

Make the Socialist Government fix these and you will make 60,000.00 more a year. If you currently make 20,000.00 a year after taxes, you can now make 80,000.00 a year! I think now we can easily pay off this debt by ending the Parasitosis and if you don't believe this, then stick with your Leftys you voted in and be grateful when they grant you a 50¢ minimum wage increase, Sucker.
Abra Cadabra!

We can eliminate all Income and Consumption taxes along with paying off the 10 Trillion debt at the same time. Even if my figures are too low we can save much more and your pay could go up a lot more than 60,000 a year. At least your pay will double if we eliminate all our crazy taxes and do nothing in my list. But you've learned enough from this book to find ways to make even more—Decide for yourself or keep listening to the PIPS in Washington.

Profit or Savings Per Year

U.S. Interest savings for everybody with National Debt paid creating 10 Trillion in Capital causing 2% long term interest rates	1000 B
Asset Sales (per year or more if wanted)	1000 B
Eliminate Interest on National Debt	253 B
Product Interest Savings	75 B
Reduce Most Welfare	300 B
Reduce Most Pork Barrel	100 B
Voluntary Social Security and Medicare	750 B
With Surplus Jobs and Medicaid reductions	201 B
Create a Competitive Business Environment	500 B
Self-Sufficient Prisons	10 B
Vice Tax increases (yippee! new taxes)	30 B
Healthcare Competition	400 B
Reduce State, Property, and Local Taxes	400 B
End Unnecessary Regulation	350 B
Fair Trade	600 B
Give Statehood or Free Possessions	20 B
Stop Profit Transfers	40 B
Reduce Foreign Aid	10 B
Bring Home More Troops, (end Imperialism, solve our own messes)	9 B
Patent Protection	50 B
Stop the International Drug Trade and Illegal Immigration	200 B
Wage Increases from Surplus Jobs	3000 B
Every year gain— well, for the next 60 years	$,$$$,$$$,$$$,$$$.$$

This is the total cost in Parasitalism we waste each year. If you think things in this country are okay now, just imagine how much better our situation should be! It's your life. Let us reward our productive

6,000,000,000,000.00[29] more every year! How would you like an extra $60,000.00 (6+Trillion \ 100 million workers) a year working the same amount and just by fixing our dysfunctional Socialism?

29 This figure could be much higher and varies depending on how successful we are at reducing Socialism. No one can calculate this and the wage inflation and wage increases from a move up to higher pay productivity jobs. The sky is the limit and it all comes down to how high a value we, as a society, wish to place on productivity and families our (Human Capital,) or, unjustly continue rewarding the Super wealthy with billions in the bank, or Asset Hoarders like the OPEC Oil Sheiks, Non Profits, Monopolies, Robber Barons, and an obese bloated Socialistic government by the People of Power. As you can see we don't need any taxes and they are just a way the socialists and their parasites control you as the "meat heads" they think you are! (Somebody wake me up from this Parasitic nightmare.)

75% CRIME REDUCTION

Stop! In the name of the **Ameriplan!**

Asset Sales
Surplus Jobs
Shrink Govt. and its Corruption
Reduce Parental Deprivation
8:00-4:30 School Hours
Extend School Year
Juveniles Tried as Adults
9:00 P.M. Curfew for Minors
Teach Morality in School (Ok, let's call it Good Citizenship)
Stronger Student Discipline
More Police Visibility
Gun Restrictions on Criminals
Ex-Policeman on every Parole Board (no early paroles, late paroles for bad behavior)
End Judicial Activism
Simplify Laws
Reduce Illegal Drug Trade and Usage
Reduce Other Vice Addictions
Capital Punishment
Reduce Teen Pregnancy
End Illegal Immigration
Reduce Irresponsible Pregnancies
Reduce Welfare
Protect Borders and Help Mexico Remove Their King Pins
Reduce College costs (how about the tuition 18 times lower when I went to school?)

NATIONAL DEFENSE (Finally, we do have a need for some responsible Government)

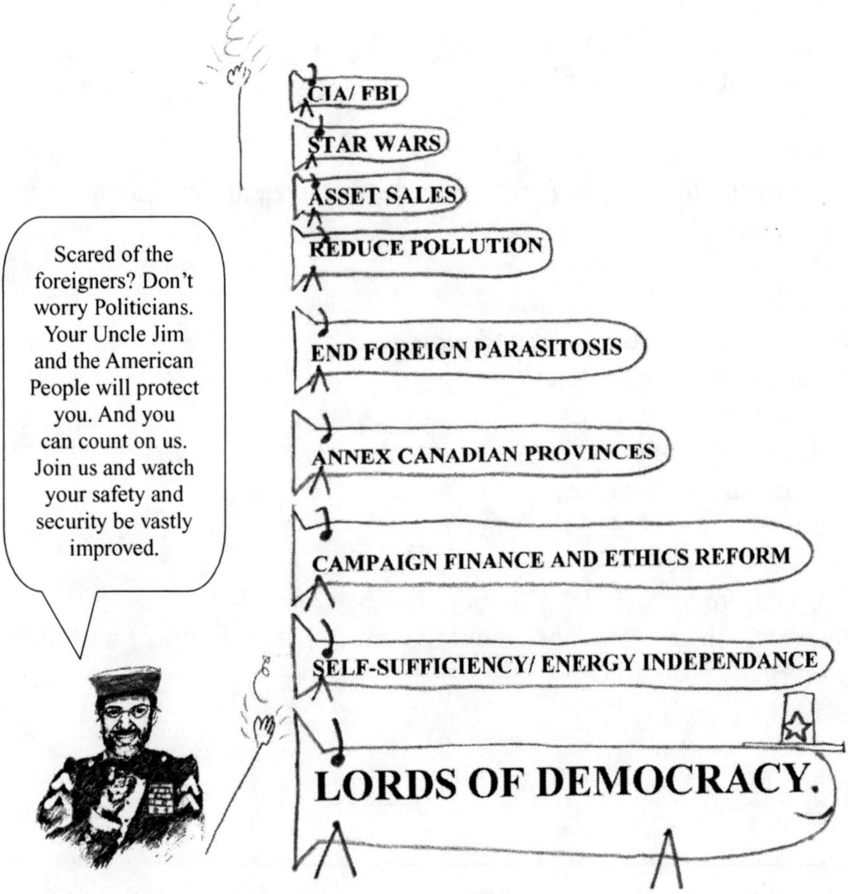
Scared of the foreigners? Don't worry Politicians. Your Uncle Jim and the American People will protect you. And you can count on us. Join us and watch your safety and security be vastly improved.
CIA/ FBI
STAR WARS
ASSET SALES
REDUCE POLLUTION
END FOREIGN PARASITOSIS
ANNEX CANADIAN PROVINCES
CAMPAIGN FINANCE AND ETHICS REFORM
SELF-SUFFICIENCY/ ENERGY INDEPENDANCE
LORDS OF DEMOCRACY.

YOU AIN'T NEVER SEEN A FRIEND LIKE ME!

14

The 70% SOLUTION

WOW! I cannot fully express the surge of joy I experienced when after many years of study in quiet solitude on long walks, I completely understood the major problem in our country, which is growing Socialism and its inevitable Parasitosis. Once you comprehend the nature of this disease, it becomes child's play to intellectually attack this virus and provide workable solutions, especially for yourself. I pray in some small way, I contribute to defeating this sickness in our society. This book is my vehicle of expression; objecting to the growing domination and sloth from the Socialist Environment we are experiencing in this country. Hopefully, in our lifetime, we will embrace Capitalism in which we all benefit in a win-win exchange without a bunch of Blood Thirsty Parasites and Predators sucking off your fruits in a win-lose Socialist exploitation for the glory of themselves. What about your glory and right to live for your own sake in freedom? **"Ask not what you can do for Socialist Government, but ask what Socialism did for you with all your money it raked in and why do we owe 10 Trillion?"** Do you want your **Pay 4 Times Higher** or do you have another 30 years to blow and then maybe they can fix something? You own this country. You decide when you're ready to quit being a host, an absentee owner milked by the Parasites, and take charge of yourself.

To solve 70% of our problems, we need to cut the cancer out of our malignant Socialist bureaucracy. Or, put another way, our Government is not competing on behalf of our people. Government is fat and sassy. It needs to shed some weight by going on a diet to reduce its obesity and stop critically injuring and harming our people. These Socialists and their Parasites got their American Dream by eating yours, running you on the treadmill, not by honest work producing wealth for themselves and our country. Their cure is a Parasiticide called ASSET SALES and we need to do this now before more baby boomers retire or we will have caused critical impairment to our economy and permanently damaged our country.

Today we can end the Socialist squeezing of our economy, choking off our freedom and stunting our potential. They did this by hoarding and consuming most of our capital, along with usurping our liberties to the point of caging us in a "Skinner's black box." These actions made our people poor, ignorant, weak, and dependent on Government. This fits in with the Socials plan to dominate us as "Beasts of Burden" and control our every move. They arrogantly know what is best, especially for them. It is true, the more they tax away our wages and freedom, the more we need them. And the more we need them, the more they can get away with Parasiting on us. This is a negative cycle that the Socialists and their Parasites will never want to end. It is also true when there are abundant resources and freedom, the stronger and more independent people will become, needing less Welfare and regulation from the Government. The Socialists and People in Power hate this because they will be out of a job and can't dominate you when you are self-sufficient and independent! To be fair, there are politicians who mean well and talk compassionately but don't see the critical awful damage their laws and taxes cause our people. Many of these inept bureaucrats never had a real job in their life. However, many in this Socialist clique know perfectly well the abuse and suffering they cause on you and your children even as they claim how much they love your children. There are some really evil people in Government who don't give a darn about you no matter what they say. Just because you are honest and fair with people, don't expect fairness from the vulture crowd as they survive by eating your flesh to the bones. We must shrink the Parasitosis by selling back to our people all our lands, buildings, etc. so we can clean their plague in our Government. This will take awhile, the Socialists in Government confiscated over 100 Trillion of our wealth. Let's eliminate our taxes so we have some money left to buy this stuff back. Make yourself a solemn oath to be done with them and their diseases today, forever.

By the one action to *sell Government assets*, we start a chain reaction sending positive shock waves into every institution and citizen in this country. **NOW?? "YES NOW!"** It is time to end the Neo-Liberalism and its negative Parasite environment based on confiscation and punishment. Let us instead strive toward a positive environment based on accommodation and reward. *Asset sales* are the tonic to strengthen our people and defeat Socialism and its Parasites as we grow our economy at 10% a year. Asset sales are the common denominator to solve our 4 major problems in the Ameriplan. But more important than our people making 4 times their current pay, asset sales create millions of jobs, reduce most of our crime, free us from debt bondage and encourage our desire for improved National Security and a willingness to respect one another and work together to solve the problems we face today. Here's how *asset sales* work . . .

As I've said before . . . . in nature the strong get stronger and the weak get weaker. Let your good buddy Uncle Jim help you to be strong. How about a sip of my tonic??? Called Asset Sales! Or maybe you are a true believer of Marx, the Leftys and their Parasites. Well, I feel sorry for you as you doom yourself and mankind in a miserable existence in decay where people are nothing but spiritual Zombies. You will be livestock to be slaughtered at the Parasites whim. Some life! It doesn't have to be this way.
Asset Sales Elixir by AMERIPLAN

GOVERNMENT'S SILVER BULLET FOR SUCCESS

Top Secret
Confidential
Ameriplan 70% Solution
Pssssssst. The little known secret to maintaining Political Power in this country for the next 60 years is destroying the Parasitic Socialism with . . . .

ASSET SALES!

If politicians could only solve one macro problem, it would have to be *Asset Sales*. *Asset Sales* cause the creation of millions of jobs (according to the "*4X Job Theory*"), drastically reduce crime (according to the "*E.&S.P.T.I.T.*"), greatly increase individual wealth (according to the "*American Pie Theory*") . . . with all of these, our citizens will be healthy, have the time to defeat Parasitalism and have the resources to fix the rest of our problems and vastly improve our National Security. Only at this point will we stop searching for the Politician's Corruption and we will respect them as Statesmen (according to the "*Political Scandal Theory*"). And don't forget the 10 Trillion debt and Social Security deficit will be paid off renewing and perfecting the *Cycle of Democracy*!

Below is the big Picture. *Asset Sales* provide incentive in our environment bringing out the good in our people according to the Behaviors of Human Nature and Natural Law.

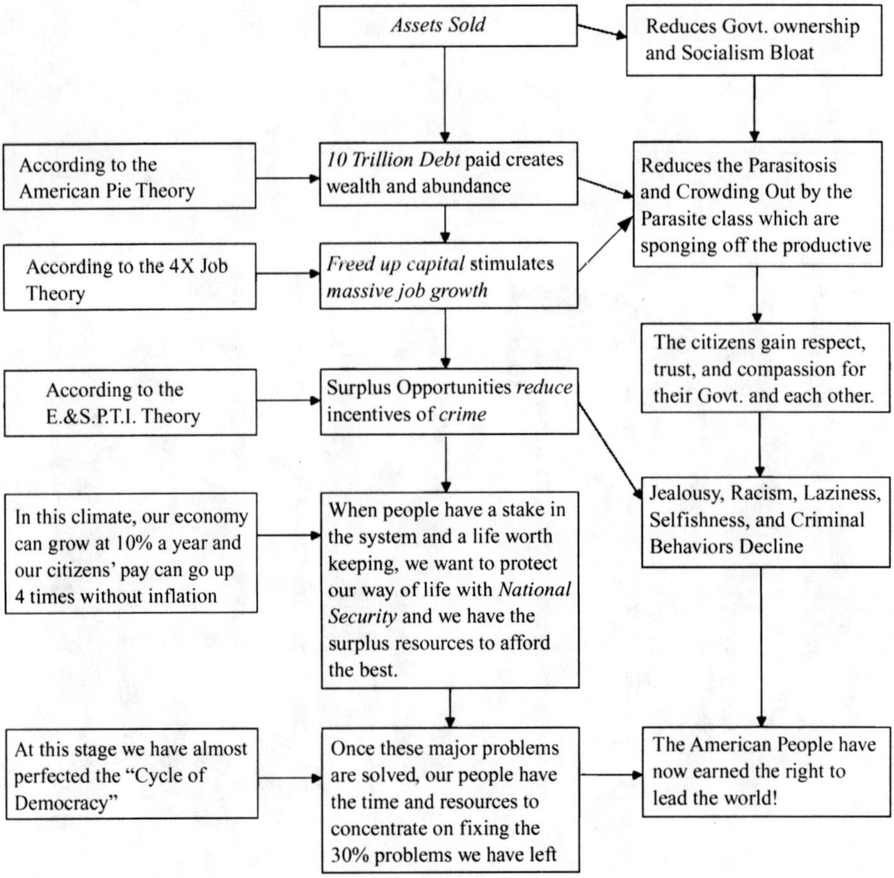
Assets Sold
Reduces Govt. ownership and Socialism Bloat
According to the American Pie Theory
10 Trillion Debt paid creates wealth and abundance
Reduces the Parasitosis and Crowding Out by the Parasite class which are sponging off the productive
According to the 4X Job Theory
Freed up capital stimulates massive job growth
The citizens gain respect, trust, and compassion for their Govt. and each other.
According to the E.&S.P.T.I. Theory
Surplus Opportunities reduce incentives of crime
Jealousy, Racism, Laziness, Selfishness, and Criminal Behaviors Decline
In this climate, our economy can grow at 10% a year and our citizens' pay can go up 4 times without inflation
When people have a stake in the system and a life worth keeping, we want to protect our way of life with National Security and we have the surplus resources to afford the best.
At this stage we have almost perfected the "Cycle of Democracy"
Once these major problems are solved, our people have the time and resources to concentrate on fixing the 30% problems we have left
The American People have now earned the right to lead the world!

Now the American Dream is a reality for most all of us! This one simple action of *Asset Sales* is essential to ensure our people prosper in a Capitalist environment. With this, we can defeat the immoral policy of using excessive taxation, borrowing, and Fiat inflation (part of Keynes Economics) to steal wealth from our productive to feed the Socialists and their Parasites. With this massive theft, is there any wonder why some of our people disrespect and treat each other so badly? Of all the solutions I've written, that we can do, none can compare to the power of this one action. Capitalism can only exist if our people have the use of our resources to grow and become strong. *Asset Sales* are the missing ingredient of true supply side economics. Don't count on the Neo-Liberals and Socialists to help you with this one because it will defeat their Parasitic system. Now will Asset Sales work forever? No. For about 60 years or until we run out of Government Assets. But remember . . . most of us will be dead in 60 years, and by then the next generation will create their economic genius. I could tell you what they should do. But why spoil it? They will discover the answer!

I want to make one last fun solution to fix our problems. We need it, and it sure would be fun to see our politicians compete. Most Patriots want small Government but we want it to be strong with the best people running it. I propose a bonus system for our elected officials to create incentive for them to do the right thing (the right thing is doing the bidding of the American people in a Limited Republic). And, so we have a limited republic we need to rope in our People in Power and amend the Constitution with 1. Balanced Budget, 2. Term Limits, 3. Abolish the Income Tax. After we amend the Constitution why not each year our Senators, Congressman, President, Vice President, Cabinet Members, and Supreme Court Justices balance the Federal Budget, without using any of the trust fund monies, we give them a 1,000,000.00 a year bonus. When these officials totally pay off the 10 Trillion debt, we give each of the current officials a $2,000,000.00 bonus for doing such a great job! This incentive pay is peanuts compared to the 40 Trillion in debts and promises the Socialists have charged on our account. Taking this strategy further, we can give 1 Million bonuses each year the Medicare and Social Security short falls are covered and when these are fully funded and the program made voluntary, we can give each official another $2,000,000.00 bonus, apiece. Once again, this is cheap compared to the unfunded liabilities we have charged to our children.

On the surface, incentive bonuses seem like a simplistic and silly idea, but when you read the following reasons you may not think this is so simple. For starters, we won't have to worry about a balanced budget amendment and the PIPS that lie saying they support this amendment then aggressively fight its passage with Parasitic excuses behind the scenes. One good thing about the nature of a parasite, they can always be bought and we can persuade the Parasites to feast on each other instead of our families!

1. With incentive bonuses, pay is based on results. We will be able to get back to our jobs knowing the officials will do

our bidding. We won't trust them blindly anymore. We've lost respect and trust but we do care. If they don't meet our objectives and goals, they don't get the bonuses and I guess they had a better reason not to pay off the debts and they are happy with their low base salary. Remember that you can barely live in Washington, let alone maintain a home state residence on 250,000.00 a year salary. You see people, our politicians are financially dependent, insecure and at risk. This is how the Parasites like it because it's easier to Parasite on weak politicians. The politicians are subject to Parasites just like us. If we fix our politicians problems, they can fix our problems. Of course this makes me wonder why the politicians haven't already eliminated income and consumption taxes. I guess because of the Perks, Paid Vacations, Pensions, and Jobs from the Parasites that greatly help. Unfortunately, these come at a very expensive price to the American people. According to the "*Laws of Nature*", when we strengthen our politicians, they are less susceptible to Parasital attacks. We will now get lower taxes and solve our major problems.

2. When we increase our officials' pay we tend to expect more out of them and we can demand excellence—you get what you pay for!
3. With Bonuses, there will be lively competition by our politicians to do our bidding, win and keep their high pay jobs.
4. With Bonuses, the best people in our country will run for office, as these will now be higher value jobs, as they should be.
5. With high paid politicians, they will not be subject to the pressures of the Lobbyist and the Parasites' grasp. Campaign finance reform will be much easier now.
6. Our elected officials look at the American people as pennywise and pound-foolish. In our country we pay some freaks that are in sports, and entertainment multimillions and we can't even cough up a million or two for our people who hold important jobs in the county? Mutual respect will return with an honest day's pay for an honest day's work. Our pay system in some industries is plain nutty.
7. With the objective to fix our tax and debt overdose, the pressure on the Parasites will force them back into productive

endeavors, producing goods and services, which are real and benefit our society instead of trying to live off their wits, eating your wallet and sucking up your time and energy. Now when our politicians spend money, they will not want to waste a penny fearing they might lose their bonus.

8. Our politicians are a mirror of ourselves. If we increase their pay it won't be long before they increase your pay and you will expect it because you are paying for the best. Or, you can always vote them out. You should pay them well so they are above tainting and corruption. Just like you want your pay higher so you are above the temptations of crime and socialism. Are you with your Yankee Doodle Patriotic Son Uncle Jim?
9. Most importantly, we get back to the philosophy of "rewarding those that produce for our country." *I call this the "Philosophy of REALISM"*. This is Capitalism and this is how it should be. With performance bonuses, our politicians will defeat the Parasites and predators for us so we can get back to our job and family.

"So why haven't our politicians created **surplus jobs, paid off the 10 Trillion, reduced crime 95% and vastly improved our National Security**, especially if it is so simple?"

The way I see it, you need to understand that our politicians are not men of vision with extraordinary talents, but ordinary people certainly just like you and me, no better or smarter. They are basically good and try to do the right things. They, believe it or not, are not leaders but followers of us! We are in the Land of the Free and Brave. We get to vote and voice our opinions to our politicians. We own this country and have the moral obligation and responsibility to step up to the plate, grab the flag, and figure out what is wrong and take charge. I am telling you, we have the vision and desire of the American Dream in our own hearts. Yes, all we ever had to do was tell them. We just got sidetracked during the Cold War then became Socialistic as we lost our way. But still, we can change the mess quick because you and every one of us is a "Lord of Democracy" in our Limited Republic. I sense a ground swell for Freedom, it's back and growing louder each day in our country. tell your politicians to end the Parasitic Socialism because you want back . . . .

YOUR AMERICAN DREAM!

Let it be said, "We left this country a better place for our children."
You can make a difference! Especially for yourselves.
(If you only believe, all things are possible.)

My Patriot, congratulations and success on your journey with all the joy and happiness you have earned.

Go get your Dream!
And use those 6 Silver Bullets to guarantee your prosperity and freedom. And tell your friends!

Hey Patriot, I hope you didn't skip to this last chapter before reading all the other chapters.

This book came to fruition because of one question that nobody could provide me the answer to. So, I took it upon myself to study Politics and Economics. The question is "**Why does it take two incomes today to support an average family**, when 30 years ago, one income provided a higher quality of life for a family in financial security, even after all of our new technology, more education, smaller families, longer hours both spouses work at a job and we borrowed 10 Trillion on top of it?" If you have read the book, you already know, but I'll say it one last time . . . "it is the growing Socialism and its inevitable Parasitalism!" Got it?

I hope you have enjoyed the Simple 70% solution to our problems. And you know it's really not simple but developed from our heritage, human nature, and with a very complex set of figures and problems (about 10,000,000,000,000.00!) Ok, so you become a master economist, I'll say it one more time! I wouldn't want anybody to not see the simple truth in front of their very eyes.

"ELIMINATE TAXES BY SELLING GOVERNMENT ASSETS TO INCREASE YOUR PAYCHECK 4 TIMES!"

And where else but here have you ever heard of one simple solution which in a POSITIVE way, will create 160,000,000 new high pay American jobs, pay off our 10 Trillion national debt in 4 years, drastically reduce most of our crime 75% and vastly improve our National Security? Is not our Governments only purpose to provide safety, freedom, and opportunity (LIFE, LIBERTY, and the PURSUIT OF HAPPINESS?) The rest is up to you Patriots.

If you liked this book or not, please contact me at my website and email me with your suggestions and ideas to help eliminate Parasitalism, with more wealth, and a freer, happier, and healthier life for you and your family. You deserve it! And now Patriot . . . farewell with my hope the AMERIPLAN may provide you guidance so you may reach your American Dream. For now, I am going back to work producing for our people, solving day to day problems and trying to help keep freedom with true Capitalism alive in this country. You can help too, with the Silver Bullets. Now go forth and empower yourself!

Join me,

Uncle Jim
(Dreamer/ Patriot)
Website: *www.unclejimameriplan.com*
email: *unclejimameriplan@yahoo.com*

Congratulations! Go with my wishes for success and happiness and may you obtain your **AMERICAN DREAM!**

We showed them, didn't we Uncle Jim!
Thanks Uncle Jim!
Ameriplan Graduation Ceremony featuring Masters Degrees in Economics

INDEX

D

E

F

V

W

Z

It is truly amazing how the Socials, with huge tax collections, could enslave us by 10 Trillion! And they have the gall to call you Mean Spirited, Uncompassionate, Nationalist, Bigot, Racist, Fascist, Protectionist, and Cruel because you can't anymore afford to pay for free healthcare for the unproductive and want tax cuts? We could have had a lottery, making 10 Million poor families millionaires! Much better than subsistent subsidies. The name calling and madness must stop! The economic experiments and fiascos with the "New Deal", Free Trade, Irresponsible Immigration, Deficit Spending, Fiat Money, Great Society, Socialism, Welfare, and all the Parasitalism over the last 80 years, have exhausted and failed! It's time to become Realists. Nobody gets a free ride anymore. Welfare for the rich, poor, political cliques and any lobbying foreign nations getting special deals is tyranny and oppression, a miserable disease forcibly extracting the fruits of labor from our hard working productive families playing by the rules. For others, unproductive Welfare is great Parasiting and sucking off another's efforts, living the life of leisure as the Hosts work longer and longer hours in vain, to pay Parasital Homage, away from their families and friends. However, with a 10 Trillion Debt, we have to do things the old fashioned way (which is the only way that works) . . . .

TO REWARD THOSE WHO PRODUCE!

Safety nets? Of course. But when we create 160,000,000 new high pay surplus jobs, we won't need Income Taxes, Welfare and a 10 Trillion drunken borrowing binge as we mortgage and destroy our children's future. Nor will the Politicians. Their Socialism is now being unmasked as the greatest rip-off in history! Get ready to take the flag. True Patriots, you've already started helping our people by buying this book. Now let us look to the future with strength from the knowledge you already had and *know* our problems are easy to solve. You just needed a little memory boost from your good Buddy Uncle Jim! Relax, dash your fears and anxieties, we *will* greet the new day with confidence.

Patriots? Are you afraid of anything or scared? Nervous with trepidation? Forget Uncle Sam! You are with me now for the rest of our lives. Learn from me and then please teach me as we re-perfect "a more perfect union."

LaVergne, TN USA
30 April 2010
181047LV00003B/1/P

9 781450 040099